HORARY ASTROLOGY

the key to scientific prediction,
being the prognostic astronomer

W. J. Simmonite, M.D., Ph.D.

with additions by

JOHN STORY

and

further edited in the light of
American experience

by

ERNEST A. GRANT

© Copyright 1950 by the American Federation of Astrologers, Inc.
All rights reserved.

No part of this book may be reproduced or transmitted in any form or by any means, electronic or mechanical, including photocopying or recording, or by any information storage and retrieval system, without written permission from the author and publisher, except in the case of brief quotations embodied in critical reviews and articles. Requests and inquiries may be mailed to: American Federation of Astrologers, Inc., P.O. Box 22040, Tempe, Arizona 85282.

First Printing 1896
Revised and edited by Ernest A. Grant in 1950
Reprinted 1985
ISBN Number: 0-86690-161-2

Published by:
American Federation of Astrologers, Inc.
P.O. Box 22040, 6535 South Rural Road
Tempe, Arizona 85282

Printed in the United States of America

PREFACE TO THIS EDITION

While cogent reasons were assigned by John Story in his Preface to the revision of the original work of Dr. Simmonite in 1896, there are more compelling reasons today why this great work on Horary Astrology should again be made available to all students of the oldest of sciences and greatest of arts.

Not only are there greater thousands of sincere students of astrology abroad today than there were either in 1849 (when we believe the original edition was first published) or 1896 when John Story published the sixth edition and amendment of the original, but the advances made through experience in dealing with the nature of the planet Neptune in astrologic and the further discovery of the planet Pluto (concerning the latter of which, however, we are in much the same position Mr. Story was, although we probably have greater knowledge concerning the influence of Pluto than Simmonite had concerning Neptune), make it highly desirable that Dr. Simmonite's great work be amplified somewhat, amended where necessary, and broadened.

This edition is presented essentially in the light of American experience. Both Dr. Simmonite and Mr. Story found their experience in England where they were largely dealing with a homogeneous population with a common hereditary background. Thus the physical descriptions and characteristics assigned by them were essentially Anglo-Saxon. In America, however, astrological experience is found in a heterogeneous population whose hereditary background, both physically and psychologically, springs from almost all races in Europe and Asia, now so intermixed that many occultists express the opinion that a new race is being developed.

In this work we have adhered as far as possible to the terminology used by the original authors, identifying our additions and modifications of the original by parenthetical expression of our views and experience. Too many authors seem to have "borrowed" from Dr. Simmonite without indicating their source material, thus basing all interpretation upon the environment of mid-Nineteenth Century environment. It should always be remembered that all astrological interpretation **must** be made in the light of environment — environment of all kinds — and the middle of the Twentieth Century is a long, long way from that of the middle of the Nineteenth Century.

This work is therefore presented with a view of being of some little assistance to students of Horary Astrology through standing on the mental shoulders of these giants of astro-lore and thus broadening our own horizons.

Ernest A. Grant

Washington, D.C.
A.D. 1950

PREFACE BY JOHN STORY

Reader, it gives me great pleasure to again publish this useful store of knowledge for the benefit of my fellowmen. The teaching and rules laid down in this book will assuredly benefit you with a little study and care. My task is now to issue to the world the Sixth Edition of "Horary Astrology," it being the true key to Scientific Prediction. The first edition was issued by the late Dr. W. J. Simmonite, M.D., Ph.D., who bid the world adieu in his Meteorological Almanack of 1862. The present volume has been very much enlarged, more than any of the former editions, and contains rules by which thousands of enquiries with regard to the future may be answered.

Let me give you one word of warning, viz.:—Exercise great care to select the right Ruler and Significator of the question propounded. This is the primary and fundamental rule, which, if violated or misunderstood, is the cause of so many of those false predictions which are taken as a basis for argument against the truth of Horary Astrology.

Astrology is the oldest and truest Science of which mankind has any knowledge, and whoso doubts its truth and reliability can prove it, if they will test it fairly and truthfully. Let them learn the nature and influence of the planets and their comingled influence in aspect to each other, then take these factors as their key and see if it will not unlock some of those serious problems which are always troubling unenlightened humanity. This is the Key to let you into Light; it will unlock those occult laws which, when once seen and understood, will bring with irresistible force such a revelation to your mind, that you will recognise it as the highest and truest that will ever be offered you on this sphere.

Look at the rapid strides Astrology has made since I republished the "Arcana of Astrology" in 1889, and this advance will continue while Neptune is in Gemini, the House of Mercury, the Ruler of Literature. Readers of my edition of the "Arcana" will remember my remarks upon this point.

Sincerely yours,
JOHN STORY

159 Cemetery Road
Sheffield, 1896

INTRODUCTION

Horary Astrology, which the author has more palatably denominated **Prognostic Astronomy**, is the sublime art of foreseeing events from the position of the heavenly bodies, the stars—which were made by Omnipotence for "**signs** of things to come, and for seasons, and for days, and for years"—at the moment the **question** is seriously propounded, or when an individual may be non-hypocritically anxious about any **important** matter, the result of any business, or any circumstance on the tapis with which he may be connected. And if the party be not an artist himself, he may by the succinct, perspicuous, and correct rules in this book, solve any question which comes within the jurisdiction of Judicial Astrology. This part of the science of Astral Philosophy is the easiest understood, and the most advantageous to mankind.

The Art of solving Horary Questions is founded upon those inexplicable or miraculous **sympathetic** properties which are universally found to exist more or less throughout the natural creation. Of these wonder-striking sympathies, there can be no doubt in the philosophic mind; but the **vegetive** soul of the world invisibly carries, and inseparably unites a specific virtue from the starry heavens between one thing and another, which goes under the nickname of **gravitation**, ever working those secret efforts, which no reflective mind can fail to warmly admire. In the present case, who is to determine what this soul cannot effect between the heavenly bodies and the animal spirit of man? working such uniform sympathies, as that a question of importance cannot start from the mind, but in a sympathetic point of time at which the planets and signs of the zodiac governing the person's birth, and acting upon the very subject that engages the thoughts and attention. Hence, the birth of the question carries the story of the whole matter in hand on its forehead! And hence, also, follows that skill in natural prediction by which the artist can satisfy, by the rules in this book, those doubts to which the mind of every man is more or less subject; by this simple and easy, but beautiful theory, as well as Abiathar the priest was by the stars of the ephod, which presumes that the same sympathetic power which causes the iron and magnet to approach each other—the waters to approach the luminaries—the planets to revolve in circles around the central god of day—which influences the needle to point to the earth's magnetic pole—which, by occult sympathy, influences the unborn foetus in the womb, and produces corresponding marks with the mother's wants and fears—the same sympathetic instinct which induces the child to approach the nipple—which induces animals to feel the approach of danger; also changes in the atmosphere, and thus to foretell rain. The same occult influence which drives the frantic herd about the pastures,, which affects the brain of the maniac, or which, circulating through all living nature, pervading all, disquieting all, even to the minutest swarms that fall in the heavy dews, when the sky means to lower, this universal sympathy is neither more nor less than the **powerful influence of the heavenly**

bodies, and is the **first** pervading cause of every anxious and ardent doubt to which the mind is subject, or upon which the mind dwells with eagerness and desire, if possible, to know the result. All instinct is but sympathy, and the same common affinity between various parts of matter, which induces rats to forsake a falling house; ants to quit their nests, carrying their young with them, before an inundation; dogs to foretell disasters by strange barkings and whinings, will enable a human being to propose a horary question at the very moment the heavens are particularly disposed to give a correct solution. Such was the feeling of David when in Keilah, where he heard that Saul was coming to besiege him, was desirous of knowing the truth, whether Saul was coming or not; and if he was, **whether the men of Keilah would be true to him, or would betray him.** And being informed they would betray him into the hands of his enemy, who was seeking his life, he fled into the wilderness of Ziph, and escaped the danger that was impending over him. Hence, Nature, in this case, is always found to accommodate herself to every emergency, by a chart of the heavens, cast at the moment when the desire is most ardent, and the querent possessed of faith on the subject. For we know **all persons,** who have any provisional care, or honest, honourable concern for themselves and others, are desirous to know, nay, frequently wonder with tremulous expectations, what shall be the event, or end, of this or that undertaking. The true issue can be known, as this Work will prove satisfactorily when solved by the rules herein. And there is nothing, be it remembered, in it, either of **black art,** or **white art,** or any other **art,** than the **Art of Truth,** consequently neither angelical nor diabolical, meritorious nor criminal, good nor evil. A person is equally as justifiable in making an enquiry in one thing as another; and to propose a horary question is an act as indifferent in itself as to ask what o'clock it is, or does it rain, that I may provide myself to go out in it so as to escape detriment. This contains nothing supernatural or devilish; for it is nature itself, operating in its usual way.

Sectarian bigots, ignorant enthusiasts, and religious hypocrites, say it is wrong to wish to know what shall befall them in this or that undertaking at a future day. Let us ask, have you not anxious desires about your future prosperity or adversity? Has not the Omniscient Creator implanted those desires? And has He not contrived and provided a supply for all our moderate wants and enquiries? And if it be essential to man's welfare to be forewarned of "the time and the judgment," that the **wise man** shall know it, that he may not be overtaken with difficulties, so as to wrong his neighbour and his friend by cheating him of his honest claim—as many religious cants, who are willing to follow blind and deceptive chance, which they blasphemously call "providence," have done within the circle of our acquaintance. These have heaved at a gnat and swallowed a camel. When they embark with their neighbour's property, let them ask what the "signs of heaven" say will be the result, and then let prudence and common moral honesty and modesty be the reins of their procedure, and then they will reflect honour on the cause of God, instead of stigma and reproach.

Very probably the medium through which the influential sympathy operates, and which causes distant portions of matter to operate on each other, may be a very fine subtle fluid, emanating through infinite space, wholly imperceptible, excepting by its efforts, and thus apparently **unaccountable**, were it not attributable to celestial agency; but which, to a believer in Astrology, appears nothing more than the ordinary and unerring laws of nature. Thus, this species of prognostication, notwithstanding the silly, commonplace gibes of imitative witlings, and the foolish ridicule of self-conceited egotists, the tyranny of priestcraft, the ignorance of godly bigots, is really founded on the same immutable laws to which the universe at large is subject.

As to the absurd and foolish idea that it is superstitious, unlawful, or sinful to study Astrology, a moment of unprejudiced and wise reflection will convince to the contrary. Prediction is deduced in a demonstrable way, according to a certain chain of causes, which, for ages past, have been found uniformly to produce a correspondent train of effects. Where, then, consists its sinfulness, or its superstition, since the whole system is founded on the result of actual observation? If Astrology, which foretells future events by the course of the stars, is either sinful or unlawful, so were the labours of the celebrated Halley, Kepler, Herschel, and others, who nightly pored over the starry heavens, gauging the firmament in search of discoveries; and alike unlawful are the labours of the present Astronomers Royal; so is the prediction of the return of a comet. Equally sinful is the calculation and anticipated eclipse of the luminaries. The Horary Figure is nothing more nor less than a chart or representation of the heavens on a flat piece of paper, and planets placed therein, and there is nothing sinful in this, any more than in the innocent young lady representing the face of the heavens at any hour on the celestial globe; and by predicting from the said configurations of the heavenly bodies, the Artist does but verify and fulfil that passage of the sacred Scriptures, which positively declares that the stars and planets were created and placed in the firmament for "**signs**" of that which should afterwards come to pass.

The Almighty Creator gave the Babylonians notice of the "**signs**" of their destruction; "For **the stars of heaven,** and the constellations thereof, shall not give their light; **the sun shall be darkened in his going forth**"; that is, shall be eclipsed, "**and the moon shall not cause her light to shine.**" (Isaiah xiii, 9, 10) This evidently meant the luminaries were eclipsed in the zodiacal sign **Virgo,** which ruled Babylon, as noticed in this work. And the fearful fall of Egypt was prognosticated by the same species of "**heavenly signs,**" which He knew the Egyptian Astronomers well understood: for "when I shall put thee out I will cover the heaven and make the stars thereof dark; **I will cover the sun with a cloud, and the moon shall not give her light.**" The "bright lights," that is, the sun and the moon, which, at the creation, God called the "**two great lights,**" "will I make dark over thee." (Ezekiel xxxii, 7, 8) Are not the behests of providence effected by means? Did not God wish them to understand these precursors of their calamity? If not, why did He use them? If such investigations are sinful now, they were sinful then, and God was the author of such sins. But, sceptic, do not charge the Almighty with folly; "let God be true, though every man a liar." The judgments which fell upon Zion, were predicted by the eclipse of the sun, and the moon, and the stars withdrawing their shining (Joel ii, 10, 30 and 31). "**I shall show wonders in the heavens and in the earth**, blood, and fire, and pillars of smoke; **the sun shall be turned into darkness,** and the moon into blood, before the great and terrible day of the Lord." (Mark xiii, 24, 25; Luke xxi, 25)

The Astrologers of the East understood the "sign," or "the star," which acted as the heavenly messenger of the "Birth of the Holy Child Jesus." And the heathen philosophers, who were all Astrologers, told the heathen world, when they saw the extraordinary eclipse of the sun at Christ's crucifixion, "that the world was about to be destroyed," or the God of Nature suffered. These Astrologers were many thousand miles from the "hill of Cavalry" at the same time. The end of the world, or Christ's second coming, will be prognosticated as follows: "the sun shall be darkened, and the moon shall not give her light," etc. (Matthew xxiv, 29, 30)

Surely after such authority as the foregoing, we shall not find many who will charge the Astrologers with sinning while contemplating such phenomena as above, nor deny the portents of the "signs of heaven." Yet I know there are some narrow-minded bigots who make man a sinner for a word—a race of unhappy fidgety mortals, "under Mercury afflicted," who with loud boastings about morals and religion, go about to condemn every look, word, action, and opinion, that squares not with their narrow, misconceived and selfish views of things. You must walk with them, or walk out of the world; for they are **perfectly right**—you must say their *shibboleth*—you must subscribe to their articles—you must observe their observances—you must kneel at their altars, bow to their gods, and listen to their councils, or you cannot be happy here, nor prepare happiness hereafter. They have chalked out a line of duty so narrow that neither themselves nor others can walk in it with safety. They, therefore, pass through life as if the ground on which they tread was composed of nothing but bogs and quagmires, and as if the azure aspect of the heavens was absolutely injurious to their sight. Could we follow them into the hidden haunts of their own hearts we should there see what sinuosities, what serpentinings, what obliquities of feelings, views, and principles, what secret longings, what mixtures and contradictions, make up their characters! Here we should detect the demon of pride lording it over the soul; there the little imps of envy and malignity riot in wantonness through the whole system. All this can never escape the experimental Astro-Philosopher, who will stand aloof from having dealings with them, and expose them and their base insinuations to the understanding of those they designingly, though "as angels of light" in appearance, wish to victimize.

Far be it from the author to suppose that there are no truly virtuous objectors to our science. I know there are many; some who think that, were it fully established in society, it might be dangerous; and others imagine that they disbelieve it altogether. But, as Sir G. Mackenzie observes, "of many who say that they do not believe in the possibility of foretelling future events, I have known few on whom it had not a very sensible effect." Those who reject the science on account of its supposed dangerous tendency, do not sufficiently reflect that no science, having its basis in truth, can really be dangerous. But what if bad men should apply it to bad purposes, is it more than is done with almost every other art or science? Have not the arts of engraving, and of good penmanship, been productive of forgery? Have not the fine arts been used for the purpose of Idolatry, and of obscenity? Has not religion its hypocrites, who use it as a cloak for their licentiousness? Have not some men prayed themselves into bigots, and others philosophized themselves into atheists?

Those who reject Astrology as an idle dream and an illusion have never seriously applied their minds to the study of it. They have entertained wrong impressions respecting its pretensions; and have imagined that the science professes to teach **more** than it really does. They have never been able to erect a figure of the heavens at any required moment of time. They know not the date on which the predictions are based. They have never watched the baneful influences of Saturn afflicting the eastern horizon; nor the benignant operations of Jupiter upon others; nor the bad aspects of their own Mercury with Uranus and the Moon. They have their Mars vitiated by aspect of Uranus, which have declared in them a certain portion of querulousness, mixed with no small share of ignorance, arrogance, and envy, eternally prompting them to find fault with what they do not understand. These persons, unwilling to be thought ignorant of any thing, pretend to be familiarly conversant with every thing; and they imagine they manifest their superlative shrewdness and incomparable dexterity by a sort of wholesale dealing in notes of interrogation. Thinking, as they do, that they individually are the emporium of knowledge, they grant nothing to their opponent; they concede no point; they admit to positions, not even for the sake of argument; they are mighty dexterous at a syllogism in their own favour; but uniformly reject the minor, the major, and the *ergo,* from every other quarter. They are generally, smatterers in some art, or dabblers in some science; and having acquired a string of technicalities, never fail to pour out a most abundant portion of them into the ears of those who may not happen to make any particular science their study. But ask these persons a question, even in their own favourite study, and for the most part the answer will be an expression of astonishment at your ignorance; but you must not look for a definite answer; most assuredly you will be disappointed if you calculate upon deriving any information of real utility from them. Are these the individuals to decide upon a question of so momentous, so profoundly philosophical, so invaluable to each man, to the millions of society, nay, to the whole world, as Astrology? a science based upon the fabric of creation; which has employed the master mind of a Ptolemy, a Thales, a Plato, a Virgil, a Kepler, a Newton, a Davy, and thousands more, whose names are immortalized by men of talent. Let those who wish to explode the science first cast their own horoscopes, or prove, from some authenticated nativity, that there is no truth in Astrology; then, and not till then, will we listen to their pompous assertions against the science; but by the time they are capable of performing the above requirement they will be fully convinced of its truth, and become converts to the doctrines which they formerly condemned.

Neither should the occasional failures of some of its professors afford any argument against the science. We are aware that to juggling nonsense and knavery of some of its professors this science owes much of the odium under which it labours. But men do not condemn the Scriptures merely because heresies, and heretical schisms, have arisen therefrom; nor do they deny the art of the physician through his own inefficiency; nor explode the whole science of chemistry, merely because the chemist fails in some of his analytical experiments. Why, then, should Astrology alone, which, of all other sciences, claims the most serious and undivided attention, become the butt of incredulity through the sins of some of its professors? Let the student make his opponents answer that question before he proceeds to argue with them. They say it is superstitious. Ask the caviller—what is **superstition**? And not one in a thousand can give you the import of the word "superstition." These are learned enemies, forsooth! They are butts for ridicule and laughter. The science has been used by designing persons as a kind of **fortune-telling** system; hence, old women of no education take it up, and some who have pretended to understand it have affected great wisdom and sagacity, great foresight and knowledge. Hence they have been regarded as a species of necromancers, objects of fear and wonder to the ignorant, of disdain and contempt to the wise and discerning. Astrology has nothing in common with magic, or any like crafty art. It deals not in mystery; for mystery and truth are, for the most part, at enmity with each other.

The true and educated Astrologer scorns all idea of secrecy in his science; those who entertain a contrary feeling know nothing about it, whilst he proceeds by certain rules, which all men may learn if they will take the pains; though he makes no pretensions of infallibility, or perfection, entirely in his Astronomical judgment, and does not hold himself accountable for the ill use which evil-disposed persons may make of these rules. His skill in Astral science, like real skill in every other branch of useful knowledge, has a direct tendency to promote a spirit of moderation and reserve; of caution and prudence, incompatible with the arrogance and presumption of either a mere pretender or an opponent.

The Author looks forward to no very distant day when stellar doctrines shall have acquired that stability of character and utility as to **again**, as in days of genuine philosophy, entitle it to universal reception, and when its advantages shall be looked to as the main auxiliaries of sound morals, rational philosophy, and true religion.

In the meantime its present indefatigable disciples, advocates, and admirers will be content to have the sneers, the contempt, the ill nature, and the ignorance of its adversaries; and guarding against precipitation on one hand and inattention and indifference on the other, will not fail to make those observations on men and manners; on cause and effect; on signs and correspondencies, as shall confirm them in principles, and endear them to the practice of Astro-Philosophical investigations.

Advice to Students

1. During your studies in the Astrologic Lore you will come in contact with wiseacres who will ask you silly questions, but take Solomon's advice, and "answer a fool according to his folly, lest he be wise in his own conceit."

2. You will soon perceive that your opponents are persons of little knowledge, or great prejudice with very small capacities, and almost incapable of reflection, without any original thoughts, or indeed any thoughts at all but what they have borrowed, and such as have made few observations of their own respecting themselves or the universe in general; men who are either absorbed in other speculations than those of nature, or who think only by permission; who would believe the legend and deny the existence of the antipodes, if others about them did the same. With them the *vox populi* is truly the *vox Dei*, while they *in toto* despise or turn a deaf ear to the *vox stellarum*. The only argument capable of convincing them is a great show of hands, and any absurd hypothesis, having the major part of the world on its side, would soon add them to the number of its disciples. But exercise your discriminating powers, and you will soon perceive that "Every prudent **man** dealeth with knowledge, but a fool will lay open his folly." (Proverbs xiii, 16)

3. You will sometimes meet with antagonists who will quote the opinions of learned men, but let them know that learning is not always united with discernment, nor real knowledge, any more than the words of a talking bird are united with ideas. Learning is a mechanical acquirement, and may be possessed by a very silly person, and of this we have numberless instances. With such men reason is useless: they would oppose custom to reason, and authorities to facts. You have the better of the world, if the opinions of great, good, learned men are to settle the question of its truth or otherwise. You have all ancient philosophers of note, physicians, astronomers, poets, mathematicians, divines, judges, kings, prophets, and patriarchs, on your side.

You have **Scripture** authorities:

Adam	Enoch	Heber	Joseph	Samuel
Seth	Methuselah	Peleg	Solomon	Daniel
Enos	Lamach	Nachor	Moses	Shadrach
Mahaleel	Noah	Abraham	Kenan	Meshach
Jared	Shem	Isaac	Tharach	Abednego
Jacob				Deborah

You have renowned **Physicians** on your side, as

Hypocrates	Partridge	Culpepper	Mathiolus	Agrippa
Avicenna	Diocles	Starkey	Foster	Gilbert
Cardanus	Bertrucius	Galen	John Dee	Dodoneus
Salmon	Gesnerus		Fernelius	Dioscorides

You can boast of immortal **Poets**, as

Homer	Pope	Addison	Lucan	Ovid
Hesiod	Pindarus	Horace	Milton	Aratus
Byron	Terentius	Propertius	Pezeliu	Shakespeare
Dryden	Persius	Horatius	Virgil	Ranzorius

You have a host of **Philosophers**, as

Anaxagoros	Naibod	Moore	Lilly	Zanocrates
Plato	Scaliger	Democritus	Tyaneus	Nostradamus
Demosthenes	Senneca	Tibertus	Locke	Ptolemy
Aristotle	Lucian	Ramus	Hipparchus	Bonatus
Possidonus	Macrobius	Pliny	Quintillian	Bacon
Cicero	Simmonides	Porphyry	Phauorinus	Meton
Anaximander	Thales		Heydon	Socrates

You have on your side **Historiographers**, as

Heroditus	Livy	Josephus	Berosus	Dion Cassius
Diodorus	Suetoneous	Philostratus	Zenophon	Mela
Diogenius	Tacitus	Polybius	Maximus	Plutarch
Suidas	Camben, and thousands more whom we could name.			

You have in your train **Christian Reformers**, as

Brentius	Luther	Zanchius	Seranus	Melancthon
Beza	Chitreus	Moringus	Oslander	Calvin
Musculus	Pintus	Bishop Hall	Cardan	J. Usher

and many others too numerous to mention in this synod of unquestionable talent and piety, who were zealous promoters of truth, wherever it could be found and exposed to the keen investigation of experience.

You have the greatest **Astronomers** that ever lived, as

Ptolemy	Napier	Kepler	Copernicus	Flamstead
Witchel	Brahe	Pythagoras	Galileo	Descartes
Wing				Newton

and an innumerable multitude of **fixed stars** of science and authority, whose names will live till the earth itself shall be dissolved, and whose discoveries shall be a boon to society as long as man shall exist. Can any other science boast of such names? No. Can the sceptic place in your hands such a list of learned men as opponents? All these themselves were Astrologers. You can proudly boast of having kings on your side of the question, as David, Alfred the Great, the Charleses, Cromwell, Napoleon, and the kings named in the sacred volume. We have pursued our catalogue sufficiently far to outweigh the scale of your opponents' authority of great men. What myriads of men have no other ground of tenets than the supposed honesty, or learning, or number of those of the same profession? But where is the original mind that does not examine, weigh, and concludingly establish himself on well-tried principles? Catechise these and they give a reason for assent, but will by the **non-originals** be considered eccentric or foolish. Oh, man, think for thyself. Let no self-interest and opinionated leaders or partisans decide for thee! Take St. Paul's advice, and **"Prove all things and hold fast that which is good."** How many will you meet with who are resolved to stick to a party in which education or interest has engaged them, and there, like the common soldiers of an army, show their courage and warmth as their leaders direct, without ever examining or so much as knowing the cause for which they contend. It is enough for most poor creatures to obey their leaders, to have their hands and their tongues, and, we may add their purses also, ready for the support of the common cause, and thereby approve themselves to those who can give them credit, preferment, or protection in that society. Ah! this mammon in all its hideous forms!

4. You must avoid the assaults of prejudice and mistake, till experience and matter-of-fact shall silence gainsayers and stop the mouth of ignorance. Be not dismayed when evil spoken of, for **"wisdom resteth in the heart of him that hath understanding, but that which is in the mouth of fools is made known."** So you perceive that your enemies no sooner open their mouths in railing, but you will easily judge what they are—what Solomon calls them. Beware of pride and self-conceit, yet never forget your dignity. Be humble and let no natural knowledge elate your minds so far as to withdraw you from your duty to that divine Providence, by whose omniscient order and appointment all things heavenly and earthly have their constant motion, but the more your knowledge is enlarged by this comprehensive science, the more you must endeavour to magnify the power and the wisdom of the Almighty God, and strive to preserve yourselves in "His favour which is better than life," having in constant remembrance that the nearer to holiness you are, the nearer your approach to God in your religious duties, the purer judgment you will always give.

5. When a question is asked, you must take it for granted that no more is meant than is asked, **and not frame questions** and asnwers **of your own.** This will not agree or sympathize with the mind of the querent, and will consequently be false prediction. Everything, however, sincerely propounded, may be answered by the same figure. Let no worldly consideration procure an erroneous judgment from you, or such as may dishonour this sacred science. Afflict not the unfortunate with the terrors of severe issue, in such cases inform them of their adverse fortune with sympathetic concern, direct them to call upon Divine assistance to avert the ill-fortune through which they have to pass.

PREFACE BY W. J. SIMMONITE, M.D., Ph.D.

A Work on **Horary Astrology** has long been a desideratum with the Students of the Astral Science. They are furnished with the object of their need. It will be found an excellent and intelligible Text Book to all my other treatises; both those bearing my name and others which I have issued bearing other names.

This small work is unshackled from prolix, conflicting rules and aphorisms. All the rules are founded upon the Author's extensive and experimental practice for twenty years; consequently may be confidently relied upon for their simplicity, conspicuity, and, above all, their variety.

As to the opponents against the science we shall say nothing here, but refer them to our Introduction, and advise those who deny its truth first to understand it; for by the time they understand they will be convinced of its truth, which truth will for ever silence them as its foes, and convert them to its doctrines, and irresistibly compel them to become its advocates.

One of the chief features of utility of this volume is, that any young lady or gentleman who is merely a tyro in scholastic acquirements may with ease surmount the apparent difficulties by a very few weeks' study, and convince himself, her self, and others, of the feasibility of foretelling the result of any important undertaking or event. In short, I may say, here is a Work which will on the one hand enable the student to silence the opponents against a Science which has outlived the lash of critics and the Bulls of the Church; and, further, teach the sincere inquirers after Astral Truths the verity of that Art, which shall stand the test of philosophic investigation and scrutiny when the world is on fire and art shall cease.

Nothing more than this volume and Astronomical Ephemerides, published annually, is required for the student to practise Horary Astrology, or answer his own or his friends' sincere questions.

That it may serve the cause of truth, and bring the reader nearer to the mind of that Being who rules the Stars, is the sincere wish of

THE AUTHOR

PROGNOSTIC ASTRONOMY
or
HORARY ASTROLOGY

1. The Zodiac being the great circle of the Sphere, is divided into 360 degrees, each degree into 60 minutes, each minute into 60 seconds, thirds, etc. (The Zodiac is not the only "great circle." As used in this sense, it means the "maximum" or "largest," viz., the circle of the meridian—to nadir and back again—or of the horizon—ascendant to descendant and back again—are "great" circles.")

2. Every Sign contains 30 of those degrees; thus, 12 Signs complete the Zodiac.

The Twelve Signs

♈ Aries	opposite to	♎ Libra
♉ Taurus	opposite to	♏ Scorpio
♊ Gemini	opposite to	♐ Sagittarius
♋ Cancer	opposite to	♑ Capricorn
♌ Leo	opposite to	♒ Aquarius
♍ Virgo	opposite to	♓ Pisces

3. There are also ten other bodies, called planets (although one of these, the Sun, is actually a fixed star, and the Moon is a satellite of the Earth); their symbols are:

♇ Pluto   ♅ Uranus   ♃ Jupiter   ☉ Sun   ☿ Mercury
♆ Neptune   ♄ Saturn   ♂ Mars   ♀ Venus   ☽ Moon

4. The Asteroids are:

    Vesta   Juno   Pallas   Ceres

(These are apparently segments of a planet which once held its orbit between those of Mars and Jupiter. Little credence, if any, is given to their influence upon things terrestrial.)

5. There are other points which must be considered, viz., ☊ The Dragon's Head, or Moon's North Node; ☋ The Dragon's Tail, or Moon's South Node; ⊕ The Part of Fortune.

Aspects

6. **The Conjunction ☌**: The ☌ is when two planets have the **same** geocentric longitude. This aspect is found to be good with good planets, but evil with evil planets. Its effects are strong in all cases.

7. **The Semi-sextile S⚹**: The semi-sextile is moderately fortunate and slightly beneficial. It consists of 30 degrees, or one sign of the zodiac; thus, suppose ♃ in 4° of ♈, and ♀ in 4° of ♉ or ♓, they would be S⚹ of each other.

8. **The Semi-square S☐ 45°**: This aspect is evil in signification with all or any of the planets, and is nothing inferior to the square.

9. The Sextile ✶ 60°: This aspect is formed when the planets are two signs distant from each other, or 60° apart, and is of a benign influence, not much inferior to the Trine.

10. The Quartile (or Square) ☐ 90°: The ☐ is a distance of three signs, or 90° asunder. It is an aspect peculiarly evil, and seldom can its malign influence be lessened by the interposition of more friendly rays.

11. The Trine △ 120°: The Trine aspect is 120° distant, or four signs between two heavenly bodies, and is indicative of good.

12. The Sesquisquare SS☐ 135°: The SS☐ is unfortunate and equally malign to the S☐; it is a ray of 135°; thus, supposing a star is 19° of ♑ and another is 4° of ♍, they are in sesquiquadrate.

13. The Opposition ☍ 180°: The ☍ is when two planets are 180° distant, or just half the space of the zodiac apart, which places them in diametrical radiation. This is an evil and unfortunate aspect.

These are the most notable and powerful configurations; and though there are others of minor importance, yet I refrain from mentioning them, as they are of very little moment in Horary Astronomy.

Orbs of Application

14. It is very seldom at the time a question is proposed that all the aspects which appear are each perfectly composed of their **exact** number of degrees. In such cases they are still in aspect as long as they continue within the moiety, or equal **half** part of their **united orbs**. This is called a **platic** aspect, in contradistinction to a **partile**, or perfect aspect; that is, when two planets or two significators are in the same degree of their respective signs, and it is necessary to observe these platic aspects whether the cooperation of the two planets is going off or coming on, as that will materially affect the matter under consideration.

Rule: Add the orbs of the two planets together, and take one-half of the sum; if the planets are beyond that distance, they are not then even in platic aspect.

Example: Suppose ♄ in 15° of ♈, and ♀ in 10°, they are then in platic aspect; for the orb of ♄ is 9°, and that of ♀ 7°, added to 9 equal 16, the half of which is 8; so they are within orb at 8° distant, and in like manner of the other planets.

The number of degrees each planet extends an influence round its body is: ♀ 5°, ♅ 7°, ♄ 9°, ♃ 9°, ☉ 15°, ♂ 7°, ♀ 7°, ☿ 7°, ☽ 15°.

Thus, ♀, which is placed first, applies to no planet except he be Retrograde; ♆ applies only to ♀; ♅ applies only to ♀ and ♆; ♄ applies only to ♀, ♆, and ♅; ♃ applies only to ♀, ♆, ♅, ♄; and so of the rest in order, as may be seen (article 3). The ☽, who is placed last, applies to all the planets as she moves round the earth in about 27-1/3 days; but no planet applies to the Moon except that planet be retrograde, and then it is called **mixed application** (or mutual application).

Persons Described by the 12 Signs

(While the following is set forth as for signs on the Ascendant, it is equally applicable to the persons represented by the various houses in Horary Astronomy. For example, should the question relate to a person represented by the IIId house, then following the descriptions herein given, the sign on that house cusp would indicate that person, and similarly for any of the other houses.)

15. ♈ ascending at the time of birth, or of a question, and uninfluenced by any planet in the Ascendant, produces a person of a dry, lean, spare body, rather tall, strong limbs, large bones, thick broad shoulders, long face, sharp piercing sight, dark heavy eye-brows, reddish and wiry hair, freckled complexion, and neck rather long. Disposition good and agreeable; temper hasty, but soon over or appeased; witty, ingenious, and quick of apprehension.

(The general physical characteristics of Aries on the Ascendant are a person of average height, sometimes slightly above; long face and neck, with bushy eyebrows; head broader at temples and tapering towards chin; eyes generally gray or grayish brown, often large and prominent, wiry dark hair, with a slight tendency to grow thin at the temples. The first Facet (5°) of Aries produces a person of slender build, average height, swarthy complexion, broad face with high cheek bones, dark reddish hair. The second Facet produces one of heavier build, long face and black hair. The third Facet gives good features, with dark complexion and medium build. The fourth Facet gives a well-proportioned body of youthful appearance, with dark brown hair, sometimes streaked with auburn. The fifth Facet produces the shortest of the Aries types, dark complexion, long face and bright eyes. The sixth Facet gives well-developed body, strong features, and generally dark curly hair.

By disposition the first Decanate (10°) produces the pioneer type who hews the pathway for mankind to follow. The first Facet makes him fearless, active and bright; ability for leadership. ingenious. The second Facet gives a resentful attitude; frequently conceited; vacillating fortune; but showy or consequential. Brings trouble upon self.

The second Decanate produces a person with a proud nature and great ambition for personal attainment. The third Facet is serious, grave, intellectual and thoughtful; they are often orators and love fame. The fourth Facet, covering the true exaltation position of the Sun makes these natives generous and refined, competent and brave; their noble spirit is indicstive of the finer natures of both Aries and the Sun; they have great tact and a sharp keen intellect with good commercial instincts.

The third Decanate produces the good scholar and teacher who possesses wisdom. Malefically aspected, these characteristics may be turned to evil purposes, for sometimes (fifth Facet) they are somewhat contrary and impulsive, or (sixth Facet) brave, indifferent to danger, but rash. Under favorable influences the sixth Facet is indicative of an ambitious and aspiring person; gains some through impulsive action.)

16. Pluto in each of the 12 signs has not, at this writing been finally determined. It will probably take a full revolution of this planet in astro-experience—sum 240 years—before final determinations can be adequately made. However, one of the finest published researches on this planet is that by Brunhubner. He has stated the following concerning this mysterious body:

("Physical: Middle to tall stature; full, oval, however, sometimes slightly angular face; stately, often pretty appearance; inclined to be corpulent; strongly developed nose, bushy eyebrows; very hairy body, lustrous, often fascinating eyes; sometimes sinister eyes; robust, great resistance, strong life-force, strong magnetism. The most important characteristic of this type is the sensuous expression, which, however, shows a certain refinement. This is the type in whose facial expression one can recognize the struggle of the two regimes—matter and spirit—in about the following manner: the lower third of the head signifies the material, the base; while in the upper two-thirds the spiritual reception already is breaking forth (polar influence of Pluto).

("Psychical: Pluto acts especially strong upon the psyche—the native is serious, morose, scheming, brooding, pondering, burrowing, with a melancholic tendency. If in harmonious aspect, he is pensive and joyful, but in inharmonious aspects, he is brooding, morose, penetrative, very reserved and taciturn. Further, such natives are passionate, sensual, covetous, always demanding, desirous, insatiable, fanatical, full of longings, peculiarities; extreme or contrary in emotional things; irresistible; are filled with a strong urge to have experiences of life; unrestraint, arrogance, ambition, obstinacy, envy, mistrust, jealousy, skepticism, pugnacious. They have sudden fits of anger, are self-tormentors, and irreconcilable; are foolhardy and fearless.)

("Mental: These natives have a desire for authority, lust of power, qualification for leadership. They are born critics with acute, outspoken ability to differentiate; outstandingly analytical; fair arbitrators, with strong suggestive personalities.")

17. Neptune in Signs will be like Venus.

(More modern research makes us disagree with Dr. Simmonite on this score. Neptune in Aries does not change the pure Aries type to an appreciable extent, except that the eyes seem to have a dreamy look and much of the healthy appearance of Aries seems to be missing. Instead of a ruddy complexion, it is more pallid. The disposition goes from one extreme to the other. It either lifts a person to the heights or casts him down. The position of Mars must be carefully noted for the lower side of its influence gives the unscrupulous liar, resourceful to the extreme and ready to undertake anything for notoriety. The higher side of the influence gives success in every undertaking of life.)

18. Uranus in ♈, or on the cusp of the house signifying the **quesited**, denotes one rather tall, auburn hair, thin in appearance, a little colour in the face, eccentric and hasty temper, and one that remembers an affront a long time; fond of learning, inquisitive, and one that does not marry early in life; given to

novels and writing; a worker in wood, an artificer, inventor, and fond of farming and cattle.

(Our experience is that Uranus produces a tall, thin, well made person, with ruddy complexion, and an active body. It gives the character great originality. The mind is very positive and not easy to overcome. They are masterful persons and born leaders of thought. Sometimes this position of ♅ leads to selfishness. Always champions of individual freedom, these natives often become revolutionists.)

19. Saturn, a significator in ♈, declares one moderate in stature, dark ruddy complexion, high forehead, good intellect, rather full eyes, dark hair, not much beard or whisker, a spare body, strong voice; given to boasting; morose, a retainer of anger; crafty, and not easily imposed upon; fond of disputation and contention, and in this he generally proves conqueror.

(Saturn in Aries produces an exceedingly clever person by his own standards. They have great ambition and will find a way in which to make themselves leaders. The positions of Sun and Mars should be carefully noted to determine whether their character will be lofty or low. It is not wise to offend these people.)

20. Jupiter in ♈ denotes a middle stature, ruddy, oval visage, light brown hair, quick piercing eyes, high nose, and often freckles or pimples on the face; a very obliging person, of a noble, free disposition; industrious; a lover of peace and tranquility. The person follows some respectable calling in life; sometimes a respectable farmer, corn dealer, or one connected with architecture, or a seller of articles over the counter.

(Jupiter here indicates one of a noble, loving disposition. It is indicative of a great benefactor for all who seek his friendship. The martian spirit is completely overcome by this position of Jupiter for they despise discord, quarreling and contention. They are fond of traveling. Their greatest weakness is a tendency to pride and egotism.)

21. Mars in ♈ portends a native of a middle size, large bones, well set, furrowed or wrinkled forehead, bold fierce countenance, rather sunburnt complexion; sandy hair, sharp blue or grey eyes, often a mark or mole above the nose, ambitious of rule, a lover of war and contest, yet generous and free spirited; ready apprehension, active fancy, and often fortunate. The natives make good butchers, druggists, smiths, and all or any business connected with fire. Combativeness large.

(Mars, of course, accentuates the ♈ character and gives a determined, resolute, daring disposition. Their self-confidence makes them care for nothing or nobody. They must be first in spite of the consequences. They are good fighters and love war. Their boundless energy and active minds and great resourcefulness makes them great pioneers of materialistic and worldly enterprise. The body is strong built, but rather bony, with a swarthy complexion and either red or sandy curly hair.)

22. The Sun in ♈ portends a middle stature, strong and well made, good

complexion, though not very clear, yellow or flaxen hair, and full eyes; one of noble disposition, full of courage and valour, delighting in warlike deeds, and gaining victory; formidable to his enemies; he raises himself in society, but is rather proud.

23. Venus or Neptune in ♈ represents a middle stature, but slender (we do not agree with this concerning Neptune, which has little influence on the pure Aries type); light hair, good complexion, a pensive aspect, with a mark or scar in the face (Venus gives pimples and skin eruptions, rather than a scar); oval visage in the 15th and 16th degrees; a lover of company, often to the querent or quesited's detriment; inprovident and unfortunate; one not fond of fast employment, and does not continue long at one branch of business; apt to change for ease. Amativeness moderate, with foolish combativeness.

(Venus in this position gives the extravagant and wasteful person, fond of a good time, sports and gambling, in which he might be successful. While they are generally ruled by their partners, they are inconstant in love. Their inner ideals are lofty, but impractical.)

24. Mercury in ♈ gives a thin and middle stature, oval face, light brown and curling hair, dull complexion, except ☿ be in the 14th degree, then clear; one quarrelsome, discontented, lying, thievish, and contentious; but if ☿ be in good aspect with ♆, ♃, or ♀ and is not afflicted by ♅, ♄, or ♂, the disposition will be much improved. In the last 5 degrees, hollow cheeks, light eyebrows, and flattish nose. (Their manner is alert and 'jumpy.')

25. The Moon in ♈ personates a middle stature, rather plump round face, light brown hair, tolerably good complexion. In disposition, choleric and churlish, ambitious of honour, but not very fortunate; often changing residence, with various mutations in life. Men generally prosper most by speculating as hucksters, selling of eatables and fruit, and other articles of consumption.

(The Moon gives a thin body in early years, but much heavier in later years. They are self-opinionated, rash, eager and active. They have many ideas, but are not always truthful. Much depends on the position of the Sun and Mars.)

Of the Sign ♉

26. Taurus alone denotes a short, stout body, broad brows, large eyes, full face, thick lips, short neck, thick broad hands and shoulders, dark curling hair, swarthy complexion; brutal unfeeling, and violent; melancholy, slow to anger, but when once enraged difficult to please; large animal propensities; this happens if unaspected by stars of a contrary nature.

(The first Facet gives medium height, dark complexion, usually dark hair, with small round blue eyes. The second Facet gives a short body but more rugged and compact, with a full face but sometimes swarthy and ill-conditioned. The third Facet also gives a short body with rather disagreeable and poor features and sullen appearance. There is a tendency toward corpulence and the hair is thin. The fourth Facet gives a body of medium height or taller, of good form. These persons are often good-looking, of fair complexion with light brown hair.

The fifth Facet gives a poor body of medium stature; the complexion is sanguine and often lymphatic; the eyes are dark. The sixth Facet gives a nicely developed body of good form; the complexion is usually dark and the hair black.

(These Taurean natives have a determined, practical and unchanging character, laborious and sometimes slow, with an inclination to laziness. They are usually honest and acquisitive. Affection, sociability and faithfulness are among its finer characteristics, but in the lower nature they are haughty and proud. An aroused temper makes them unreasonable and prejudiced.)

(The first Decanate gives ambition for personal success, which usually comes late in life. The likes and dislikes are strong, but a fondness for ease and comfort remains always strong. The first Facet steadies the nature so that success comes through concentration and determined fixity of purpose. There is much discontentment. The second Facet gives the pouting nature; being exceedingly sensitive they frequently bring sorrow upon themselves. They are subject to despondency and occasionally are shifty and unsettled.)

(The second Decanate gives highly developed intuition, discrimination and practical business ability, but the blend of the Virgo influence with this decanate also gives a critical character. While the higher vibrations give fine character, keen appreciation and excellent ability in the commercial world, the lower vibrations cause the native to be over-acquisitive and selfish. The third Facet indicates one subject to many temptations in life. Although fine looking, they are careless and indifferent and may become envious and ill-natured. The fourth Facet often brings out the lower side of the second Decanate for energy and courage seem to be lacking unless strongly aroused. There may be some innate psychic power. The are often faithful, affectionate and loyal.)

(The third Decanate increases the intellectual ability at the expense of intuition. Ambition is greater, but the influence of early environment remains fixed throughout life. If the fifth Facet is indicated, these persons often have a tendency towards deception, subtlety and degeneration. They are selfish and lack conscientiousness. In the influence of the sixth Facet, difficulty is also found because of the looseness of character. Temperance in all things should be the motto of these persons for excesses and intemperance are strongly indicated.)

27. Concerning Pluto *see* article 16.

28. (Neptune in ♉ is one of its best positions for physical beauty. It gives a great charm and curiously winning smile. Taurus in itself has a certain inherent beauty which is further developed by ♆ .

29. Uranus in ♉ represents a person of mean stature, rather stout, not very handsome, dull complexion, and brown hair, large gustativeness, grey eyes, one somewhat conceited, fond of money; in actions, secret and eccentric.

(Uranus increases the height in all signs; in Taurus the person is at most of only medium stature, with dull dark complexion. The position of the Sun should be carefully noted in nativities. Uranus is an unfavorable influence here upon character unless it receives strong favorable influences from other planets. Its spasmodic action does not blend with the fixity of Taurus and thus stimulates unorthodoxy in the lower nature.)

30. Saturn in ♉ denotes a body heavy and clumsy, lobbing walk, dark hair, generally inclined to vicious actions; determinate in prosecuting any movement in connection with contention; destructiveness large.

(Saturn in this position gives an ungraceful, awkward and at times outright clumsy body with sallow complexion and dark hair. There is a strong materialistic tendency, with selfishness and a desire for gratification of the senses.)

31. Jupiter in ♉ personates a middle stature, stout and well-set body, strong and compact, not very handsome, brown curling hair, swarthy or yellow complexion; wise, discreet, free disposition, and humane, but a lover of the opposite sex. (Jupiter here gives material success.)

32. Mars in ♉ gives a middle stature, well set, dusky complexion, brown hair, which is rough or coarse, brown full face, and sometimes a mark or scar on the throat or face; a treacherous, false, dissembling person; gluttonous, luxurious, and debauched; given to gambling and betting wagers; generally fond of keeping ale houses, victualling houses, and other places of sportive amusement. Abusive amativeness.

(Mars here decreases the height, giving an obscure dark complexion with large mouth, broad face and dark hair. It gives a treacherous disposition, combative and war-like; they bring trouble to themselves and everyone with whom they are associated, unless the horoscope as a whole shows balance and highly developed moral qualities.)

33. The Sun in ♉ rather short, well set, dark complexion, wide mouth, broad face, Roman nose, strong and athletic. He or she is confident, has much self-esteem, and is not a little proud; delights in contention; having plenty of combativeness, generally becomes conqueror.

(The Sun in ♉ gives confidence without reason. The pure joy of overcoming and winning causes much strife for these persons. It gives great endurance. The body is short with a rather broad and fleshy face, large nose and mouth; the eyes are grey or hazel and the hair dull brown.)

34. Venus in ♉ denotes a comely person, mean stature, fleshy body, well made, ruddy complexion, dark eyes, but not clear, luxuriant brown hair, and of beautiful character; the temper is mild, winning and obliging, the disposition is kind, humane, and engaging, beloved by everyone, and generally fortunate. The native is often engaged in teaching, or selling articles across the counter, as drapery, grocery, confectionery, etc. If they are trades they follow those that are clean and ornamental, as joiners. Philoprogenitiveness good and **pure**.

(Venus in ♉ gives dark brown hair and blue or gray eyes; good moral character, with a kind and obliging disposition; they live largely for others and are held in high esteem.)

35. Mercury in ♉ gives a middle stature, corpulent, and well set, swarthy sunburnt complexion, short thick brown hair; in condition, slothful, gluttonous, and wanton; large gustativeness; fond of sexual intercourse, to his detriment and misfortune. He follows light and trifling callings by way of living.

(Mercury in ♉ is not a good position, for it slows up the mental processes and causes fanciful illusions.)

36. Moon in ♉ gives a corpulent, well set person, low middle stature, dull complexion, brown or black hair, but disposition mild, peaceable, ingenuous, obliging, and rather proud, but of sober carriage; just in all his actions, and consequently gains the respect of all with whom he is familiar; he also most easily attains preferment suitable to his station in life. Good developments of amativeness and philoprogenitiveness, especially if the Moon be unafflicted.

(The Moon in ♉ sometimes gives a short body, but usually one of medium height which is compact and well-proportioned. The skin is smooth, though sometimes dark, but the features are generally clear-cut and neat. Alan Leo tells us that this is probably one of the best positions for the Moon rising, especially when well aspected by Venus for "there is often a great comeliness and personal charm." The changeableness engendered by the Moon seems to disappear when it is found in this fixed position. The native is somewhat mooding, brooding frequently over fancied wrongs, and the feelings are very personal. It also accentuates the desire for ease and gives an indolent disposition if afflicted.)

Of the Sign ♊

37. Gemini represents a tall upright body, well set, complexion good, though not clear; bright eyes and good sight; long arms, fleshy hands and feet, strong chest, brown hair; acute wit, ingenious, a fluent tongue, apt discourse, but not very faithful, being in disposition fidgety, curious, petulant, changeable, light, and trifling.

The first Decanate of ♊ gives lighter hair than the rest of the sign, with the first Facet slightly darker than the second. The first Facet gives a slender build, dark complexion and shifty gait. The second Facet increases the size of the body, gives a good complexion and jovial expression. The third Facet produces a rather short body, very dark hair and ruddy complexion with soft features. The fourth Facet increases the bodily build, giving a refined appearance. The eyes are brilliant and the complexion clear. The fifth Facet gives a well-built body, tall and inclined to be slender. The face is narrow and has a sort of jaundice appearance, while the hair and eyes are both dark. The sixth Facet gives a well-formed body with good features. The complexion is usually pale and the hair dark and glossy.)

38. (Neptune rising in ♊ increases the height and gives the body a graceful appearance. The complexion is either light or pallid in appearance, the eyes are large and expressive. Sometimes it tends to corpulence. Neptune here also tends to sensuous conduct. Certainly in the lower types their associations are evil and often irresponsible. They are very seldom intentionally harmful to others, although kleptomania is one of its characteristics under malefic configurations. They are good at mimicry and are natural-born chatterers who talk a great deal without saying anything. Under favorable influences, however, they may rise high in life and prove to be geniuses. There is musical ability and a talent to

produce poetry.)

39. Uranus in ♊ personates a body tall, well-proportioned, dull sanguine complexion, brown or dark eyes, dark hair, oval face, intelligent looking countenance; in manners blunt and prompt, especially if ♊ be not ill aspected by the ☽; the mind is somewhat scientific, but not profound.

(Our experience in America is that while Uranus rarely gives a dark-skinned sun-tanned type of complexion, it usually gives light hair and eyes. Uranus here gives a fondness for science. Mentally alert and quick of thought, these persons are generally far ahead of others in thought. Frequently this position of Uranus indicates a genius.)

40. Saturn in ♊ denotes a rather tall stature, dark sanguine complexion, oval visage, well proportioned, dark brown or black hair; ingenious, not very fortunate in his transactions; his manners rather unpolished and perverse, and therefore warily to be dealt with; a tolerably good husband, and he is often employed in managing business for another, in writing, ordering, and superintending.

(These natives are usually large or raw-boned. Saturn overcomes to a large extent the variable influence of Gemini and gives an ability for concentration on mental pursuits. Particularly is this true if in an aspect to Mercury, for then profoundness of thought is shown. However, the overcarefullness brought on by the methodical plodding of ♄ may cause hindrance to success. The moral nature is frequently warped and the nature suspicious.)

41. Jupiter in ♊ personates a well compact, plump body, full middle stature, sanguine complexion, but not very clean; brown hair, full expressive grey eyes, graceful deportment, affable, courteous behaviour, gentle, mild, obliging, but too fond of the opposite sex; fond of learning, but never acquiring more than ordinary. If between five and fifteen degrees the native will be rash, a bad husband or wife, unsettled, and often an enemy to himself or herself, then very unacceptable to others. Men are generally connected with writings, and are employed as bookkeepers, clerks, lawyers, preachers, etc. The moral region is good and beneficially developed.

(Jupiter gives a kind disposition and indicates an obliging person of good moral character. They are very judicious and are fond of female company. Jupiter in this position also gives a fondness of science and philosophy, and a desire to lift philosophy from the field of abstract mental processes to concrete mental understanding. Poetic and literary ability is also shown, but much here depends upon environment.)

42. Mars in ♊ portends a person rather tall, well-made, light complexion in the first ten degrees, but generally good in any part of this sign, brown hair, except in the first and second Facet, when the hair will be flaxen; very unsettled in most affairs, yet ingenious in many things, though unfortunate in all and generally lives in a mean condition, shifting here and there, exercising his wits for a livelihood, and not continuing in any calling which he served his apprenticeship; wishes to be a mason, farmer, cowkeeper, etc.

(The hair generally has a reddish tint to it, particularly when near the cusp of the Ascendant, and the complexion is often swarthy. Mars gives a wandering and unsettled disposition in this sign. Arguments and disputes are common to these natives, for they love to argue for the sake of argument rather than the ascertainment of truth.)

43. The Sun in ♊ represents a well proportioned body, a full middle stature, sanguine complexion, brown hair; in disposition affable and courteous; he is subject to be controlled by others, and is frequently imposed upon on account of his passive turn of mind and procedure.

(Inclined to early baldness; large eyes. The mental contentment of these persons is so great that they are not easily offended. They are fond of change and travel and have a strong inclination to both science and art. They make good salesmen as a rule because of the blending of personality with talkative ability. Frequently they have literary ability.)

44. Venus and Neptune in ♊ portends a person of above the middle stature, rather tall, slender, and straight, brown hair, moderately clean complexion, hazel eyes (see 38 re Neptune); disposition charitable, honourable, liberal, easily wrought upon, and rarely guilty of a dishonourable act. Venus afflicted by ♄ or ♂, then the native is dissipated, mischievous, adulterous, and if a female, she is unchaste and blameable; and if married will deceive her husband, more especially if ♀ be in ♊ in the wife's nativity. (*see* Arcana)

(Venus gives a loving disposition. These persons seem to be carefree. They are just and merciful with an innate ambition to be charitable. The duality of Gemini and the amiability of Venus cause inconstancy in love-affairs, very often have two sweethearts at the same time. This position of Venus often brings more than one marriage.)

45. Mercury in ♊ gives a full statured person, upright body, well made, brown hair, a good complexion; in disposition, ingenious, a good orator, lawyer, bookseller, or some other calling connected with the pen. Self-interested.

(The influence of other planets on Mercury must always be carefully noted. Mercury increases the fondness for the arts and sciences. It gives a good disposition, and a fondness for learning. Frequently these persons become human encyclopedias. Particularly good judgment is indicated if the vibrations of Saturn or Jupiter are favorable. The influence of Saturn may make them profound in their thought. Poetical or musical ability is generally shown when Mercury is found here.)

46. The Moon in ♊ portends the native tall and well formed, upright and comely; brown hair, good complexion. The quality of the mind subtile, crafty, ingenious, ill-disposed, and generally unfortunate, unless other testimonies assist. If the ☽ be in good aspect of ☿, ♃, or the ☉, then the party will be charitable and sincere, gentle and obliging, genteel in manners, and much respected by the opposite sex.

(These natives are usually highly nervous in appearance; the nature is lively, much given to change. Usually these people are very shallow and almost incessant talkers. The arms and hands are always in motion when speaking. Note particularly the positions of Venus and Saturn for they may give stability otherwise lacking.)

The Planets in ♋

47. Cancer denotes persons, when uninfluenced by aspect or position, of short stature, that latter fifteen degrees rather taller and stouter, and the upper part of the body more thick and better set than the lower; little eyes, pale and wan complexion, oftentimes distorted teeth; brown hair, and winning voice; females are liable to have many children; and it generally gives men a feminine appearance.

(The first Facet gives a body of medium height, full and fleshy with dark brown hair. The second Facet shortens the stature, gives a small face, good forehead and blue eyes. The third Facet gives average height, dark hair, small nose with a pallid complexion. The voice is often shrill. The fourth Facet gives an awkward body, dark complexion with grey eyes. The fifth Facet also gives a poorly made body, out of proportion, with brown or platinum hair. Sometimes there is an inclination to slenderness. The sixth Facet gives a short body, long face, large eyes and nose. There is an inclination to obesity and the skin is often freckled.

(These persons have a strongly developed maternal instinct and love the home life. They are sensitive and domestic, and frequently in both male and female charts indicate a fondness for the culinary art. They are hypersensitive and while too easily influenced by friends are distrustful of strangers. They brood a great deal, both over the past and fear of the future for they are highly imaginative and fanciful. While there is a certain amount of changeableness, they usually have a deep sense of fidelity. They are very sensitive to criticism and their feelings are easily hurt.)

(The first Decanate gives a receptive and tenacious disposition. Moral instincts are strong and their whole lives are bound up with domestic ties and impressionable attachments. Environment plays an important part, but their greatest pleasure comes from giving comfort to family. Sometimes they go to extremes and are over-cautious and exacting in their requirements. The first Facet gives tact and alertness, but a suspicious nature. Anger and resentment are easily provoked. The second Facet gives vanity, a consciousness of their own ability, and a fondness for adventure and romance. There is also oratorical ability.)

(The second Decanate gives psychic and mystical tendencies, with control over the sensations. They have many varied experiences in life. It increases tenacity and gives a love of power. Conventionality is a prime requisite of their lives. The third Facet inclines the native to be combative through his selfishness, but frequently they have a sense of quiet endurance. The fourth Facet gives a tendency to despondency, obstinacy and often they are self-willed. They are also deeply affected by environment.)

(The third Decanate gives a hospitable and sympathetic nature. They have a keen desire to acquire knowledge. With this decanate rising, and the Moon afflicted, the native may be over-anxious, hysterical and hypersensitive with a tendency to obssession. If the Moon is well aspected, the disposition is kind, the mind is active and they are useful workers for the good of humanity. They have much curiosity. The fifth Facet lends to self-esteem and makes the native somewhat talkative. Sometimes they are the victims of their own foolishness. Their psychic nature makes them particularly sensitive to sensation. The sixth Facet produces the person who can be relied upon. They are shrewd, active and high-spirited. They have much patience and deep religious feeling.)

48. (Neptune gives the watery appearing, thin-skinned body, the skin is pale and colorless and the hair is straight, light brown in color. The native is highly emotional; smiles or tears come readily. Their temper is exceedingly unreliable and they are highly and easily influenced by others. Under affliction they are parasitic.)

49. Uranus in ♋ represents a short stature, dull pale complexion, sad brown hair, thin face, sharp nose, small eyes; disposition jealous, slothful, eccentric, malicious, fond of recreations, and often puts the best side outwards; seems to be what he really is not; thievish and other ill qualities, except ♃, ☽, ☿, or ♀, cast a good aspect to ♅. He confines himself to no fast employment.

(American experience differs much from Simmonite. Uranus increases the height, the native is not so stout and the hair is usually a little lighter. Uranus does give unreliability in this position, but the native invariably comes before the public. These persons are thoughtless for the feelings of others and change their residence often.)

50. Saturn in ♋ personates one of sickly constitution, brown hair, thin face, pale complexion, subject to jealousy and malicious actions, which are mitigated by the good aspects of the benevolent planets ♃ ☌ ♂. The native will be imprisoned some time of life.

(Saturn shortens the stature, with an ill-formed and disproportionate body. These natives are often ugly for there is nothing pleasing in either form or expression of the body. The disposition is malicious. Selfish ambitions will be satisfied at the expense of anything or anybody.)

51. Jupiter in ♋ gives a person of middle stature, pale fleshy face, rather corpulent body, dark brown hair, oval face, a busy loquacious person, intermeddling with all persons; conceited in his or her own abilities; a favourite among women; fortunate by water, and delights to be thereon. He makes sailors, spirit or wine merchants, publicans and beersellers.

(Jupiter here gives much ambition. These persons aim at high attainments. They are pleasant associates and desire to have an interest in everything. The exaltation of Jupiter here increases the benefic influence.)

52. Mars in ♋ gives a short person, dull complexion, thick brown hair; disposition servile and stupid, sottish and idle, shallow and trifling; never closely employed, but fond of leisure and loitering.

(Mars in ♋ gives a contentious disposition. These natives have great activity but they are restless. They have a constant passion for notoriety and crave authority.)

53. Sun in ♋ gives a little body, unhealthy countenance, not very handsome; brown hair; disposition harmless, innocent, cheerful, and a lover of the opposite sex; an admirer of sports and pastimes, music, dancing, and such kinds of recreations; but not fond of labor, neither mindful how he performs any employment. He does not generally follow any calling or trade.

(The Sun gives a pleasant and agreeable disposition, free and jovial. The sensitiveness is somewhat overcome so that they do not easily take offense. They are great entertainers.)

54. Venus or Neptune in ♋ represents a short statured person, fleshy body, round face, pale complexion, light hair; ♀ between 24 and 30 degrees, changes the colour of the hair to a redder appearance, and a little hue in the face; in disposition, lazy, slothful, inconstant, yet puts the best appearance outside, but not to be depended on; employed in selling confectionery, wines, ales, etc., and other articles of consumption, and in these he prospers, but in nothing else.

(Neptune does not shorten the body as much as Venus. Venus gives a round face, smooth skin, light brown or platinum hair and blue eyes. Venus also unsettles and makes the disposition changeable. It is hard to depend on these people. They love good company, but vanity and idleness are characteristic. They are kindly to others and desire popular esteem.)

55. Mercury in ♋ personates a low or short stature, dull complexion, sad brown hair, thin face, sharp nose, and small eyes; disposition dissembling, sottish, thievish, except ☿ happens to be in good aspect to the ☽ and ♃ ; but if ♃ be in ♍ or ♊ , then the native is a vagabond, etc.

(Mercury alone gives small, mean-looking person, with sharp eyes, and nose, and thin face. Note aspects. Mercury here gives a remarkable memory, the blend of its mental attributes and Cancer's emotional character indelibly imprinting the mind. They are, however, inclined to be deceitful, crafty and sometimes malicious.)

56. The Moon in ♋ represents a plump middle stature, well proportioned, round full face, brown hair, pale dusky complexion; disposition changeable, jocular, merry, harmless, free from passion, and generally well beloved; fortunate in most affairs, yet changeable in his resolves. The native is fond of traveling, water, sailing, and often does best at seaports, or in any part of Scotland; he does well as a fishmonger, or any calling connected with the water and liquids. He may turn publican, or brewer, or beer seller.

(Moon in ♋ gives a short body, small round face, and what Alan Leo calls a "crab-like or rabbit-like expression, the septum of the nose appearing to view below the nostrils with many slight sensitive lines on either side of the nose." The skin has large pores. There is close attachment to home life and domesticity and the fortunes are associated with him. However as the Moon indicates the public, there is a connection in that sphere and success with public matters relating to the home. Frequently it gives much close association with the mother, even after maturity.)

The Planets in ♌

57. Leo represents a large body, but the first six degrees will be lower and stiffer, broad shoulders, pleasant countenance, sometimes austere, full eyes, yellowish or flaxen hair, rather curling, large head, high forehead, good complexion, strong and active; in disposition resolute, unbending; but if the ☉ be afflicted a mere coward, hasty in temper, yet often generous, free and courteous; the latter part of the sign produces a weaker body, with lighter hair. Male natives are fond of ease and pleasure.

(The first Facet gives a body of medium height, broad and well-formed. The features are clear-cut and the hair is brown. The second Facet gives medium height, fine clear skin, light hair and eyes. The third Facet gives a broad body, husky, and strong, with a pale complexion, dark hair, dark eyes and full beard. The fourth Facet gives a tall slender body, light hair, pale complexion but a well developed physique. The forehead is strong and forceful appearing. The fifth Facet gives a large well proportioned, fine manly body, with full face and sharp eyes. The sixth Facet gives a slender build, dark eyes and hair. The upper part of the body is well proportioned, but the legs are short.)

(The first Decanate of Leo gives a sincere character, honorable and magnanimous, but much pride. There is great organizing ability and a love of authority and power. Unless other indications contradict, success comes early in life. The lower side of this influence brings downfall through indiscretion and surrendering to passionate impulses. As a matter of fact, the emotional side of their nature presents grave danger of demoralization through passion and sensuality. The first Facet inclines these natives to daring, rather than courage, and gives them an imperious and bombastic demeanor. They are highly magnetic, with much pride and self-esteem, and boastfulness. The second Facet gives a more harmonious and peaceful nature for those persons are kind and generous. They are also very attractive and neat in their dress. Their courteous manner commands respect.)

(The second Decanate adds dignity to judgment and diplomacy, although there is a liability to go to extremes making the native more demonstrative and at times rebellious. The philosophical side of the nature is more fully developed. The third Facet gives a revengeful tinge to character for these natives never forget a wrong. Chastity is the key to this facet if of high vibration, and through this quality love and wisdom may be obtained. In the fourth Facet we find a harmonious nature, although sometimes selfishness and undesirable ambitions produce hypocrisy.)

(The third Decanate strengthens the will-power, thus increasing the persistence. The head and heart work together uniting the intellect and the emotions. The emotions are thus stabilized by the intellect and success is much more certain. The fifth Facet gives good understanding and adds loyalty, sympathy and sincerity to the character. The sixth Facet lends itself to pleasure so that gambling should be avoided because of the union of head and heart.)

58. (Neptune in ♌ decreases the size, but it also gives romantic and brilliant eyes. Neptune also lends romance to the nature and gives extravagant ideals and romantic ideas. These natives are excellent at mimicry.)

59. Uranus in ♌ portends a person of a rather upright genteel make, tolerably good complexion; high broad shoulders, strong bones, brown or auburn hair, fullish eye, and Roman nose; hasty temper, ambitious, and proud. The qualities of the mind are philosophic, ingenious, learned, inquisitive; but eccentric, difficult to please, and secretive.

(Uranus in ♌ tends to make the hair and beard light or sandy; gives an independent disposition with much resoluteness. Passions are strong and subtle, but these natives are generous. It is an influence for genius.)

60. Saturn in ♌ a moderately large stature, broad round shoulders, wide chest, light hair, large bones, grave aspect, large perceptive organs; stooping walk. The quality of the mind tolerably good, generous but passionate; not very courageous or valiant when put to the test. The trades most fit are bricklayers, farmers, shepherds, masons, porters, carriers, potters, etc.

(American experience is that Saturn in ♌ gives a bony, firmly set, square-built body of medium height. These people never become stout. There is much ability and capability for managing and controlling large enterprises. Great powers of concentration of both mind and will are inherent.)

61. Jupiter in ♌ represents a strong person, tall and well made, light brown or yellowish curling hair, ruddy complexion, full eye, rather comely appearance; noble minded, courageous, magnanimous, lofty; delighting in warlike actions, a terror to his enemies; one that scorns to bend, contending for honour, mastership, etc. He often produces persons who are workers in wood.

62. Mars in ♌ gives a well proportioned body, sanguine or sunburnt complexion, large eyes, short limbs, and a brisk cheerful countenance; a lover of the opposite sex, inclined to boasting; delights in recreations and warlike exercises, as shooting, riding, and fighting; loves decent apparel, and is generally beloved; in disposition noble, free spirited, and endeavours to please. This denotes masons, joiners, smiths, cutlers, and manufacturers of steel.

(Mars in ♌ gives a hasty temper, love of firearms and surgical operations. These people are ardent lovers, but often mistake passion for love and intensity for depth.)

63. Sol in ♌ gives a strong well made body, light brown hair, sanguine complexion, prominent eyes, full face, with a mark or scar on it; in disposition a just person, faithful to his or her friends, punctual in the performance of promises; ambitious of honour, a respectable person holding office under government, and superintends in common course of life.

(These people retain youthful appearance late in life. The Sun adds dignity to character and makes the native faithful, just and courteous. It gives ambition for honor. When badly aspected, particularly by Jupiter, it makes the person proud and domineering.)

64. Venus or Neptune in ♌ personates a tall stature, well made, clear complexion, round face, full eyes, light flaxen or red hair, and freckled face; in disposition moderately faithful, soon angry, but not lasting, generous and free, but rather proud, often indisposed, a good humoured person. In selling over a counter he is generally employed.

(Venus in ♌ gives a proud and haughty disposition, with much passion. However, these persons are kind and generous but too much given to pleasure. They are ardent lovers and are fully persuaded of their own ability.)

65. Mercury in ♌ gives a large body, swarthy complexion, brown hair, round face, full eye and high nose; in disposition hasty, proud, conceited, ambitious of honour, a boaster, and subject to contention. They are mostly fond of being employed in public situations, where many men are employed.

(These people are usually good mimics and have ability for the drama. It also gives an ability to write love romances and adventure tales, as well as some artistic ability.)

66. The Moon in ♌ personates a tall stature, strong and large boned, large eyes, full face, sanguine complexion, light brown hair; lofty, proud aspiring disposition, ambitious of honour, desirous to rule, abhors servitude, and rarely proves a fortunate person. His most proper trade is that of a fishmonger, etc.

(The Moon in ♌ gives flexibility and adaptability to the tenacious and fixed qualities of ♌ for these natives appear impulsive and enthusiastic where their own interests are involved.)

The Planets in ♍

67. Virgo alone denotes a person of mean height, slender stature, but very neat, and decently composed, dark brown hair, round visage, not very beautiful, yet much admired, small shrill voice; all the members inclined to brevity, and the person is witty, discreet, of a pleasant conversation, studious, and given to learning.

(The first Facet of ♍ gives a slender body, brown eyes and hair with an intellectual appearing forehead. The second Facet increases the height and gives a good complexion with light brown hair and eye. The third Facet gives a rather strong body, blue or grey eyes, light curly hair and good features with a clear complexion. The fourth Facet gives a slender body, round face, good forehead and dark eyes. The fifth Facet gives a long face, thin lips, broad nose and nostrils. The sixth Facet gives a well-built body, inclined to be small, but sprightly and the complexion is fair.

(Virgo gives a quiet, modest and reserved character. There is great adaptability and sense of obedience, but lack of self-confidence in the pure type, and some pessimism. Because of the analytical qualities of Virgo there is a desire for reform, but usually it is due to lack of understanding of the views of others rather than originality in thought. The mind is usually logical and has a great capacity for detail. The pure type of Virgo is inherently honest, being acclaimed by some astrologers as the only sign of the zodiac having this quality. The opinions are very changeable. The analytical qualities of Virgo often give a scientific type of mind and many of the world's greatest scientists have this sign prominent.)

(The first Decanate of ♍ gives a quiet, reserved, retiring and receptive disposition. There is much perseverance but no determinative ambition. Selfishness is somewhat overcome by sympathy for others. These persons are orderly, critical and self-centered, and are difficult to understand at first. They are not lazy, but will live by their wits if possible, rather than work. Physical effort is distasteful to them. The first Facet makes them mentally proud but full of tact and subtlety; the second Facet gives honesty, sincerity and refinement.)

(The second Decanate arouses the independence of the nature and the practicality of these persons makes them well adapted to business life where their success comes through practical common-sense methods. This decanate also gives some musical ability and somewhat artistic temperament. The third Facet gives an amiable and refined disposition with scientific tastes; they are generally pleasant and agreeable. The fourth Facet gives a fondness for the arts and sciences, a fluent speech and much prudence and discreetness.)

The third Decanate accentuates the practicality and business characteristics. To this is added intuition. It is a fortunate decanate for fate. Great determination is shown and because of this they are usually successful. The fifth Facet gives a sincere and affable disposition. They are intellectual and anxious to accomplish some good in the world. Their best position, however, is in serving others. The sixth Facet gives an artistic ability which is frequently submerged by the materialism of these persons. They are not only anxious to build wealth for themselves, but they become anxious for the affairs of others.)

68. Concerning Pluto, *see* article 16.

69. (Neptune in ♍ gives a short stout body, sensitive eyes and thin light hair. Neptune fills the native with all kinds of schemes. They are demure and retiring and no one ever knows their character thoroughly. In lower vibrations, this position produces a deceptive individual, interested only in illicit pleasures, or it produces thieves.)

70. Uranus in ♍ represents a tall proportioned body, dark complexion, oval face, brown or black hair, good sized head, and austere countenance; the quality of the mind is clever, learned, acquiring knowledge by different means, though abrupt, and cares not for the foolery of fashion; generally employed in scholastic callings, such as teaching, writing, superintending, an excise officer, etc.

(Uranus here gives a genius for music, statistics and fine details. The research of Uranus added to the analytical nature of Virgo makes real students of these persons. It also gives journalistic ability and a taste for science.)

71. Saturn in ♍ represents a tall spare body, swarthy complexion, dark hair, long head and face; in disposition melancholic, retaining anger; a projector of curiosities to little purpose; studious, subtle, reserved, and determinate. He follows light business, as pawnbroker, a broker of some description, and one who deals in articles over a counter.

(Saturn here makes a scholar. These persons love to read and study, particularly melancholy subjects. They are painstaking and thorough in all they undertake.)

72. Jupiter in ♍ gives a full sized person, well made, and handsome, dark hair, ruddy complexion, not clear or fair, but well proportioned altogether, choleric, ambitious of honour, boasting and studious, yet through rashness subject to losses. In business clever, and able to perform his duty in any calling in which he may be engaged. He signifies schoolmasters, editors, printers, accountants, lawyers, clerks, bookkeepers, etc., also gardeners and workers on the land.

(Jupiter gives compactness to the body, dark hair and a sort of scientific expression of countenance. It gives an even tempered disposition, thrifty and ambitious of both honor and position. These persons rarely marry and because this is one of the poorest positions for Jupiter, they are rarely successful.)

73. Mars in ♍ personates a middle stature, well proportioned body, dark brown or black hair, swarthy or sunburnt complexion, generally a mark or scar on the face; in disposition hasty, proud, retains an injury, not easily pleased, and from his precipitate procedure is obnoxious to error and dissipation.

(Mars gives an energetic and capable disposition, but these people are not affable. They are busy workers and make useful servants, but must be judiciously managed as they are easily offended and somewhat resentful. They are intellectually disposed.)

74. The Sun in ♍ denotes a tall, slender stature, well proportioned, good complexion, much dark hair, cheerful and convivial, fond of singing and other pleasing recreations which delight the ear and palate; in the last degree thin face and dark hair.

(The Sun makes these persons ingenious, but not ambitious. There is a degree of selfishness here which generally grows late in life. They are severe with those who offend them. The body is well developed and the hair is dark brown.)

75. Venus or Neptune in ♍ gives a tall, well proportioned body, dark complexion, oval visage, and sad brown or black hair; mind ingenious, a good speaker, aspiring turn of mind, but often unfortunate in his undertakings, unless he hold a good position, which is better than business. (*See* article 69 for Neptune.)

(Venus in ♍ gives a well composed body with an indifferent complexion, usually dark hair or eyes. The disposition is subtle and cunning, very ingenious and active. They will always take care of their own interests; have a high sense of refinement in dress and personal habits and look with disdain on those not expressing such refinement, unless seriously afflicted when they will be careless about dress and appearance.)

76. Mercury in ♍ makes the body tall, slender, and proportioned, dull

complexion, dark brown or black hair, long face and austere countenance; quality of the mind changeable, fidgety, yet ingenious and accomplished.

(Mercury increases the height and gives ambition otherwise lacking. It quickens the intellect and gives a scientific trend to mental attributes. Well aspected it gives a fluent tongue and they always have something to discuss. This position of Mercury also keeps these natives well occupied. They are always occupied and have plenty to do.)

77. The Moon in ♍ personates a tall stature, rather dark ruddy complexion, oval face, and dark brown hair; ingenious, reserved, courteous, melancholy person, seldom well disposed, and generally unfortunate, petulant and sottish, talkative and boasting.

(The Moon gives medium height and a very neat appearance. The hair has a brown tinge to it, but the skin has a jaundice appearance (yellowish-brown). The features are small and delicate. They are quiet and demure in disposition, neat and orderly in their methods and always just as precise in ideas.

The Planets in ♎

78. Libra alone denotes a person tall and elegantly formed, round face, having beauty, rather slender, lank auburn or flaxen hair, generally blue eyes, fine clear red and white complexion in youth, which in old age becomes pimpled; courteous, friendly disposition, just and upright.

(The first Facet gives a tall body, with pale complexion, grey eyes and auburn hair. These persons are very good looking. The second Facet gives a tall body, with an inclination to stoutness, particularly after 27 years of age. The hair is light, the eyes blue and the complexion clear. The third Facet produces a person of medium height, with a dark complexion and smooth skin. The features are very attractive, the forehead is strong appearing, the eyes grey and the hair usually dark. The fourth Facet gives a slender build, with clear complexion of permanent beauty and with greenish-grey eyes. These persons are very magnetic. The fifth Facet gives a good form, a person of beauty. The complexion is fresh and the eyes dark blue. The sixth Facet gives a tall, graceful, beautiful, well-developed body, with light brown eyes and hair.)

(The first Decanate gives an affectionate disposition. They are very susceptible to the influence of companions and have little ability to change circumstances. They are keen of observation, generally refined and truly artistic. The nature is very sympathetic. There is a tendency to physical laziness and they are somewhat disposed to depend upon others. They are fitted for mercantile pursuits for they have good judgment in valuing merchandise. The first Facet gives fluency of speech and good understanding. They are favored by others. The second Facet makes the native serious and discreet.)

(The second Decanate accentuates the sympathetic side of the nature and increases the intuition. These persons love approbation. They are sometimes called eccentric, due to the blending of the influence of Aquarius, the sign of this decanate. They also have a fondness for occult and mystical subjects, but can seldom stay fixed upon a given subject long enough to accomplish a purpose. The third Facet gives diplomacy and ambition, but results must be accomplished through mental effort rather than physical. These natives are studious and shrewd. The fourth Facet gives prudence and depth of perception. The nature is quiet and thoughtful with scientific tendencies.)

(The third Decanate is rather unfortunate for it weakens the influence of the sign as a whole. The chart as a whole must be studied carefully for there are strong tendencies to produce an exceedingly foolish person, notwithstanding fine personality. The fifth Facet gives a good disposition and generous nature, but it is frequently too generous for the native's own welfare. The sixth Facet gives a noble, virtuous and honorable character, much to be admired and respected. Education is essential to success in the sense that the mentality must be developed.)

79. Concerning Pluto *see* article 16.

80. (Neptune usually gives great beauty in this position. The native is tall, has a beautiful skin and has large languid eyes, light blue in color. The ideals are lofty with visionary notions. There seems to be a lack of practicality. The intuition is highly developed and eloquence and compassion are characteristic. In lower types, sexual indulgence and morbid cravings are indicated.)

81. Uranus in ♎ describes a person rather tall, upright stature, comely appearance, moderately stout, smooth brown hair, oval face, sanguine complexion, high forehead, grey eyes; in disposition mild and kind, the quality of the mind learned and accommodating, faithful and trustworthy. He follows a clean, light business.

(Uranus here gives a hot temper and independence, both of which bring unfortunate conditions into the married life. However, the eccentricity of Uranus is largely overcome in this position.)

82. Saturn in ♎ portends a person of middle stature, good looking, brown hair, oval face, large nose, high forehead, tolerably clear complexion, opinionated of himself, rather extravagant, fond of debate and controversy, and often comes off victorious.

(Saturn here sometimes causes the hair to be black. Saturn also shows his best characteristics here as a lover of justice, intense loyalty and devotion to duty. The personality is somewhat reserved, independent and cold.)

83. Jupiter in ♎ indicates a body slender, tall and handsome, upright oval face, light brown hair, full eyes, fair complexion, but sometimes pimpled or freckled on the cheeks, yet a prepossessing appearance; disposition and temper mild, winning, and obliging, fond of recreation, much esteemed; fortunate if in good aspect with ☉, ☽, or ♀.

(Jupiter gives a beautifully formed body inclined to stoutness after the 28th birthday. The disposition is loving; a large circle of friends, particularly of the opposite sex. Jupiter here gives worldly success and popularity, for the ambition of Sagittarius is coupled with the fine personal qualities of Libra.)

84. Mars in ♎ personates a tall stature, well proportioned body, oval

face, sanguine complexion, light soft brown hair; the beginning of the sign to the first ten degrees, hair wiry or reddish; disposition cheerful, but rather conceited, fond of dress and fine outside, much attached to the opposite sex, and warmly beloved by them, and from whom he often is maligned when connecting himself with imprudent characters. His wife is rather often wild who has this position in his nativity.

85. The Sun in ♎ gives a tall, straight, upright body, full eyes, light hair, rather handsome face, ruddy complexion, a slight rash or pimple on the face; in disposition fond of talking of warlike affairs, yet a great coward, and not to be trusted as a friend, weak in his attachments, and not altogether given to speaking the truth.

(The Sun gives a body of medium height, straight and upright when walking. The complexion is usually very fair, the eyes large and blue and the hair light brown. The disposition is amiable, but affairs throughout life are rather unfortunate as these people are too yielding under pressure. They do not have the stamina to stand upon their own feet but must lean upon others.)

86. Venus or Neptune in ♎ represents a tall, upright elegant person, oval face, rather beautiful, sanguine complexion, often freckled, brown hair, and beautiful dimples; disposition obliging, fair in his dealings, much respected. They signify drapers, tailors, confectioners, grocers, druggists, musicians, barbers, etc. ♀ ☌ ♂ a tobacconist, ♀ ☌ ♅ a tailor of a respectable character. (For Neptune *see* article 80.)

(Venus, of course, accentuates the higher qualities of this sign and finds its fullest expression here, so that the disposition is exceedingly fine. They love respectability for its own sake and are courteous and obliging in every respect. The love-nature is polarized toward the higher emotions and is elevated to the plane of the mind. They marry for companionship's sake.)

87. Mercury in ♎ gives a tall but not thin handsome person, light brown hair, sanguine complexion; disposition just, virtuous, prudent, a lover and promoter of learning, and happily qualified with natural abilities; fond of light reading, such as novels, romances, poetry, etc.

(Mercury in ♎ gives medium height and a proportionate body, blue eyes. They love virtue and morality; are eloquent and make excellent companions.)

88. The Moon in ♎ gives a tall, well made body, with smooth light brown hair, fine red and white complexion, and handsome face; disposition pleasing, a lover of mirth and recreations, respected by the opposite gender, liable to dishonour in courtships, unless ♀ be well placed and the ☽ in good aspect of ♃, ☉, or ♀ ; denotes publicans, hair dressers, hatters, music sellers, umbrella and parasol makers; also female tailors.

(The Moon here usually makes the eyes a true grey with a wistful look. The personality is likeable, exceedingly adaptable. These persons are refined and concerned only with the higher emotions. They are easy and courteous in speech, always concerned about the companion, whether in social gatherings, in business or in marriage. It is one of the best positions of the Moon for personality.)

The Planets in ♏

89. Scorpio when uninfluenced by any planet denotes a person strong, robust, and corpulent, broad face, middle stature, dusky complexion, brown curling bushy hair, dark eyes, thick neck, coarse hairy legs, often bow legged; active, thoughtful, and reserved in conversation.

(The first Facet gives a body of medium height, sometimes inclined to be short, with a full round, ruddy face. The complexion, particularly in the first three degrees, inclines to be fair, carrying over some of the influence of Libra. The second Facet inclines to a short body, but firm, strong and generally stout. The hair has a reddish tint to it, but is usually chestnut in color. The eyes are either dark or dark grey and very quick. The third Facet gives a well-proportioned body, either tall or of medium height. The hair has a tendency to be light, but the darker shades usually prevail, while the eyes are of a greyish blue. The fourth Facet gives a tall body of slender build, with dark hair and ruddy complexion. The eyes are usually dark or brown. The fifth Facet gives a short well-proportioned body, an oval face with pallid, but well outlined features. The sixth Facet gives a well made body, generally short or tall, one extreme or the other, with reddish hair and a ruddy complexion.

(There are two distinct types of Scorpio people which were referred to by the ancients as "Scorpio with the sting" and "Scorpio without the sting." The first of these, the lower type, are a vindictive, "know-it-all" type who will never admit when they are wrong. The disposition is mean, although outwardly they appear to be of very fine character. They are not to be trusted for their own ends must be gained. They are frequently over-sexed. The higher plane of this type is as lofty as the lower type is low. They are courageous, proud and dynamic. They have a personality which commands respect, and their executive ability is tremendous. While they are not lovers of hard work, they do work hard in order to succeed. In both types their likes and dislikes are pronounced. They never waiver. There is some lack of tact and diplomacy which may involve them in difficulties, but because of their dynamic energy they usually succeed.)

(The first Decanate gives an active mind and body. The dynamic energy is accentuated because of the double Mars influence of this decan. In the higher type these persons will sacrifice much for their fellow man and will labor hard to pursue knowledge as they understand it. In the lower type this effort is directed towards their own selfish aims with a jealous tinge to protect self. The first Facet is highly magnetic in personality and individuality. They are usually generous and pleasant company. They have much confidence, will-power and intuition and the character is inclined to be sincere. The second Facet gives a generous disposition with a strong will, but a lover of justice. They are usually fond of mystical things.)

(The second Decanate well-aspected gives prominence and power. In the higher type these people love justice and give good judgment in considering matters of an abstruse nature. The disposition is thoughtful, discreet and generous in those having the third Facet ascending. While somewhat critical, they have the intellectual ability to justify honest criticism. The fourth Facet gives more tact and diplomacy than the other portions of Scorpio. These natives have a thoughtful nature and very strong character.)

The third Decanate of Scorpio is sometimes referred to as the "fatalistic decanate." It is not so much "fate" as it is their own vacillating nature. This decan is highly emotional and has a peculiar combination of critical sarcasm. These natives are not good managers of their own affairs. While the fifth Facet sometimes gives good judgment of human affairs, it does not give it as it relates to self. The disposition appears to be good, but their extreme fondness for the opposite sex often brings them into difficulty as the personal-moral nature is not too strong. They also have a desire for magical and occult subjects. The first half of the sixth Facet gives a fairly good character and a very positive intellectual nature. The last half surrenders completely to the emotional senses and they are too easily led into sensual pleasures.)

90. Concerning Pluto *see* article 16.

91. (Neptune in ♏ gives a body of middle stature, thick dark hair, dark muddy complexion and mysterious appearing eyes. Neptune does not usually show its better nature here. It has a tendency to cause depravity in sex matters. Its influence on character is mysterious and gives depth to the feelings. Strongly benefitted by other planetary positions, its higher qualities are manifest by research and investigation into occult, psychic and spiritual matters. The sex nature is very strong.)

92. Uranus in ♏ portends a mean stature, well set, broad make, long face, dark complexion, dark hair and whiskers, broad shoulders; disposition honourable, faithful, firm and conscientious; the mind ingenious, thoughtful, but reserved, and fond of employment.

(Uranus in ♏ increases the height somewhat, and gives a strong body with broad shoulders. The hair, eyes and complexion are all dark, although if Uranus is close to the cusp it sometimes gives a fair complexion. While many astrologers, particularly of the old school, believe Uranus to be exalted in Scorpio, many of those who have carefully studied its influence here do not accept it as a fact. It does give intensity to character, but it also increases the passions. These natives are difficult to understand and appreciate. They have good reasoning abilities and are capable of debate, research and study, particularly as it relates to medical and physiological matters.)

93. Saturn in ♏ represents a person of mean stature, thick trussy body, broad shoulders, dark hair, strong constitution; disposition surly and contentious, a retainer of anger, often to his or her own detriment, not willing to yield when in error. He works in metals or minerals.

(Saturn shortens the height, but gives the native a thickset, dark complexion. This type has a stealthy look. The disposition is jealous, inclined to be quarrelsome. It gives great ambition, but the pride is so narrow that success is hard to attain. It also gives an ability for psychic research.)

94. Jupiter in ♍ represents a stout compact body, middle stature, full eyes, dull complexion, and brown hair; disposition proud, lofty, and ambitious; one that desires rules, and if ♃ be in the angle the native is fortunate among nobles, great men, and soldiers; a person of great stability for his own purposes; temper rather turbulent; in all his actions selfish, and therefore ought to be warily dealt with. He makes gardeners, quarry masons, colliers, excavators, and railway labourers.

(Jupiter inclines to fleshiness and medium height. The complexion and eyes are frequently very dark or florid. Under affliction, the native often appears to be bloated. Jupiter is not in a good position here for it gives a boastful disposition, resentful and with highly developed egotism. The mind is good and success usually attends it in a material way.)

95. Mars in ♍ signifies a well set middle stature, rather corpulent, broad face, swarthy complexion, and dark curling hair; in temper ill humoured, passionate and revengeful; in disposition determinate, rash when put to it, and revengeful, but the quality of the mind is ingenious, active in gaining knowledge; fond of warlike engines; in arts and sciences ready apprehension and inventive. A worker in metals, tin-men, smiths, and artificers.

(Mars here gives the face a flat appearance. The hair is usually red or dark brown, and the hair either curly or kinky. While Mars is exceptionally strong in this position, it usually brings forth the baser side of the nature, lending deceit, quarrelsomeness and vindictiveness to the character. Good surgeons, police officials and soldiers are here shown if the strong character is of the higher type, although this is to be taken in consideration with the Xth house influence as well.)

96. Venus in ♍ denotes a stout, well set, corpulent body, broad face, dusky complexion, and dark hair; in disposition debauched, yet a despiser of females under pretense of chastity, opposed to marriage, subject to contention and envy; guilty of many vicious actions, especially if ♀ happens to be in ill aspect of ♄, ♂, or ☋. If he marries he is disposed to strife, contention, jealousy and probably through this diabolical principle may cause his wife's death. He gambles, and makes any shuffle rather than work for an honest livelihood.

(Mars here often gives a sort of battleship grey appearance to the eyes. It is about the only position in which Venus gives a quarrelsome disposition. Venus here gives a bossy nature and an envious disposition. It is not good unless other planetary positions counteract it.)

97. Mercury in ♍ gives a mean stature, well set, broad shoulders, swarthy complexion, brown curling hair; disposition subtle, a lover of the opposite sex, given to pleasure and loose company, yet careful of his own interest; often he is thievish, a liar, and crafty, and subjects himself to trouble through his deceits; in mind he is clear and ingenious, fond of inventions. He is given to drunkenness and other dissipated and abominable practices. He ought to be shunned as a companion.

Mercury in ♍ gives height to the body, well built and strong. These natives do not like to be left alone.)

98. The Moon in ♍ gives a short, thick, fleshy body, dark brown or black hair, dark complexion, ill disposed, treacherous, malicious, brutish, and sottish; imprudent and thievish, concerting with ill characters. If a woman she is generally infamous. If ☽ receives the good aspect of ♃ or ♀, the disposition is improved, but still unfaithful; a retentive memory, and the organ of firmness good; a lover of friends and children. Most fortunate as fishmongers, green grocers, hawkers of articles of consumption, also in huckstering and marketing.

(Mars here in a male chart gives a much more solid and stronger built body than in a female chart. It tends to give weight to the male with poor features and frequently a deformity in the nose. In the female the body is generally small, the eyes large with a sort of hollow expression. It is essential to note the position of the Sun in all cases. This is not a very good position for the Moon for unless the influence of the Sun is beneficial, the nature is somewhat uncertain and treacherous or unreliable. There is a tendency to violent changes in relationship to others. False pride is generally manifest and there is an unforgiving or resentful attitude.)

The Planets in ♐

99. Sagittary endows the native with a strong, active, and well formed body, tallish, face rather long, but handsome, fine clear eyes, ruddy or sunburnt complexion, chestnut coloured hair, growing off the temples; subject to baldness; generally a straight Grecian nose; jolly, daring, intrepid, active, bold, generous, fond of horses and hunting.

(The first Facet indicates a tall, broad-shouldered person, with strong features, brown eyes and light brown hair. The face is rather long and the complexion is often freckled. The body is quick in its movements. The second Facet gives a body from medium height to tall, but strong and well-built. While the eyes are inclined to be dark, the hair and complexion are usually light. The third Facet gives a body of medium height, inclined to stoutness. The mouth is small, the features clear and light complexioned and the eyes grey. The fourth Facet gives a tall, heavily built body; the features are strong and clear-cut, while the hair is brown and the eyes either hazel or grey. The fifth Facet gives a medium to tall body, slender, but strong and well-built. The eyes are light blue; the hair either light brown or yellow in some cases. The face is usually long. The sixth Facet gives a tall body, inclined to stoutness. The features are clear and pleasant. The eyes are dark grey or blue and the skin smooth and fair.)

The first and foremost characteristic of most Sagittarians is their enthusiasm and ambition. They are jovial, hospitable and good-natured. Unless seriously afflicted in their moral character, they are just and truthful, generous in their relations with others, but serious in their desire to accomplish. They are peculiarly fond of ritual ceremony. Athletic competition and all forms of outdoor sports command their interest. Their primary weaknesses are impulsiveness and over-optimism, but these often give them success. The gift of learning is theirs and they find great success in law, philosophy and religion. While they are ruggedly built to endure hard work, they usually accomplish most in mental positions.)

(The first Decanate accentuates the general qualities of Sagittarius. The mind and body are both exceedingly active. They will sacrifice much for their fellowmen. The first Facet gives both a good mind and disposition, with honesty and trustworthiness as strong characteristics. Benevolence and acquisitiveness are the keys of this facet. The second Facet gives a love of others. The moral nature is highly developed as a rule for their religious spirit is strong and they are primarily interested in matters related to abstract thought.)

(The second Decanate, having an Aries-Mars influence, quickens the temper, but it gives great endurance. They will accomplish in the face of any odds, even though, under affliction, it be in the wrong direction. The third Facet increases the vitality. The nature is generous, open and free. These natives take the world into their confidence and are often too expressive for their own good. The fourth Facet is not so strong. It sometimes gives an effeminate disposition causing the native to be a misfit. Consequently they are frequently not as sincere as other portions of this sign.)

(The third Decanate gives the ability of leadership. Here we have persons who find favor with the masses and are able to exercise power and authority with discretion. It is frequently a strong position for ecclesiastics who attain high positions. In the fifth Facet there is sometimes a disposition to practice deception. These natives desire fame and public acclaim. Deception is usually in the sense that they pretend to be more than they really are. For this facet the positions of both Jupiter and the Sun should be carefully noted. The sixth Facet gives a serious disposition. While there is great activity in their lives, occasionally it operates on their passions. They do, however, have such a strong influence from both the Sun and Jupiter that they accomplish great good in the world.)

100. Concerning Pluto *see* article 16.

101. (Neptune in ♐ gives a tall, well-built body, sometimes inclining to fleshiness, but rugged appearing. The eyes are large, the features clear-cut and fair. There is a peculiar blending of the ruddy complexion of fire signs and the pale complexion of water signs. Neptune, peculiarly enough, has an unusual influence here in that it gives an engaging personality. It inclines to a study of religion, philosophy, and occult matters. In its lower vibrations, however, it does as much harm as it does good in its higher nature. These lower types still have the resourcefulness given to higher types, but it is directed to "wildcat" schemes, Utopian and communistic ideas "and other frothy enterprises," as Alan Leo put it many years ago.)

102. Uranus in ♐ delineates a person tall or full sized, genteel make, fair complexion, brown hair, not fleshy, strong boned, and rather thin face; one hasty, but soon reconciled; moderately careful; well disposed and not covetous; rather proud, but strives after honourable things; fond of recreations, but no spendthrift; a sincere friend, but a perpetual foe to his opponents. A joiner, modeller, architect, timber merchant, cabinet maker, etc.

(Uranus here usually gives a light complexion; hair either light brown or golden; the eyes clear, either light blue or grey, with a peculiar gleam which invites friendship. Uranus in this sign is a sign of genius or latent ability which if developed brings great honor. Art, science, and philosophy are their true fields of thought and advancement.)

103. Saturn in ♐ gives a large person, brown hair, good make, tolerable complexion, not stout, but rawboned; obliging, careful, choleric, precipitate in making promises he or she cannot conveniently perform without prejudice; a lover of his friends and merciful to enemies; the native generally buries father or mother. He makes a good farmer or dealer in cattle, etc.

(Saturn's usual stern qualities are somewhat modified in this position, for these people are kind, courteous and benevolent. They will brook no offense against themselves and will quickly retaliate. However, when once they have returned the offense, they are quick to make friends again and admit their error. This is a strong mental position for Saturn as it gives a natural love of learning, whether scientific, philosophical or ecclesiastical.)

104. Jupiter in ♐ personates a fine tall stature, upright, well made, oval face, fine eyes, chestnut hair, and thick beard; disposition noble, free, obliging, affable; an admirer of females; magnanimous, industrious, and friendly. He mixes with religious persons. ♃ in ☌ or △ of ♂ renders the native of good credit, and prosperous in marital enterprise.

(Jupiter here gives a healthful ruddy glow, heavy body, with the head inclined to appear large but well proportioned and with features that command respect. They are sincere, affable, and just. This position of Jupiter brings success in almost any field of endeavor.)

105. Mars in ♐ produces a tall, compact, well made body, oval face, brown hair, sanguine complexion, quick, penetrating eyes, cheerful in company, but hasty temper, merry, active, courageous, talkative, delights in decency and elegant appearance. In aspect to ♂ a chemist, surgeon, duelist; he is choleric, proud, lofty, and daring.

(The hair is usually dark brown or red and the eyes brown. Mars here gives a happy-go-lucky disposition. These natives are usually good-natured, loving entertainment and association with others. They are also fond of travel, outdoor sports and excel in them because of their dynamic active and ambitious nature. They lean more to physical effort than mental for they are inclined to be superficial.)

106. Sun in ♐ describes a tall, handsome, well proportioned body, oval face, sanguine complexion and light brown hair; a very lofty, proud spirited person, aiming at great things, and does not like to give way to others; one who performs some honorary distinctions in life. ♂ or ♃ here renders the native daring, one that will rule over other persons in the same calling of life.

(The Sun in ♐ increases the stature; body strong and wellbuilt; the face is oval; complexion fair and sometimes sanguine, while the hair is either light brown or golden. It gives great ambition for honor. The disposition may be inclined to be too proud and at times actually haughty, although they have great diplomacy. These natives are frequently talkative and sometimes argumentative, not so much for the sake of argument but for the development of thought. They love competitive sports in which they usually excel. In religion they go to extremes, either decidedly religious or an evangelical type, or absolutely anti-religious.)

107. Venus or Neptune in ♐ personates a tall, handsome, well proportioned body, oval face, sanguine complexion and brown hair; ingenious, but rather proud, a little passionate, curious temper, fond of recreations, and very obliging; often the querent and his friends are at variance, nevertheless the querents marry advantageously, gain by their partner, or by their father or grandfather. ♀ , ☌ , or △ of ♃ denotes the love or friendship of superior persons. (Concerning Neptune *see* article 101.)

(Venus gives a medium to tall body, strongly built with pleasing expression on face. The skin is smooth and fair, the eyes grey or hazel, and the hair light. There is a strong tendency to stoutness as the years advance. Venus gives a pleasing disposition; a great deal of pride, but a willingness to subordinate self. There is some tendency to a passionate nature which under affliction may produce excesses.)

108. Mercury in ♐ describes a person of tall stature, well formed, not corpulent, rather spare, large bones, plenty of nose, oval face, ruddy complexion; passionate, but soon appeased, delights in chases, not prudent in judgment, neither very fortunate, rash in his actions, to his detriment; forward in youth, but does not improve progressively. ☿ ☌ ♂ passionate; ☿ ☌ ☽ , stupid.

(Mercury here makes the body quick in its movements. Likewise, the character and mind are active but tend to be shallow. Always full of ideas, these persons are exceedingly intelligent concerning inconsequential matters. Tendency to be conceited and vain.)

109. The Moon in ♐ gives a handsome person, oval face, sanguine complexion, brown hair, open and generous disposition, rather hasty and ambitious, honest and kind; fortunate and much respected. In good aspect of ♀ or ♃ fond of amusements; has great power among kindred; fond of females' company, yet virtuous, sincere in friendship, high spirit and good abilities.

(The Moon inclines to a tall body, but stout or fleshy, strong and active, with the muscles standing out. Eyes are frequently dark blue, large and pleasant appearing; the neck is usually long. The Moon gives oratorical ability. It is often indicative of real wit for the mind is quick and subtle. They are marvellous entertainers and very seldom remain fixed in either position or residence, although both the Xth and IVth houses should be carefully noted concerning these. The disposition is lovable and they are very expressive of their affections. The changeability of the Moon plus their great ambition and self-confidence sometimes brings about their downfall through having their "fingers in too many pies.")

The Planets in ♑

110. Capricorn shows a short, slender person, long thin visage, thin beard, dark hair, long neck, narrow chin and breast, weak knees, crooked, ill formed legs; mind subtle and witty, but changeable.

(The first Facet usually gives a tall, slender body, with well-formed features, generally dark, although this facet sometimes gives a very fair complexion, particularly in the second half. The second Facet gives a small body, usually with a dark complexion, rather long face, but good features. The third Facet produces a large-boned type, medium to tall. The body is strong and muscular. This facet gives a more commanding appearance than any other in Capricorn. The fourth Facet gives a body of medium height, but generally with a clear complexion. The hair is light brown and the eyes are also brown. The fifth Facet gives a body of medium height, well proportioned and of good appearance. The complexion inclines to be fair rather than dark and the features are clear-cut. The sixth Facet gives a body of medium height, well proportioned with blond complexion and hair.)

(Capricorn is the most egotistic or self-esteemed sign of the zodiac, but it is a quiet egoism usually expressed in desire for possession. It gives a strong will and a great deal of patience. The character is persevering and practical. It is also the most cautious and most secretive of the signs. Under affliction it inclines to melancholia, but look to the position of Mercury. Capricorn is slow to make friends and is highly resentful toward enemies.)

(The first Decanate gives an ambitious, self-reliant nature, serious and inclined to melancholia, but with keen insight into the future. The first Facet gives balance to the judgment and intellect, as well as high ideals. The second Facet does not give such a strong nature, but ambition gives a powerful driving force. This in turn sometimes causes these persons to attempt to accomplish more than they are capable of attaining.)

(The second Decanate decreases ambition, but gives a steadfastness and powerful endurance. These natives are more sympathetic and kind but incline to conservatism and orthodoxy. Quiet plodding, thoroughness for detail and fixity of purpose are characteristic. The third Facet strengthens the character and gives tact and diplomacy. These natives are ever seeking knowledge. The fourth Facet gives a deep, but easy-going disposition. Environment influences their actions a great deal.)

(The third Decanate increases the influence of environment and decreases self-reliance. Its influence is largely upon the mind so that education is essential to success. In some types these natives are timid and distrustful of others, but there is a great desire to be of service to humanity. The position of Mercury is important. The fifth Facet is usually an indicator of success in mundane affairs. There is a tremendous power of mental acquisitiveness. The mind is not only receptive, but has a peculiar ability to retain—a veritable walking encyclopedia. The sixth Facet gives a weak nature, often vacillating to such an extent that failure inevitably follows. There is also a servile, dependent attitude which is not favorable to advancement.)

111. Concerning Pluto *see* article 16.

112. (Neptune in ♑ is highly idealistic. The native is a great planner for things hard to obtain. In the advanced types this expresses itself either through politics or economics. They have good minds for mathematics, as well as their application to mundane and philosophical matters. In the lower types this position of Neptune may produce depravity through drink, primarily, as well as association with low type individuals. Neptune gives a body medium to short, stout and small-boned; complexion dark, hair black and thin, but silky; eyes battleship grey or dark blue.)

113. Uranus in ♑ gives a lean person, middle stature, dark or black hair, plenty of whiskers, thin face, dull complexion, little eyes, and striding walk; disposition reserved, secretiveness large, firm in his dealings and procedure; one that may be depended upon for his promises; a farmer, or having to do with railways; butchers, and business that requires strength.

(In American experience Uranus increases the height slightly, gives a fairly well-built body. The hair is light, the forehead high and the eyes bright and steely in appearance. The neck is thin and the face generally long. He has a fine opinion of self. These natives are either of a very lofty type of mind and character, or ostentatious, haughty and proud. Positions of other planets in relation to Uranus are important.)

114. Saturn in ♑ personates a lean, rawboned body, dark hair, middle stature, sallow complexion, small eyes, long, lean visage, and awkward stooping gait; one who is peevish, discontented, covetous, yet respected by persons of honour, sound mind, of few words, a lover of employment; connected with the earth, by which he profits; retains anger, and is of great gravity. ♄ ☌ ☽ portends poverty; in △ of the ☽ he is changeable, jealous and mistrustful; ♄, ruler of the VIIth, the native does not marry early; vexations and troubles in marriage, suffers much anxiety, and in danger of losing his life; he is also liable to contention with enemies; in ☌ of ♃ grave and serious; in △ he would be fortunate as a farmer, excavator, potter, plasterer, and other heavy dirty trades. In bad aspect of ♃ he suffers from religionists.

(Saturn gives a tall slender body, with long face and sallow complexion. The eyes are generally small and the hair dark. Saturn gives a melancholy nature; quiet, reserved and resentful, these natives have little to say. They are usually diplomatic and have tremendous power of concentration of both physical and mental effort when it will assist to attain success. Their ambitions are slowly aroused, but hard to satisfy.)

115. Jupiter in ♑ declares a low, middle stature, pale complexion, not much beard or whisker, thin face, little head, dark brown hair, rather darker than beard; mind ingenious but peevish, inactive, helpless, and not very fond of

work. Jupiter unafflicted the native will be miserly, and will appear poor and indigent, although plenty laid up in store; if in the VIIth he overcomes his enemies, and marries tolerably well. He is honest and discreet, whose person is far above rubies, and portends happiness in the querent's latter days. ♃ ☌ ♂ the querent is bold, proud, magnanimous; in bad aspect ill-natured, subtle, ungrateful, ambitious, fond of war and quarreling. ☽ ☌ ♃ petulant and chaneable.

(Jupiter here inclines to more weight than is usual for Capricorn. Jupiter gives success in public matters with the general attitude condescending and disdainful of others.)

116. Mars in ♑ gives a small stature, lean body, little face, little head, lank black hair, and dark complexion; ingenious mind, good disposition, witty, shrewd, and penetrating, generally successful in his undertakings. In the VIIth the wedded partners will be hasty, many bickerings will arise between them. Mars in the VIIth, it is never well to trust to friends, for they will turn malignant enemies. In ✶ or △ of ♄ he is prudent and cautious, yet bigoted in religion. Should aspects befriend ♂ he is likely to gain wealth; in ☌ of ♀ too fond of women, and not always very particular as to their respectability; in ☌ of ☽ fond of traveling, and danger of dying a violent death. He will do well in keeping cattle, etc.

(Mars gives pinched features here; the hair is usually dark with a reddish tint. However, Mars gives a good disposition in this position. The mind is clear, active and ingenious. They are usually fortunate and accomplish a leading position in life, even if they have to plot and scheme to attain that end. Dynamic energy added to self-centeredness is certain to push one forward.)

117. Sun in ♑ represents a mean stature, not well made, spare, thin body, oval face, sickly complexion, brown soft hair; in the first Facet, light brown hair, the party is just and honourable, a tolerable temper, yet very hasty at times, gains love and friendship by his agreeable conversation. In old age honoured, although in his younger days he will expose both reputation and estate by the means of lewd women; fond of taking short journeys to visit friends. In △ of ♃ he gains money; in △ of ♄ he is ostentatious and conceited, he would be successful as a farmer; in △ of ☽ he is proud and aspiring; in ☐ or ☍ of ♄ cowardly and treacherous.

(The Sun here decreases the height; gives a resolute and determined disposition. It overcomes some of the selfishness of Capricorn by increasing benevolence and consideration of others. The morals are usually lofty, but there is fondness for female association of a high order. Political ability is also a characteristic of this position of the Sun.)

118. Venus or Neptune in ♑ gives a mean stature, pale, sickly complexion, dark hair; if in the first Facet, sad brown hair, generally a person fond of enjoyment, a lover of women, not fortunate, subject to sudden changes in life, and strange catastrophes. In the VIIth the marriage will be happy, but the wife will be irritable and a little extravagant; many enemies, both public and private, but they are unable to injure. In ☌ of ♄ or ♂ he is wretched and debauched.

If a man of property he often wastes most of it by gaming or pleasure; in ✶ or △ of ♃ the person is virtuous and incapable of fraud or malice; if in △ or ✶ of ♄ shy and retiring in his manners; in ✶ or △ of ☿ ingenious and good natured; in □ or ☍ of ♂ treacherous and inconstant; if it be a female she is a prostitute, or very shameless. (For Neptune *see* article 112.)

(Venus tends to medium height with a pale complexion. There is a contrast between the complexion and the hair and eyes, both of the latter appearing dark brown. Venus here gives a great ambition to attain everlasting fame. It desires to accomplish without great effort and without competition. In fact in competition with others it will cause the native to devote his effort to mental success by subtle means. In the lower type this will produce a drunkard, as well as one who while always boasting of his own success and accomplishments, has accomplished nothing worth talking about.)

119. Mercury in ♑ personates a lean stature, bow-legged, thin face, dusky complexion, brown hair, helpless, sickly, and dejected, peevish and unfortunate; in ☌, □, or ☍ of ♃ or ♂ public enemies, calculating and covetous, capable of learning, and very artful. I should avoid these as companions or friends.

(Mercury here produces a small thin body with dull complexion. If Mercury be well aspected it gives great diplomacy. The mind is generally narrow in its outlook, however, and under affliction is tricky and crafty.)

120. Moon in ♑ personates a low stature, thin, small weak body, thin face, dull complexion, dark hair, weak in the knees, idle, dull and debauched in his conduct; yet if the ☽ receives the friendly rays of the ☉, ♃, or ♀ from good places of the figure the disposition is therefore improved; ☽ in the VIIth sorrow in youth. He never marries early, but follows vicious and disgraceful courses. The querent despairs of the matter in question, nor does he care much about it.

(The Moon in this position decreases the height, giving a long thin face, rather "hatchet faced" with a prominent nose. The skin is sallow and unhealthy looking in appearance. The position of the Sun is important. The Moon here gives a crafty nature. It produces a timidity which causes the character to be cautious and subtle that its own interests be cared for.)

The Planets in ♒

121. Aquarius describes a person short, well set, robust, strong, healthy, rather tall, never short (*sic*), delicate or fair complexion, long face, clear, but not pale; somewhat sanguine, hazel eyes, sandy or dark flaxen hair; generally an honest, benevolent disposition.

(Aquarius on the Ascendant gives a body of average height or above, very strongly built and rather inclined to be angular. The face is long and oval, the complexion clear; the eyes are light blue with blond to light brown hair and dark blue with dark hair. The arms are frequently long, with a short-waisted body. A healthy glow in appearance. Their bodies are exceedingly positive and on occasion give forth an electric discharge beneficial when used in the treatment of disease.

(The first Facet gives a tall body, with ruddy, healthy complexion and usually penetrating eyes with either light or dark brown hair. The second Facet gives medium height with small features and a tendency to dark complexion. The third Facet gives a tall body, well built, with a clear complexion and small features. The eyes are sharp and bright blue generally, and the hair light brown. The fourth Facet gives medium height, small features with dark complexion. The fifth Facet gives medium height, but with a thin well built body. The complexion is fair and clear, the hair and eyes both light in color. The sixth Facet gives a tall well built body, with good complexion, generally light. This facet gives a really handsome form.)

(The general character as indicated by Aquarius is frankness, honesty and stability. These natives have much originality, are fixed in opinion, but are reasonable and recognize the viewpoint of others. They make good companions for they are cheerful and good natured, but sometimes rather silent. There is also a nervous type of Aquarius which seems to be increasing in numbers with the advance of western civilization. They are sometimes spasmodic, and under affliction, are uncertain and undependable. They have a great gift for making friends and their interests generally tend toward progressive and occult matters.)

(The disposition as shown by the first Decanate is refined, sympathetic and humane. They are largely governed by their associates for while of fixed character, they accept and absorb influences readily. The high standard of refinement and purity of the better side of this sign is difficult to attain, but those who do respond to its higher vibrations "live in pure mind apart from all lower sensational and animal tendencies." The first Facet gives an amiable, easy disposition which is liable to bring many temptations. The second Facet is also easily led and fond of pleasure. They are frequently unreliable and easily fall into habits which are not conducive of developing the better side of their nature.)

(The second Decanate is more stabilizing in its influence. It inclines to intellectual attainments, although it does not give great depth. They make excellent linguists, and are frequently good teachers. The third Facet gives a quick, active nature, fond of discussion, and these natives are usually capable speakers. The fourth Facet has a tendency to develop some conceit in the nature for they always have a good opinion of their own abilities. These persons are ingenious and make excellent companions.)

(The third Decanate further improves the stability, giving balance and good judgment. The tastes are more refined, and in charts of high vibration the mystical side of life is prominent with a gift for clairvoyance. This is a decanate of celibacy, although the native is affected deeply by love affairs and marriage. Artistic ability is here indicated, as well as ability for the stage and elocution. The fifth Facet gives both a high moral character and intellectual ability. The sixth Facet acts in a double manner. At times it inclines to give a just, honest and sincere nature, while others born with it rising are sometimes cunning and deceptive. Much depends on the character developed in early years of life.)

122. Concerning Pluto *see* article 16.

123. (Neptune gives a body of medium height, fair complexion and abundant light hair. The eyes are usually light blue, large and appealing. Neptune in Aquarius is an excellent influence for art, music and sociology if other influences in the chart corroborate. In the low types, however, Neptune here makes the native a parasite, shiftless and always dependent on others.)

124. Uranus in ♒ represents a middle stature, rather fleshy, clear complexion, a good sized head and face, and brown hair; in disposition honourable, faithful, and punctual in promises; the quality of the mind firm, ingenious, steady in speech, patient and industrious; yet one that does not marry early. A mechanic, an inventor of items of machinery, and things connected with railways, etc.

(We disagree with Simmonite concerning Uranus in Aquarius; it gives a tall, angular body, well-proportioned, with light brown hair and clear-cut features. The eyes are large and lustrous. Uranus here gives independence and ingenuity. The character is somewhat eccentric and given to odd pursuits and investigations. These people have a keen sense of values and are interested in the great humanitarian problems of our age.)

125. Saturn in ♒ portends a strong stature, large head and face, corpulent, dark brown hair, clear complexion, sober and graceful deportment; if ruler of the first or sixth, frequently indisposed. Affable and courteous, profound wit, able in art or science, and naturally a person of a pregnant genius, by which he gains wealth. ♄ ☌ ♀ in the VIIth he marries a woman of an opposite temper and disposition to himself. If in ✶ or △ of ♃ sober, wise, and religious. ♄ afflicted by ♂ the native is base, envious, and quarrelsome.

(Saturn in ♒ gives a body of medium height, complexion dark and hair black. It gives much self-reliance. They frequently make good diplomats and detectives for they have an ability to ferret out the truth and to keep things to themselves until the proper time.)

126. Jupiter in ♒ personates a middle stature, well set, brown hair, a little red tinge, clear complexion and rather corpulent; disposition cheerful and affable, hurtful to none, but obliging to all; delights in moderate recreation; just and merciful to enemies, in short, a good humoured, laborious, industrious person, rarely guilty of extravagance, but generally of a very commendable disposition and deportment. In ☌ of ♄ he is careful and gains wealth; in ✶ or △ he is possessed of an inheritance, or houses may fall to him; ♃ in ✶ or △ of ♂ bold, proud, presumptuous; in ☐ or ☍ the native is rash and adventurous; ♃ in ☌, ✶ or △ of ♀, courteous disposition, fond of the female sex, and rises to preferment and honour.

(Jupiter gives a "happy-go-lucky" disposition. These natives enjoy themselves to the fullest extent, but particularly seek out respectable companions. They seem to imbue all with whom they associate with their own pleasant disposition.)

127. Mars in ♒ personates a body well set, rather tall, corpulent, fair

complexion, and sandy hair, turbulent spirit, too much addicted to controversy, often to his own detriment, if other testimonies do not occur. If he have brethren they will die before him. ♂ in ✶ or △ of ♀ the native is kind, gentle, and courteous, yet too fond of women's company; in ☌, □, or ☍ of the ☉ he aims at high things, but too frequently falls into trouble and misery; if ☉ is lord of the VIth, VIIth, or VIIIth danger of death by means of a fall, or a wound with a weapon; if lord of the Xth he is very likely transported, or at least imprisoned; if in ✶ or △ of ♃ the native is cheerful and merry, of a jovial disposition and just; one of good fame, and obtains the favour and good will of worthy persons.

(Mars gives a body of medium height, well-proportioned and strong. While the hair is usually red, it is sometimes either sandy or platinum blond. These natives are usually handsome. However, Mars gives a quarrelsome disposition here. They delight in argument and in making themselves appear different from other people. It is not a good position at all, although strong beneficial vibrations from other planets can overcome this.)

128. The Sun in ♒ prognosticates a middle stature, well made, yet corpulent body, round full face, clear complexion, and light brown hair; disposition moderately good, cheerful and of good conversation, but subject to ostentation, and desirous to bear rule, yet free from malicious actions; clever at most handicrafts if he is employed in them. ☉ in ☌, ✶, or △ of ♃ or ♀ religiously disposed, he obtains the love of women, by whom he is benefitted; but if the □ or ☍ of ♃ the native wastes his patrimony, is lofty, proud, and pragmatical; ☉ in □ or ☍ of ♂ danger of the loss of an eye, rash in all actions, and squanders away his substance. The querent is employed about foundries or railways.

(The Sun in ♒ gives an ambitious and aspiring disposition. They glory in authority and love to rule for they must be foremost in all activities of life. Progressive interests command their attention particularly in the fields of art, science and sociology.)

129. Venus or Neptune in ♒ gives a handsome person, reasonably corpulent, clear complexion, light brown or flaxen hair; in △ of ♃ a perfect beauty; in disposition just and commendable, affable and courteous, inclined to no vicious actions, one that loves civil recreations, quite obliging. ♀ afflicted by ♄, if a female, she is unchaste; the native is poor and of a timorous spirit; ♃ in □ of ♀ a flatterer; if a professor of religion, a hypocrite, and generally joins society for the sake of gain, or to mingle in youthful society; ♀ afflicted by ♂ given to strife, debauchery, and wickedness; ♀ in bad aspect of the ☽ a more vulgar, sordid creature, deceitful, and subject to misfortunes, especially for and among women; ♀ in ✶ or △ of the ☽ the native arrives at honour, and becomes very popular, but is inconstant, and performs no great actions; ♀ ☌ ☉ the native is proud and prodigal, liable to consumption and hectic fevers, frequent crosses and vexation. (Concerning Neptune *see* article 123.)

(Venus in ♒ gives a fine body, well proportioned with fine clear skin, blond complexion, blue eyes. Venus gives a courteous disposition always interested in the welfare of others. This is one of the most unselfish positions of any planet. There is a deep sense of the needs of humanity and a keen desire to assist in some way. These people are peacemakers and detest evil in any form.)

130. Mercury in ♒ personates a body of the middle size, rather fleshy, full face, clear complexion, brown hair, and a prepossessing countenance; disposition obliging, humane, and charitable. The quality of the mind ingenious, witty, inclined to the study of arts and sciences, and apt to find out many curious inventions. To be prosperous they ought to be employed as bookkeepers, teachers, clerks, secretaries, travellers, and other businesses connected with the pen. In ☌ ♅ astrologers, ministers and lecturers, but of an eccentric character. In ✶ or △ of ♄ the native is selfish and determined in his or her own way, parsimonious, and churlish; in good aspect of ♃ or ♀ courteous, prudent, and amorous; in good aspect with the ☽ mutable, a lover of inventions and novelties; but ☿ , afflicted by ♄ or ♂, unfortunate, poor, selfwilled and treacherous, and not fit for a companion.

(Mercury increases the height, and unless aspected by an exterior planet, gives a slender body. The face is long and usually the cheekbones are high. The disposition is good, generous and kind, inducing respect. The influence of Aquarius on Mercury here is to stabilize the mental attributes so that these people are often geniuses.)

131. The Moon in ♒ describes a middle stature, corpulent but well formed; brown hair and clear complexion; disposition affable, inoffensive, and benevolent. Mind ingenious; a pregnant brain, fond of learning, and a good genius. Trade, a shipwright, painter, merchant, etc. The ☽ in ☌ , ✶ or △ of ♅ or ☿ , then fond of learning and travelling. The ☽ ☌ ♃ or ♀ , gives prudence, and aims at high and honourable things, strives to oblige and serve his acquaintances, but the ☽ afflicted he is jealous, suspicious, and mistrustful, fond of tavern company.

(The Moon gives medium height, large eyes, but small features usually; the face is long and usually the cheekbones are high. She also gives an ability to rule other people, but the nature of the native is difficult to understand. They maintain their own way of life at all times, but sometimes are wayward and perverse. Those people have many hobbies and an interest in the mystical and obscure. It is a good position for astrologers.)

The Planets in ♓

132. The sign ♓ , shows a short person, thick set, pale, delicate complexion, fleshy face, and rather large thick shoulders, stooping gait, clumsy step, dark hair, illshaped head, not very well made, sleepy looking eyes, and large eyebrows, short arms and legs; the native holds the head down when walking; disposition timid, dull and phlegmatic.

(The first Facet of ♓ inclines the body to more height than any other portion of ♓ . The build is heavy, shoulders broad, hair thin, and the eyes are sunken and watery. The second Facet also gives a heavy body with brown hair, inclined to be thick. While the body is fleshy, it also appears bony. The third Facet gives a short plump body with good features and a rather healthy glow. The complexion has a soft velvety appearance. This facet often produces freckles. The fifth Facet gives a medium, but well proportioned body, strong and muscular appearing. The eyes are usually light and the hair chestnut in color. The sixth Facet gives a short stout body. Contrary to other portions of ♓, the features are dry, the complexion ruddy and robust looking. The hair is usually dark.

(The watery influence of ♓ gives uncertainty to the character. There are really two types, one which is very affectionate and good natured and another which is indolent, imaginative and parasitical. These people do not care much about work and only work sufficiently to accomplish what is necessary. They love a life of ease. They have a very sympathetic nature and are willing to express it in their relationship to others provided it requires no great effort. They are very adaptable.)

(The first Decanate of ♓ is very impressionable, restless and anxious. Environment and associations control the native more than innate will-power. The emotions are strong and as a result they suffer a great deal. The disposition is kind and generous and Pisceans often will do anything for a needy friend. As a rule, they are romantic and sentimental, although occasionally they may go to the other extreme and display cold nature. These natives are very receptive and are secretive or mysterious to the extreme. On the whole this is the most favorable of Pisces' decans for these people tend to find favor with those in superior positions, but too frequently the lack of self-control proves detrimental. The first Facet gives a subtle disposition to an irresolute person who lacks decision. They often lead a dual life. There is an inclination to study and some mediumistic ability. The second Facet increases the facility for study and as a result gives a person of good understanding. A prudent nature is also given with much patience. These natives are generally thoughtful and fond of the arts and sciences.)

(The second Decanate is more stabilizing in character, but there is a lack of self-confidence. These persons have a keen desire to be the channel for good. They are economical and careful. Their adaptability becomes an asset rather than a liability for their principal inborn desire is to be of value to humanity. The third Facet increases those positive characteristics and they are just and honorable. While the disposition is at times unstable because firmness is lacking, they have great self-reliance and will not hesitate to make decisions. The fourth Facet seems to influence in a peculiar way. While there is internal indecision, outwardly they appear to be decisive and firm. They are sincere and faithful and express good judgment.)

(The third Decanate generally shows forth the weaker side of ♓ for these natives are often jealous and selfish. Material side of life is emphasized, particularly as it relates to pleasures through which emotional expression is found. The sense of proportions are poor and this is sometimes interpreted as a lack of fear of consequences. The truth of the matter is that they do not sense the consequences. The ♏ influence on this decan is inimical to moral development unless other configurations overcome it. The fifth Facet gives a carefree, generous disposition. They talk too much and are very fond of company. They are very impressionable and will agree with any viewpoint. When the higher nature is strongly developed these natives show very strong character. The sixth Facet is very contradictory. Sometimes they are bold, combative and conceited, while at other times they lack these qualities and are entirely affected by surroundings, are dreamy, mediumistic and subservient.)

133. Concerning Pluto *see* article 16.

134. (Neptune in ♓ gives a short stout body, but the appearance has a sort of pearly complexion. The eyes are deep set and usually of light blue color. The appearance of these natives is generally inspiring. Here Neptune in its higher vibrations gives a humane, sensitive and impressionable nature. There is a deep love of poetry expressed in every avenue of life. These people are idealistic and inspirational. In the lower types, however, they are lazy, addicted to drink and parasitic in nature.)

135. Uranus in ♓ personates one of a middle stature, pale complexion, oval face, dark brown curling hair, high forehead, inclined to be plump or fleshy, and moderate beard and whisker. The temper malicious, but not without cause; a lover of female company, and sometimes addicted to drink; disposition just in his actions, rather fond of debate; ingenious, but somewhat mutable in his resolves, and generally fortunate. He does best in following a trade in which he sells articles of consumption, as beer, bread, huckstering, fishmonger, and seller of all kinds of liquids.

(Uranus in ♓ increases the height of the body which is stout. The complexion is pale and the hair is usually brown, either light or dark. Uranus generally brings out unfavorable characteristics when placed in this position. The nature is very peculiar and eccentric. They are vacillating and undependable.)

136. Saturn in ♓ represents a middle stature, pale complexion, dark brown hair, a good sized head and face, full eyes, and not good front teeth, active in his movements, but waddling walk; disposition contentious, malicious, fickle, not to be trusted as a friend, treacherous, though with a good outside. The disposition improves as the native grows older. Employment—butcher, farmer, having also to do with railways, metals, and other things connected with the produce of the earth. The ☌ of ♄ and ♂, portends many sorrows; ♄. ♂ ☉. liable to losses, the native subject to be cheated in his property; in ☌ or ill aspect of ♀, he is dishonoured by females, and is libidinous; in ☌ or ill aspect with ☿, self-conceited, and fond of mysteries; in ill aspect of ♃, trouble and vexation; but the good aspects of ♄ and ♃ denote gravity, fond of travelling, desirous of seeing new things, and he will gain by merchandise.

(This is not a good position for Saturn for in charts otherwise benefic, these natives are generally unfortunate so far as worldly gain is concerned. It gives a good mind, however, exceedingly devotional. In any case these people are difficult to understand. They are exceptionally secretive and live very much to themselves. There is some hypocrisy and in charts of low vibration, a strong inclination to drink and vice.)

137. Jupiter in ♓ describes a low stature and fleshy, dull complexion, brown hair, sometimes flaxen; disposition dull and stupid, deceitful, idle and worthless; sottish, debauched, and a bad husband or wife, and much addicted to lustful depravities. Businesses which the native ought to follow to be most successful are those of a ship-carpenter, painter, whitewasher, halft-presser or knife-hafter. Mars here afflicted by ♄ the party signified is a sloven, dissembler, especially if this sign be on the house of question; more especially if ♀ be in ♊, in the Vth, disposing of the ☽, lady of the VIIth, renders the party not only a notorious whoremonger, but also a thief and liar, and so much the worse should ♃ be in ♍. Mars in ✶ or △ of the ☉, then he may meet with preferment, and may gain by a nimble tongue in good aspect with ♀; he is too much given to females.

(Jupiter in ♓ gives a body of medium height, stout but with a healthy appearance and moderately good looking. The face is full, the hair dark and the forehead prominent; a lover of music, of good company, of pleasure. The character is usually strong and there is a great deal of ambition. The disposition is studious and these natives usually will search out to the bottom of things.)

138. Mars in ♓ describes a mean stature, rather short and fleshy, dull complexion, but pale; disposition dull, artful, stupid, often debauched, inclined to drink and to be idle. If ♂ be with ♃, the disposition is improved, more benevolent and industrious. Mars with ♀, then very prodigal, much addicted to the opposite sex; but if with ♄ cruel, he suffers from his dishonesty; but in ✶ or △ of ♄, then grave, cautious and cowardly. If ♓ ascends with ♀ in ♊, in the Vth, disposing of the ruler of the VIIth, the querent is a notorious liar and thief, and so much the worse should ♃ be in ♍.

(Mars gives a short body, generally very stout. The complexion is usually ruddy with hair light brown, having a reddish tint. Mars here gives a hypocritical disposition. Blending the fire of ♂ with the duality of watery ♓, we find an inclination to vicious habits, excessive drinking, association with low company, etc. Of course, this may be modified in a horoscope of high vibration.)

139. The Sun in ♓ signifies a short fleshy body, round face, a good complexion, light brown or flaxen hair; disposition fond of gaming and feasting, a lover of the female sex; yet a person very harmless to others, and who injures none but himself and family, which he often does by his extravagance and prodigality.

(The Sun gives a body of medium height, stout and with fairly good complexion. The face is round, the hair light brown and thin. The Sun gives a hospitable and generous nature. Strong fondness for water and these people frequently make good swimmers. It overcomes the lower characteristics of Pisces to a large extent and gives some ambition. There is a strong tendency to religious matters in this position.)

140. Venus or Neptune in ♓ portends a middle stature, rather plump and fleshy, full face, with a dimple in the cheek or chin, good complexion and brown hair; disposition just and mild, peaceable and ingenious, somewhat mutable in his resolutions, yet moderately fortunate in the world. The business best to follow is that of a seller of eatables and drinkables, and such things as decorate or ornament females. (Concerning Neptune *see* article 134.)

(Venus in ♓ bestows a pleasant disposition, peace-loving to the extreme. It gives balance to understanding and a harmonious temperament.)

141. Mercury in ♓ shows a person stiffly made, pale, sickly complexion, and hairy body; disposition repining, disconsolate, yet a lover of women and addicted to drinking, and consequently a nuisance to himself, family, and neighborhood, and indeed a pest to society, as all Mercurial persons are when that planet is found there, significator, in the signs ♓ and ♐.

(Mercury does not increase the height to an appreciable extent here. The face is pale and thin, the eyes usually grey and the hair dull brown. This is not a very strong position for Mercury for the mixture of its mental attributes with the emotionalism of Pisces gives a fondness for gratification of the senses. They are exceptionally fond of the opposite sex and through this do not rise in life unless the chart otherwise shows great moral stamina.)

142. The Moon in ♓ describes a person of a mean stature, pale countenance, light brown hair and plump; disposition idle, dull, evilly disposed, and often unfortunate. Fishmongers, tripesellers, and such like are indicated by this position. The ☽ in ☌, ✶, or △ of ♀ or ♃, the disposition is improved and the body is more active. The ☽, here, afflicted by ♄, the person will be in danger of losing an eye, and he is subject to many crosses. In good aspect of ☉, he aims at honourable procedure.

(The Moon here inclines the lower portion of the body to be ill-formed and the native clumsy. The features including the eyes are soft and mild, but poorly formed and languid. The personality is refined and pleasing. There is deep sympathy and ability to express the emotions through intellectual channels. These people make good doctors and nurses for their personality is thus expressed as soft and gentle. There is too frequently, however, an inferiority complex which produces timidity to the extreme and gives strong forebodings of evil which usually never materialize.)

143. Many astrologers make sad confusion in describing the form of any person. Their rules are too intricate to admit of clear definition, and too contradictory to be easily and perspicuously reconciled. The sign on the cusp of the house signifying the quesited, and the sign intercepted, if there be one, their lords the planets any way aspecting; and to those some add the luminaries, and the stars that aspect them; all these are significators of the form of the body as well as the mind. I am certain no human intellect, however acute, can form a correct judgment of anyone's appearance from so many conflicting testimonies.

Rule: Take the planet which rules the house of inquiry, and the sign in which he is posited, together with any planet in the sign of the cusp of the houses, and judge of the appearance and quality of the person quesited. If there be no planets in the sign of the cusp of the house signifying the inquiry, then judge solely by the lord of that house, and the sign in which he happens to be. Never mind aspects, neither conjunctions, nor any other. There is, however, some slight modification to be made; for when a planet is direct, judge just as the foregoing describes; but if the planet be retrograde, the person will partake somewhat more of the description given by the sign, independent of the planet, and this must be attended to; for the planets being in their exaltation, or fall, detriment, or accidental abilities, have been fully provided for in considering the appearances.

Disposition Produced by the Planets

Pluto ♀
144. Concerning Pluto *see* article 16.

Neptune ♆
145. (♆ is dual in its influence on disposition and character. In the one type it produces the idealist, the religionist, mystic, psychic, the dreamer who is sometimes too visionary. In the other it produces the irresponsible, lazy, indecisive individual without moral stamina. Under affliction they are deceptive, intriguing, dishonest. This is the planet of mimicry and oft-times these people ape others, are parasitic and dependent upon others through a lack of initiative themselves.)

Uranus ♅
146. ♅ denotes an eccentric person, far from fortunate, always abrupt, and often violent in his manners. When well dignified, he gives sudden and unexpected changes in life of a beneficial character, full of inventions and novelties. When ill dignified, he causes remarkable and unlooked for losses, a violent temper, and a very bad husband or wife, and misfortunes by public bodies.

Saturn ♄
147. ♄ when well dignified, as in ♑ or ♎, is profound in imagination; in his acts, severe; in words, reserved; in speaking and giving, very sparing; in labour, patient; in arguing or disputing, grave; in obtaining the goods of this life, studious and solicitous; in all manner of actions, austere; a true friend, except influenced by others, which is not often the case.

148. When ill dignified, as in ♈ and ♋, he is envious, covetous, jealous, mistrustful, timorous, sordid, outwardly dissembling, sluggish, suspicious, stubborn, a contemner of women, a liar, malicious, murmurer, never contented, and over repining.

Jupiter ♃

149. When well dignified, as in ♐ and ♋, the native is magnanimous, faithful, bashful, honourable, aspiring at high matters; in actions, a lover of fair dealing, desiring to benefit all persons, doing glorious actions; honourable and religious, sweet, affable conversation, indulgent to his wife and children, reverencing age; a reliever of the poor and full of charity; liberal, hating all sordid actions, just, wise, prudent, grateful, and virtuous.

150. When ill dignified, as in ♊ and ♍, he wastes his patrimony, suffers anyone to cozen him, is hypocritically religious, tenacious and obstinate in maintaining false tenets, ignorant, careless, regardless of the love of his friends, a gross, dull capacity, systematical, chasing himself in company, insinuating and stooping where no necessity is, in order to gain and retain good opinions of others; a bad husband. Most sectarian bigots have ♃ ill dignified, as when in ♊ or ♍ especially.

Mars ♂

151. ♂ when well dignified produces a fearless, violent, irascible, and unsubmitting person, naturally delighting in war, or contention, but in other respects prudent, rational, and even generous, or magnanimous. Generally very conscientious.

152. When unfortunately dignified, the native is wholly destitute of any virtue, prone to violence, boasting, quarreling, pride, treachery, robbery, murder, treason, and every species of cruelty and wickedness. He is not so violent in ♉ or ♎, although in his detriment he is the worst in ♋ and ♑.

Sun ☉

153. When well dignified, the disposition is noble, magnanimous, yet proud and lofty, but humane, a faithful friend, and a generous enemy scorning to use advantages which may be given over his opponents, generally of few words, but very pompous and magnificent, fond of dress, ornaments, and decorations of all sorts, extremely partial to costly jewels and splendid attire.

154. When ill dignified, as in ♋ and ♒, the native is both proud and mean, arrogant and submissive, a tyrant, and yet a sycophant, empty, vain, a great talker, restless, a vain boaster, uncharitable, despotical, unfeeling, selfish, ungenerous, unamiable, disliked on account of his arrogance and ignorant pomposity.

Venus ♀ and Neptune ♆

155. Venus or Neptune, when well dignified, the temper is even, quiet, placid, graceful, engaging, fair spoken, sweet, merry, and cheerful, amateurs in music, dancing, and accomplishments out of the ordinary way; the native is much inclined to jealousy. (Concerning Neptune *see* article 145.)

156. Venus, ill dignified, the native is lewd, idle, profligate, shameless, timorous, and lascivious, especially if in ill aspect to ♄, ♂, or ♅; and if a

female she will be a drunken creature, a notorious thief and liar.

Mercury ☿

157. ☿, well dignified, as in ♊ and ♍, represents a subtle political brain and intellect, an excellent disputant and logician, arguing with learning and discretion, a searcher into mysteries and learning, sharp and witty, learning almost anything without a teacher, ambitious of being exquisite in every science, desirous to travel and see foreign parts, of unwearied fancy, curious in occult knowledge.

158. When ill dignified, as in ♐ and ♓, the native is a phrenetic person, his tongue and pen against every man, wholly bent to fool his estate and time in trying nice conclusions to no purpose, a gambler, a great liar, coxcomb, boaster, prattler, cheat, busybody, newsmonger, and is false, a tale carrier, easy of belief, constant in no place or opinion, pretending all kinds of knowledge but void of real learning, a trifler. If the native prove a divine, then a more verbal person, frothy, of no judgment, easily perverted, unprincipled, constant in nothing but idle words and bragging.

Moon ☽

159. Luna, when well dignified, as in ♋ or ♐, the native has manners, is a lover of science, a mild searcher and delighter in novelties, naturally inclined to remove his habitation, unsteadfast, caring for the present times, timorous, prodigal, and easily frightened, loving peace, and to live free from the cares of life. If a mechanic he learns many occupations, and tampers with many ways in which to trade.

160. When ill dignified the native is a vagabond, an idle person, stupid, hating labour, a drunkard, of no forecast, delighting to live beggarly, careless, and is discontented.

Employments

Pluto ♀

161. (We are in agreement with the view expressed by Charles E. Luntz in his excellent work *Vocational Guidance by Astrology* (page 40) wherein he says:
> It is hazardous at present to use ♀ as a significator of occupation.
> His comparatively recent discovery, combined with the obscure nature of the planet, make it advisable to ignore him in vocational selection, except in connection with death and things appertaining to it. Thus he undoubtedly governs Undertakers, Embalmers, Cemetery Associations, Life Insurance Salesmen and other workers, and all occupations connected in any way with the end of life.

Likewise, in the researches of Clement Hey, FAFA, he found that Pluto was probably a greater benefic than Jupiter. He made actual tests of this planet by making purchases of commodities for resale when this planet mundanely dominated a chart for such moments and found it of value in sales work. While Mr. Luntz assigns rulership of Pluto to Scorpio, Mr. Hey assigns it to Aries. Undoubtedly when final determination is made, it will probably be found that Pluto is directly related to both these signs. *See* article 16.)

Neptune ♆

162. (Neptune has rulership over vocations dealing with liquids, such as distillers, chemists, oil and oilwell workers, gasoline station attendants, pharmacists; in addition it has to do with musicians, poets, occultists, fishing and fish marketing, poets, anaesthetists and detectives. It also rules astrologers with a primary interest in the esoteric side of the science; naval officers and enlisted men.)

Uranus ♅

163. ♅ signifies antiquarians, astrologers, phrenologists, teachers, chemists, lecturers, sculptors, metaphysicians, mesmerizers, and all uncommon students.

(We do not agree that chemists come under ♅, but rather ♆. Uranus also rules such vocations as chiropractors, naturopathists, clairvoyants, all manner of positions having to do with electricity, radio and automobiles. It rules telegraphers; public utility employees, particularly telephone; scientists; inventors; engineers.)

Saturn ♄

164. ♄ signifies husbandmen, clowns, and all employments of old men, curriers, bricklayers, miners, tinners, potters, plumbers, maltsters, sextons, scavengers, hostlers, carters, chandlers, gardeners, cowkeepers, shepherds, shoemakers, duers, excavators, and tanners.

(♄ rules real estate salesmen, builders, stoneworkers and monument buildings, coal, wood and ice men; watch and clock makers; instrument makers; religionists.)

Jupiter ♃

165. ♃ signifies judges, senators, counsellors, lawyers, preachers, professors, doctors of the civil law, bishops, priests, ministers, cardinals, chancellors, clothiers, woollen drapers, and civilians.

(♃ rules all phases of publishing, editing, advertising; with Capricorn—all positions related to horse racing and hunting.)

Mars ♂

166. ♂ signifies generals, colonels, captains, or any soldiers having command, all manner of soldiers, physicians. apothecaries, surgeons, chemists, gunners, butchers, bailiffs, hangmen, thieves, smiths, bakers, armourers, watchmakers, tailors, cutlers, barbers, dyers, cooks, carpenters, gamesters, and accord-

ing as Mars be strong or weak.

(♂ rules barbers, boxers, all manner of workers in iron and steel, officers of the law, firemen, guards and detectives, wrestlers, locksmiths and mechanics generally.)

167. The ☉ signifies kings, princes, emperors, etc., dukes, marquises, earls, barons, lieutenants, deputy lieutenants of counties, magistrates, gentlemen in general; courtiers, justices of the peace, high sheriffs, constables, superintendents, stewards of noblemen's houses, the principal magistrate of a city, town, or country village, even a petty constable, where no better is; goldsmiths, braziers, pewterers, coppersmiths, excisemen, the minters of money.

(The Sun rules Presidents, the ranking officer of any organization, vocations having to do with wealth such as bankers, stock exchange employees and speculators, workers in gold, jewelers, etc.)

Venus ♀ and Neptune ♆

168. Venus signifies musicians, gamesters, silkmen, mercers, haberdashers, linendrapers, painters, jewellers, players, embroiderers, lapidaries, women tailors, choristers, fiddlers, pipers; when joined with ♆, ballad singers, perfumers, seamstresses, engravers, upholsterers, limners, glovers, and such as sell these commodities which adorn women, and those sold over a counter. (Concerning Neptune *see* article 162.)

Mercury ☿

169. ☿, when well placed, signifies astrologers, philosophers, mathematicians, secretaries, officers of state, travellers, sculptors, poets, lawyers, printers, teachers, divines, orators, ambassadors, commissioners, artificers, and all ingenious clever persons. When ill dignified, he represents scriveners, clerks, pettifoggers, vile persons, cunning in acting mischief, thieves, carriers, messengers, footmen and servants.

(☿ also rules bookbinders, accountants, bookkeepers, transportation employees of all kinds, storekeepers and salesmen; all kinds of employment requiring speech and/or writing as a primary requisite; editors; notaries public; stenographers; messengers, etc.)

Moon ☽

170. The ☽ signifies sailors, navigators, travellers, fishermen, fishmongers, brewers, publicans, milkmen, letter carriers, coachmen, huntsmen, messengers, mariners, millers, maltsters, watermen, boatmen, navy officers, inferior servants, and dealers in all kinds of fluids, midwives, nurses, and hackneymen. (*Note:* Simmonite undoubtedly assigns some Neptunian pursuits to the Moon.)

(The Moon also rules all vocations having to do with restaurants, saloons and taverns, including waiters; domestic employees, particularly women, brewery and distillery workers; fishermen, etc.)

Local Places Ruled by the Signs

171. **Aries**—Denotes pasture ground for cattle, sandy, hilly grounds, hiding places for thieves, and unfrequented places. In houses it denotes the covering, ceiling, or plastering; stables for small cattle, lands recently ploughed, lime and brick kilns, and the eastern part of the above.

172. **Taurus**—Denotes stables, cowhouses, places for holding furniture or cattle, pasture grounds at a distance from houses, grounds lately cleared of bushes, and sowed with wheat, trees that are not far off, cellars and low rooms.

173. **Gemini**—Denotes wainscot, plastering and walls, coffers, chests, trunks, barns, storehouses for corn, hills, mountains and high places, playhouses, dining-rooms, schools, nurseries, and places for learning.

174. **Cancer**—Denotes seas, and great navigable rivers, lakes, canals, brooks, springs, wells, marshes, ditches, sinks, sedges, trenches, sea banks, washhouses, cellars and pumps.

175. **Leo**—Denotes haunts of wild beasts, woods, forests, dens and deserts, rocky, inaccessible places, castles, forts, parks, kings' palaces, fireplaces in houses, chimneys, furnaces, ovens and stoves.

176. **Virgo**—Denotes studies, libraries, bookcases, closets, dairies, cornfields, gardens, hayricks, malthouses, storehouses of butter, cheese, or corn, and barns.

177. **Libra**—Denotes detached barns, outhouses, sawpits, cooperages, inner chambers, attic stories, grounds near windmills, mountain tops, sides of hills, chases, commons, barren, stony or sandy ground, and places having a pure, clear, sharp air.

178. **Scorpio**—Denotes places where vermin and reptiles breed, sinks, drains, stinking pools, ruins near water, muddy swamps, quagmires, marshes, gardens, orchards, vineyards, kitchens, larders and wash-houses, moors, and places where rubbish is laid.

179. **Sagittary**—Denotes stables for war horses and receptables for great cattle, hills and high lands, any rising place, and the fireplaces in upper rooms.

180. **Capricorn**—Denotes cowhouses or receptacles for calves, toolhouses, or places for lumber or old wood, ships' storehouses, sheep pens, fields, fallow or barren fields, thorny, bushy places, dunghills or places for soil, dark corners near the ground or threshold, and low houses.

181. **Aquarius**—Denotes quarries of stone or mines of metals, or any place recently dug up; hilly uneven grounds; vineyards, sources of springs or conduits, roofs and eaves of houses; windows and places for machinery; surgeries and lecture rooms.

182. **Pisces**—Denotes marshy grounds full of springs where waterfowls breed; rivers and ponds full of fish; moats, water mills, old hermitages, and those places in houses near where the water is, as pumps, cisterns or wells.

Local Places Ruled by the Planets

183. Concerning **Pluto** *see* article 16.

184. (**Neptune**—rules hospitals, infirmaries, jails, prisons; all forms of liquids, the sea, seashore; caves and mysterious places; seaplanes landing places.)

185. Uranus—rules railways, steam engines, banks, gas vessels, asylums, infirmaries, dispensaries, railway stations and offices, bastiles and workhouses.

(Modern experience disagrees with Simmonite on rulership of infirmaries, dispensaries, asylums, bastilles and workhouses, assigning these to Neptune. Uranus also rules aeroplanes.)

186. Saturn—delights in deserts, woods, obscure valleys, dens, caves, holes, sepulchres, church yards, ruinous buildings, coalpits, sinks, wells, muddy, dirty, stinking places, and nuisances of every description; in aspect with ♅ , or in ♈ or ♍, very dirty places in houses.

187. Jupiter—denotes churches, oratories, palaces, gardens, altars, synods or courts of justice; wardrobes and magnificent abodes, or neat and curious places, woods, orchards and bushes.

188. Mars—denotes all those places appertaining to fire or blood; laboratories, furnaces, distilleries, bakehouses, ovens; smiths', cutlers' and butchers' shops, and such like.

189. The Sun—denotes princes' palaces, magnificent buildings, dining-rooms, towers, splendid apartments, and costly houses.

190. Venus—denotes beds and bedchambers, dancing and dining-rooms, gardens, fountains, wardrobes, banqueting houses, theatres, etc.

191. Mercury—represents, symbolically, schools, common halls, or public convened assemblies, places where lively games are held, as tennis and racket courts, fairs, ordinaries, markets, bowling greens, the hall, study, libraries, counting houses, pulpits, attorneys' and clerks' offices.

192. The Moon—represents the sea, the ocean, large lakes or bodies of water, fountains, fields near the sea, seaports, rivers, pools, fish ponds, brooks, bogs, docks, springs, common sewers, wharfs, etc.

Things Ruled by the Planets

193. (Concerning **Pluto** *see* article 16. Pluto also probably has rulership over sewers, alcoholic liquors, atomic energy, informal machines, marshes, etc.)

194. (**Neptune** rules all liquids and gasses, motion pictures, sedatives of all kinds, boats and marine objects, seaplanes, narcotics.)

195. Uranus shows coal, machinery, coins, baths, fish ponds, all things used in employments where danger is in the using thereof.

(Fishponds more properly are under Neptune, while automobiles, airplanes, and instruments of travel are related to Uranus.)

196. Saturn shows lead, iron, things of dark colour, wool, black garments, heavy materials, agricultural implements, wheelbarrows, spades, shovels, farm houses, and their outhouses.

197. Jupiter has rule over honey, oil, silk, men's clothhing, merchandise, horses and domestic fowls.

198. Mars denotes arms, pepper, brass, silver, red clothes, red wines and red things; sharp instruments, cutlery, cutting instruments, horses for war, warlike engines or instruments (and automobiles or machinery of all kinds).

199. The Sun gives gold, brass, yellow apparel, diamonds and valuable things.

200. Venus governs women's apparel, rings, ornaments, brooches, earrings, etc.; white cloth, bedding, and white wines; ♀ and ☿ joint rulers, denote metallic ornaments; ♀ and ♂ brooches and external ornaments, trumpery.

201. Mercury shows money, bills, paper, books, pictures, party coloured dresses, etc.; scientific instruments, penknives, inkstands, and all other things useful for the writing table, and for school.

202. The Moon signifies all common commodities, such as crockery, poultry, washing instruments, and silver-plated articles.

Countries and Cities under the Influence of the Twelve Signs of the Zodiac

Lest thou lift up thine eyes unto heaven, and when thou seest the sun and the moon, and the stars, even all the host of heaven, shouldest be driven to worship them, and serve them, which *the Lord thy God hath divided unto all nations under the whole heaven.*
— Deut. 4:19

203. Aries—*Countries:* Britain, Galatin, Germany, Lithuania, Lower Poland, Burgundy, Denmark, Palestine, Syria or Judea, especially Lebanon, and near Damascus. *Cities and Towns:* Naples, Capua, Verona, Florence, Brunswick, Padua, Marseilles, Cracow, Saragossa, Utrecht, and Leicester.

204. Taurus—*Countries:* Persia, Mozendaran, Media, Azerbaijan, Georgia, Caucasus, Asia Minor, the Archipelago, Cyprus, Poland, Ireland, White Russia, and Holland. *Cities and Towns:* Dublin, Mantua, Leipsic, Parma, Franconia and Palermo.

205. Gemini—*Countries;* Tripoli, Armenia, Lower Egypt, Flanders, Lombardy, Sardinia, Brabant, Belgium, the West of England, and the United States of America. *Cities and Towns:* London, Versailles, Mentz, Loraine, Bruges, Cordova and Nuremburg.

206. Cancer—*Countries:* North and Western Africa, Anatolia, near Constantinople, Scotland, Holland, Zealand, and Mengrelea. *Cities and Towns:* Amsterdam, Cadiz, Constantinople, Venice, Genoa, Tunis, York, St. Andrews, New York, Berne, Milan, Lubec, Vincentia, Madenburg, Manchester the 29th and 30th degrees.

207. Leo—*Countries:* Italy, Sicily, France, Puglia, the Alps, Bohemia,

Chaldea, the coast of Sidon and Tyre, Capadocia, Apulia, and Lancashire. *Cities and Towns:* Rome, Bath, Bristol, Prague, Taunton, Damascus, Ravenna, Bolton-le-Moors (especially the last ten degrees), Portsmouth and Philadelphia (Chicago).

208. Virgo—*Countries:* All Turkey, Croatia, Mesopotamia, Babylon, Assyria, the country between the Tiber and the Euphrates, Greece, Livadia, Thessaly, Corinth, Morea, Candia, Switzerland, and the Lower Silesia. *Cities and Towns:* Jerusalem, Navarre, Paris, Basel, Padua, Lyons, Toulouse, Heidelberg, Reading, Bagdad and Cheltenham.

209. Libra—*Countries:* China, Japan, and the parts near China; Bactrianna, the vicinity of the Caspian, Usbeck, part of Thibet, Livonia, Austria, Savoy, Upper Egypt and Oasis. *Cities and Towns:* Antwerp, Lisbon, Frankfort, Spirios, Fribourg, Vienna, Gaeta, Charlestown, Suessa and Plazenza.

210. Scorpio—*Countries:* Algiers, Bavaria, Barbary, Catalonia, Fez, Judea, Jutland, Morocco, the kingdom of the Moors, and the country about Norway. "The Natives are pugnacious, indifferent to danger, regardless of blood, and careless of each other." *Cities and Towns:* Frankfort on the Oder, Ghent, Liverpool (about the 18th degree), and Messina.

211. Sagittary—*Countries:* Cape Finisterre, Arabia, Dalmatia, parts of France between La Seins and La Garrone, Hungary, Italy, especially Taranta; Morovia, Province in France, Slavonia, Spain and Tuscany. "These inhabitants are lovers of freedom, simplicity and elegance." *Cities and Towns:* Avignon, Buda, Cologne, Narbonne, Naples, Rotenberg, Stutland, Sheffield, especially the 17th and 18th degrees; Toledo and Volterioe.

212. Capricorn—*Countries:* India, Khozassan, Cireran, Macian, Punjab, Macedonia, Thrace, Morea, Illyria, Bosnia, Albania, Bulgaria, Stiua, Romandiola, Saxony, Hesse, Mexico, Mecklenberg, Lithuania. *Cities and Towns:* Oxford, Prato, Brandenburg, Tortona, Constance, Mayence.

213. Aquarius—*Countries:* Stony Arabia, Prussia, Red Russia, Poland, Lithuania, Tartary part of Muscovy, Circassia, Tartaria especially Ursbeck, Walachia, Sweden, Westphalia, Piedmont, Azania and Abyssinia. *Cities and Towns:* Hamburg, Bremen, Trent, Saltzburg and Ingoldstadt.

214. Pisces—*Countries:* Portugal, Calabria, Normandy, Gallacia in Spain, Egypt, Fozzan, the desert of Zara, Nubia, and the southern part of Asia Minor. *Cities and Towns:* Alexandria, Ratisbon, Worms, Seville, Compostalo, Silicia and Tiverton.

Signification of the Twelve Houses

215. First House: Answers questions concerning the state, health, circumstances, accidents, mind, form, and stature of the querent, the state of a ship at sea, voyages, fathers of kings, sickness of enemies, journeys of children, friends of brethren, and the success of any enterprise.

216. Second House: Answers questions concerning lent money, wealth or poverty, loss or gain by traffic, prosperity or adversity, loss or gain, moveable goods, money employed in speculation, or suits of law, or what the VIIth house denotes; it shows a man's friends, trade of children, private enemies of brethren, and our first brother or sister, the death of wife or husband, partners, sweethearts and public enemies.

217. **Third House**: Answers questions on brothers, neighbours, short journeys, removing of manufactures, brothers, sisters, cousins, rumours, epistles or letters, children of friends, sickness of kings, friends of children, private enemies of fathers, messengers, children's trade and honour, churches, clerks, long journeys of lovers, husband or wife, sects, dreams, mutations, churches, and the trade of servants.

218. **Fourth House**: Solves questions concerning fathers, land, houses, estates, towns, cities, castles, entrenchments, hidden treasures, gardens, orchards, and fields. It denotes the house or tenement of the querent, and the issue of every undertaking; dead men's goods, substance of brethren, children of private enemies, sickness of friends, trade of public enemies, purchasing or hiring land, trade of husbands; things mislaid.

219. **Fifth House**: Answers questions relating to children, pregnancy, health of sons and daughters, personal effects of fathers, success of messengers and ambassadors, ammunition or strength of a place besieged, pleasure, charters, lotteries, brethren of brethren, death of monarchs, private enemies of servants, clubs, hills, our second brother or sister, and a person's first child, bettings, horse and foot racing, games, dancings, music, and merriment.

220. **Sixth House**: Resolves questions that appertain to servants, small cattle, the recovery of a sick person, the real state of the disease, whether of long or short duration; particulars relating to uncles, aunts, kindred of the father's die, stewards, tenants, shepherds, farmers, substance of children, brethren of fathers, death of friends, long journeys of monarchs, private enemies of wives, day labourers, and brethren or sisters' short journeys.

221. **Seventh House**: Answers questions concerning marriage, lawsuits, whether property lost will be recovered, love affairs, description of the person the enquirer will marry, theft, and describes the person of the thief, fugitives, or runaways, offenders escaped from justice, grandfathers, whether it will be well to remove, contracts, whether favourable or not, speculations in the funds or shares, etc., whether to buy or sell at given periods, partnerships in trade, fines, pleas; in battle who is victorious, children of brothers or sisters, death of private enemies; in physics the physician; defendants in lawsuits; our third brother or sister, and our second child; banks, bonds, men with whom we have common dealings, in astrology it signifies the artist. Uranus, Saturn, Mars or the Moon ill placed therein shows unfortunate marriage.

222. **Eighth House**; Answers questions concerning deaths, legacies, wills, property of a partner, wife, husband, or enemy; labour, sorrow, brethren of servants, sickness of brethren, dowry of wife or husband, substance of a second brother or sister, or of a public foe.

223. Ninth House: Solves all questions concerning the safety, profit, and success of voyages and travels; clergy, benefices, preferment in the church, advowsons, success of books, insurance, science and learning; kindred of wives, health of fathers, children of servants, or tenants; our grandchildren, our third child and our fourth brother or sister.

224. Tenth House: Answers inquiries concerning kings, nobles, magistrates, and masters; honour and preferment if attainable; the gaining of office, appointment or employment. It denotes the mother- or father-in-law of the querent; the business for which a man is most fit, substance taken away by thieves, children of servants, private enemies of friends, lawyers, sickness of children generally, gains by long journeys or by arts and sciences.

225. Eleventh House: Answers inquiries relative to friends, the trusts, flatterers, expectance or desire; perfidy of friends, ambassadors and advisors, the substance of monarchs; sickness of servants, death of fathers, enemies of children, our brother or sister's long journeys, our enemies' enemies, our fifth brother or sister.

226. Twelfth House: Answers questions concerning tribulation, sorrow, affliction, imprisonment, persecution, malice, secret enemies, suicide, treason, assassination, large cattle, relations on the mother's side, banished persons, the substance of friends, sickness of wives or husbands, death of children, trade of brethren, blasphemy, foetus of animals previous to birth, servants' enemies, mother's first brother or sister, short journeys of mothers, or master or mistress.

A Diagram Exhibiting the Principal Significations of the Houses of the Heavens

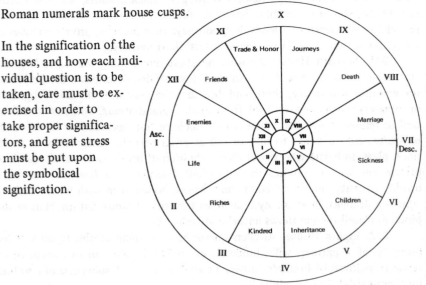

Roman numerals mark house cusps.

In the signification of the houses, and how each individual question is to be taken, care must be exercised in order to take proper significators, and great stress must be put upon the symbolical signification.

Explanation of the Diagram

This is called a horoscope or Figure of the Houses. These houses are distinguished by figures (Roman), and are either angular, as E., S., W. and N. or by I, X, VII and IV; succeedent, as II, V, VIII and XI; cadent as III, VI, IX and XII. At E. the Sun rises; at S. the Sun souths, or is on the meridian; at W. the Sun sets; at N. the Sun is on the nadir, corresponding to midnight, being the opposite point the Sun possesses at noon. Angles are of the greatest power, next the succeedents, and lastly, cadents are the weakest. The Xth is the South angle, the Ist the East angle, the VIIth the West angle, and the IVth the North angle.

227. Colours Ruled by the Planets

♀ Probably dark hues generally
♆ Turquoise blue and sea colors
♅ Plaids, checks and mingled colors
♄ Black and green
♃ Red mixed with green; ash colored

♂ Fiery red or scarlet
☉ Yellow, inclined to purple
♀ White and purple; bluish
☿ Light blue, azure, or dove colour
☽ White or light spotted cream "

228. Compound Signification

♅ ♄ Green plaids
♅ ♃ Green and red plaids
♅ ♂ Red plaids
♅ ☉ Green and purple plaids
♅ ♀ Blue and white plaids
♅ ☿ Light blue plaids
♅ ☽ Fine checked plaids

♃ ☉ A deep shining red
♃ ♀ A greenish grey
♃ ☿ A spotted green
♃ ☽ A high coloured green
♂ ☉ A deep red or scarlet
♂ ♀ A light red or crimson
♂ ☿ A tawny red or brick colour

♄ ♃	Dark green spotted with dark red	♂ ☽	A light red and glistening
♄ ♂	Dark reddish brown—a tawny	☉ ♂	Olive colour
♄ ☉	A blackish orange & shining bronze	☉ ☿	Light grey
♄ ♀	A light grey	☉ ☽	Light yellow or green
♄ ☿	A dark blue or grey	♀ ☿	Purple or light mixture
♄ ☽	A deep russet or grey	♀ ☽	Light blue, or bluish white
♃ ♂	A tawny light spotted	☿ ☽	Buff or fawn colour

The meaning of this is that, when a planet is in the house of another, you are to judge of him as mixed with that planet; thus, ♄ in ♌, the house of the ☉, would denote the dress of the quesited to be either dark yellow, or bronze colour. Every artist may form his system as he thinks best, and where the sympathy is very strong, no doubt some information may be obtained respecting the colour of their dress, if the artist thoroughly understands his own system.

229. Colours of the Zodiacal Signs

- ♈ White mixed with red
- ♉ White mixed with lemon
- ♊ White mixed with red
- ♋ Green or russet
- ♌ Red or green
- ♍ Black, speckled
- ♎ Black or dark crimson, or tawny colour (pastel shades)
- ♏ Brown
- ♐ Yellow or green sanguine
- ♑ Black or russet, or a swarthy brown
- ♒ A sky colour with a blue
- ♓ White glistening colour

Observe that if the significator be ♄, in his own house ♑, and not in close aspect with any other planet, the querent or quesited will be dressed all in black, because both planet and sign rule that colour. But if he was in the first, which rules white (230), he would have some white about his person; also, if it was ♂, who rules red, and in ♏, which rules brown, he would denote a rusty, dirty, reddish, brown, but if he was in ♌, which rules red and green, and ♃ was in close aspect, there would be much green, as well as red, about the dress, and so of the others.

230. Miscellaneous Signification of the Houses

H	Colours	Gender	Property
1	White	Masculine	Good
2	Green	Feminine	Good
3	High Yellow	Masculine	Moderate
4	Red	Feminine	Evil
5	Dark	Masculine	Pleasurable
6	Dark	Feminine	Evil

H	Colours	Gender	Property
7	Blue brown	Masculine	Moderate
8	Black	Feminine	Evil
9	Green and white	Masculine	Good
10	Red and white	Feminine	Good
11	Deep Yellow	Masculine	Good
12	Green	Feminine	Evil

231. When and What Time Will the Event Happen?

It is generally very difficult to judge of time with accuracy. The limitation of time is taken either by house and sign, or by aspect. To ascertain the number of days, weeks, months, or years, consider the degrees and minutes between the body or aspect of the significators, and according to the number of degrees which are between their aspect, even so many days, weeks, months, or years will it be before the matter inquired after is accomplished or destroyed. Observe in what house and sign the applying significator falls. Succeedent houses give weeks, months, or years as the sign is movable, common or fixed, and cadent houses give months, in movable signs, years in common, and unknown in fixed signs. Great south latitude prolongs the time, great north latitude often cuts it shorter; if the significators have no latitude the exact time is made simply by the aspects. Degrees and minutes of latitude, if it be south, should, it is said, be added to the time, but if north, subtracted from it, as north latitude shortens the time of an event, and south latitude lengthens it, but I have not much opinion of this.

Transits show the progress of the matter, and point out the most probable time in which the matter may be terminated, and that is the time to judge of. The good or evil days are those on which the transits are good or evil. Mixed application gives, instead of years, say months; for months, weeks; and for weeks, say days.

232. Of the Measure of Time

Angles	Succeedents	Cadents
Moveable Signs ♈ ♋ ♎ ♑ Give Days	Moveable Signs ♈ ♋ ♎ ♑ Give Weeks	Moveable Signs ♈ ♋ ♎ ♑ Give Months
Common Signs ♊ ♍ ♐ ♓ Give Weeks	Common Signs ♊ ♍ ♐ ♓ Give Months	Common Signs ♊ ♍ ♐ ♓ Give Years
Fixed Signs ♉ ♌ ♏ ♒ Give Months	Fixed Signs ♉ ♌ ♏ ♒ Give Years	Fixed Signs ♉ ♌ ♏ ♒ Unknown

Example: Suppose ☿ in 14° of ♈ in application to a △ of ♃ in 16° of ♌, and ☿ being in an angle, the distance between the partile and platic aspect being 2° denotes that two days would elapse before the event promised by ☿'s application would take place; and had the same aspect happened from a succeedent house the time would have been two weeks; and had it been from a cadent house the time would have been two months. When a thing is denoted by any approaching aspect the proper day to undertake the business is on the day of the aspect.

233. Where and Which Way Is the Quesited?

Wherever the significator is, there is the thing; the house where the significator of the thing is posited shows the quarter of heaven or point of the compass which way the thing may be. If the house and sign cohere this judgment is so much the more firm; if they disagree consider the position of the ☽ and with what she agrees most, and give judgment from her. If the Moon agrees neither with the sign nor house in which the significator is posited, then consider the ☉ in the same manner as before you consider the ☽, and judge accordingly. The distance is discovered from the proximity or distance of the significators to body or aspect, considered as they may happen to be either angular, succeedent, or cadent, respect being had to their latitude, whether little or great, north or south. Great latitude shows obscurity, and great difficulty in finding what is sought for; if the latitude be north it shows difficulty only, not impossibility; but if south, then all the labour of seeking will be vain, unless the significators be angular and near the aspect.

234. The Signification in Houses

Houses

The Ist, East	The Vth, N. by W.	The IXth, S. West
The IId, N. by E.	The VIth, W., N.W.	The Xth, South
The IIId, North E.	The VIIth, West	The XIth, S.E. by S.
The IVth, North	The VIIIth, S.W. by S.	The XIIth, E. by S.E.

Directions by Signs

♈ East	♋ North	♎ West	♑ South
♉ S. by E.	♌ E. by N.	♏ N. by E.	♒ W. by N.
♊ W. by S.	♍ S. by W.	♐ E. by S.	♓ N. by W.

(American experience, and particularly the researches of that eminent Horary Astrologer Pearl I. Markowitz, MAFA, is not in accord with Simmonite's statements. In the foregoing, the Xth to the IVth houses all are set forth as related to the direction **east**, while the IVth to the Xth houses are all **west**. These should be reversed. Thus, the IIId house becomes North West. The North and South directions are correct. The cusps of the angles represent the four points of the compass, West, North, East and South. A planet in the IVth, for example, if it be significator and conjunct the Nadir, indicates the quesited is North, but the farther from the angle in the IVth house it may be indicates farther to the East of North. If it be in the IIId, then it is west of north. Care should also be exercised in the directions by signs for it seems illogical to consider any of the six northern signs as representing a southerly direction, or contrarily, the six southern signs representing a northerly direction. If Capricorn represents the South point, then Aquarius, corresponding to the XIth house, would seem to represent the direction E. or S.E. by South. Further research seems necessary.)

235. At What Distance Is the Quesited?

The significator angular, and without latitude, shows short distance; if it has north latitude, some furlongs; if south, some miles. The significator succeedent, and without latitude, shows some furlongs; if it hath north latitude, some miles; if south, some leagues. The significator cadent, and without latitude, shows some miles; if it hath north latitude, some leagues; if south, some degrees. But these rules are chiefly to be considered in things having life. If it be required to know the number of miles, or degrees of distance, consider the number of degrees and minutes between the body or aspect of the significators, and according to the number of degrees between ☌ , ✶ , ☐ , △ , or ☍ , so many miles or degrees is the thing sought aftter distant from the place whence it was lost, or from the person making inquiry. The significator

    In ♈ , ♋ , ♎ , or ♑ for every degree, two miles.

    In ♊ , ♍ , ♐ , or ♓ every degree, half a mile.

    In ♉ , ♌ , ♏ , or ♒ every degree, quarter of a mile.

(In our own experience this rule does not seem to be as accurate in its applicability as we should like.)

236. Is the Subject of Inquiry to Be or not?

All Questions concern either things past, present, or to come, so the matter supposed either once was, now is, or may be hereafter. Here the first thing to be attended to is the perfection or destruction of the matter under consideration. First by ☌ , when the lord of the ascendant and the lord of that house which signifies the thing demanded is hastening to ☌ , and in the first house, or in any angle, and the significators meet with no prohibition or refrenation before they come to perfect ☌ , then judge that the thing sought after shall be brought to pass without impediment; the sooner if the significators be swift in motion, and strong; but if this ☌ of the significators be in a succeedent house it will be perfected, but not so soon; if in cadent houses, with infinite loss of time, some difficulty, and much shuffling.

237. Aspects of ✶ or △ —

Things are also effected when the principal significators apply by ✶ or △ where they are essentially dignified, and meet with no malevolent aspect to intervene ere they come to perfect ✶ or △.

Aspects of ☐ or ☍ —Things are also produced to perfection when the significators apply by ☐, provided each planet has dignity in the degrees wherein it is, and applying, otherwise not. Sometimes it happens that a matter is effected when the significators apply by ☍, but then there is mutual reception by house, and the ☽ separating from the significator of the thing demanded, and applying presently to the lord of the ascendant. I have seldom seen anything brought to perfection by this way of ☌ but the querent had rather the thing had been undone; for if the question was concerning marriage the parties seldom agree, each party repining, laying the blame on their covetous parents, as having no mind to it themselves; and if the question was about portion or money, the querent did recover his money or portion promised, but it cost him more to procure it in suit of law than the debt was worth; and I have seen it happen in many other things.

238. Translation—Things are brought to perfection by translation of light. When the significators both of the querent and quesited are separating from ☌, ✶, or △ of each other, and some other planet separates himself from one of the significators, of whom he is received either by house or joy, and then this planet applies to the other significator by ☌ or aspect before he meets with the conjunct or aspect of any other planet, he thus translates the force, influence, and virtue of the first significator to the other, and then this intervening planet (or such a man or woman as it signifies) shall bring the matter in hand to perfection.

Consider of what house the planet interposing or translating the nature and light of the two planets is lord, and describe him or her; and say to the querent that such a party shall do good in the business of, etc., viz., if lord of the IId a good purse effects the matter; if lord of the IIId a kinsman or neighbour, and so on of all the rest of the houses.

239. Collection—Matters are also brought to perfection when the two principal significators do not behold one another, but both cast their aspects to a more weighty planet than themselves, and they both receive him in some of their essential dignities, then shall the planet who thus collects both their lights bring the thing demanded to perfection, which signifies that a person somewhat interested in both parties, described and signified by the planet, will perform that which otherwise could not be performed; as many times you see two fall at variance, and of themselves cannot think of any way of accommodation, when suddenly a neighbour or friend accidentally reconciles all differences, to the content of both parties; and this is called collection.

240. General Method to Be Observed in all Questions—The Ascendant represents the person of the querent, the IId his estate, the IIId his kindred, the IVth his father, the Vth his children, the VIth his servants, the VIIth his wife, the VIIIth the manner of his death, the IXth his religion and journeys, the Xth his estimation or honour, mother, trade, etc., the XIth his friends, and the XIIth his secret enemies; also understand that when one asks concerning a woman or any party signified by the VIIth house, it shall be her ascendant, and signify her person, the VIIIth house denotes her estate, the IXth her brethren and kindred, the Xth her father, the XIth her children, the XIIth her sickness and servants, the Ist her sweetheart, the IId her death, the IIId her journeys, the IVth her mother or trade, etc., the Vth her friends, the VIth her sorrow, care, and private enemies. Let the question be of or concerning a churchman, minister, or the brother of the wife or sweetheart, the IXth house shall represent each of these, the Xth house shall signify his substance, the XIth his brethren, and so in order; and so in all questions, the house signifying the person or matter of inquiry is their or its Ist house, the next the IId, etc., around the whole of the houses.

241. How Persons and Things Are Frustrated and Detrimented – Things and persons are hindered by frustration, prohibition, refrenation, etc. When the significators apply to ☌ or other good aspect, and before the aspect is completed another planet aspects one of the significators, then the thing is hindered or frustrated. Consider the nature of that planet, of what house he is lord, and then judge the quality of the impeditor; if lord of the IIId a relation or neighbour, if the IVth the querent's father, and if the Vth, children. Things are also hindered by refrenation, also by aspect □ or ☍ without reception, and no planets transfer the light of one to the other from them; by reason of some questions or quarrelings disgust was taken, and so the matter is destroyed; or if one of the significators be applying to an infortune, or he be weak, or cadent, and behold not the lord of the house, or the cusp of the house of the thing demanded. The aspect to the cusp is better than to the lord of the house. If the significator, as above, be joined to an infortune, or retrograde, combust or cadent, then observe whether mutual reception intervene, which shows the perfection of the matter, though with much labour and solicitation. If there be no reception the affair will come to nothing, though there may have been much probability of its performance.

242. Whether the Question Be Radical or Fit to Be Judged – The Astrologer, before he delivers judgment, will consider whether the figure is radical and capable of judgment. The question is not radical, Ist, when only the first or second degree of ♒, ♓, ♈, ♉, or ♊ ascend, then do not venture judgment unless the querent be very young, and his corporature, complexion, and the moles or scars on his body agree with the quality of the sign ascending; IId, if 27 or more degrees of any sign ascend it is not safe to give judgment, except the querent's age correspond with the number of degrees ascending, unless the figure be set when any event happened, as a person went away at such a time precisely, to learn the result; here you may judge because it is not a propounding question; IIId, it is not safe to judge when the ☽ is in the latter degrees of a sign, especially in ♊, ♏, or ♑. All matters go hardly on (except the principal significators be very strong) when the ☽ is void of course. You must always be wary when, in any question, you find the cusp of the VIth house is afflicted, or the lord of the VIIth retrograde or impeded, and the matter at that time not concerning the VIIth house, but belonging to any other house. It is an argument that the judgment of the Astrologer will give no contentment to the querent, for the VIIth house generally signifies the artist. When the testimonies of fortunes and infortunes are equal defer judgment; it is not possible to know which way the balance will turn; however, defer your opinion till another question better inform you.

243. Of the Time of Erecting a Horary Figure
a. Many disputes have arisen about the proper time for the figure of a

horary question to be erected. Some think the moment when the querent is first seen by the artist; others when he salutes him, others when he inquires of him, etc. But the proper time is the hour and the minute when the querent feels the most anxious about the matter.

    b. If a person apply to the Astrologer the figure must be erected for the minute the querent proposes his question.

    c. If a letter be sent to an artist the time of the letter being received is not taken notice of, but the moment the artist reads the very question.

    d. In sickness the time must be taken when the person first spoke to the physician concerning the disease, whether the querent is the afflicted party or not.

    e. If a parent bring the water of a child, though the child cannot speak, the Ist house represents the child, and not the Vth, and so of the rest.

    f. If it be not a question but a sudden event, take the moment of its commencement, as the setting off on a journey, beginning a letter or any business, etc., or when you first discover the loss of an article. In all these cases the first impression on your mind is the time and moment for the figure.

    244. Is the Matter Good or Evil?—Consider the house to which the thing or quesited belongs, its lord, and the planets therein; also consider the house signifying the end of the matter, its lord, and planet or planets therein; and if the house signifying the thing be fortified by the presence or beams of good planets, or if ☊ be there located it shows good, but the contrary indicates evil.

    245. Is the Report True or False?—If any planet be in the house signifying the matter concerning which the report is, or the ☊ be there, or the lord of such house be angular, or in ☌ or aspect of any planet, then the matter or report is true; but if the report was good, and the said significator or planet posited in the said house be either retrograde, slow of course, combust, peregrine, or cadent, in evil aspect of a more weighty planet, or in ☌ with ☋, or if the ☋ be posited in the said house, any of these signifies the report is false. The ☽ angular generally signifies the report to be true; the report be evil, especially if she be in evil aspect; or good if she be in good aspect with ♃ or ♀. The ☽ in fixed signs, and in ☌ with ☊, shows truth; but moveable, void of course, and in ☌ with ☋, showeth falsehood.

    245. A Table of the Essential Fortitudes and Debilities of the Planets

	Essential Fortitudes				Debilities	
Signs	Planets Houses	Exaltation	Triplicity	Powerful or Joys in	Detriment	Fall
♈	♂	☉	☉	☉	♀	♄
♉	♀	☽	♀	♀	♂	♅
♊	☿	☊	☿	☿	♃	☋
♋	☽	♃	♂	☽	♄	♂
♌	☉	♆	☉	☉	♅	•
♍	☿	☿	☽	☿	♃	♀
♎	♀	♄	♄	♄	♂	☉

	Essential Fortitudes				*Debilities*	
	Planets			*Powerful*		
Signs	*Houses*	*Exaltation*	*Triplicity*	*or Joys in*	*Detriment*	*Fall*
♏	♂	♅	♂	♂	♀	☽
♐	♃	☋	♃	♃	☿	☊
♑	♄	♂	♅	♄	☽	♃
♒	♅	•	♄	♅(♄)	☉	♆
♓	♃	♀	♆	♆(♃)	☿	☿

a. The first column shows the Twelve Signs of the Zodiac.

b. **Lords of Houses**—In the second are the Planets and the signs opposite each, which denotes that the planet is Lord or Lady of that sign; where ♂ is placed denotes his house to be ♈ ; ♀ Lady of ♉ , and so of the rest. Four of the planets, ♅ , ♄ , ☉ and ☽ have each one house; the other planets each two houses. A planet in his own house is strong, and is a powerful significator, unless he be retrograde, combust, or afflicted by any malevolent planet or aspect.

c. **Exaltation**—The third column shows in which sign each planet has its exaltation; thus, the ☉ in ♈ is exalted. If a planet be in the sign wherein he is exalted, you may consider him essentially strong. If the significator be in his exaltation, and no way impedited, but angular, it represents a person of haughty condition, and arrogant, assuming more to himself than is due.

d. **Triplicity**—The fourth column tells you which planet governs each triplicity; for if a planet be in any of those signs which are allotted to him for his triplicity, he is also strong, but in a less degree. A planet in his triplicity shows the querent tolerably endowed with the goods and fortune of this world; one well descended, and the condition of his life at the time of the question to be good, but not so much so as the former dignities.

e. **Joys or Very Powerful**—The fifth column shows you in which sign each planet is most powerful. The efficacy of these has been proved by repeated experience, and they must be considered with attention.

The foregoing are the essential dignities of the planets and are good.

f. **Detriment**—In the sixth column, over against ♈ is found ♀ , being in ♈ , is an opposite sign to her own house, and so is said to be in her detriment. This is an evil position.

Every planet has its detriment opposite to its own house, and its fall opposite to its exaltation.

g. **Fall**—In the seventh column, in juxtaposition is found ♃ over his head, fall; that is, ♃ when in ♑ , is opposite to his exaltation, and so is unfortunate, etc. When the lord of any question is in his detriment or fall, he is then very evil, and no good generally comes of the matter in hand.

247. **Of the Dragon's Head and Tail**—The Dragon's Head ☊ , is of the conjoint nature of ♃ and ♀ , but the Dragon's Tail ☋ is feminine, and of a malignant tendency. As before stated, they are two imaginary points, diametrically opposite each other, where ☽ crosses the Ecliptic, or path of the ☉ . These points are moveable at the rate of three minutes and eleven seconds daily,

or nineteen degrees and twenty minutes in a year; moving round the Ecliptic in eighteen years and two hundred twenty-five days. The ☽, therefore, at every lunation, crosses at a different place, and an eclipse never occurs but when she is in or very near these points; an eclipse of the Sun when the Moon is in her Ascending Node, and one of the Moon when she is in the Descending Node.

248. The Part of Fortune ⊕ —This is also an imaginary point in the Zodiac, and is rejected, together with the Dragon's Head and Tail, by some modern professors of the Astral Science. It may demand less of our attention than the two Nodes, but in questions concerning money, lotteries, bills, etc., it is particularly useful, especially when the testimonies for and against are equal, then the Part of Fortune can alone decide.

The reason why such a point has any symbol appears to be that the ☉, the ☽, and the eastern point of the horizon, being the prime conduits through which the streams of life flow, this seat of the Part of Fortune is the harmony of all three, concentrating and uniting their natures in one point, which, when it is found to fall among fortunate stars, is indicative of good, and if it be found in the first, fifth, or eleventh house of the figure, then it promises success in health, wealth, honour, offspring, etc.

249. To Erect a Figure of the Heavens—First erect a figure of the Heavens; divide the sides into two equal parts; then draw the lines E. to S., from S. to W., from W. to N., and from N. to E.; the next the inner square, and draw lines from all the angles, and you have the figure erected.

(Here Simmonite is giving directions for drawing the square form of horoscope, but present day students simply use the wheel with the 12 houses already indicated. Likewise, in what follows he is explaining the early method of calculating the horoscope itself. The student who reads these lines is undoubtedly familiar with the mathematics of chart calculation.)

Problem: To Insert the Signs in the Figure
Rule 1. Look in Simmonite's Astronomical Ephemeris for the Sun's Right Ascension, which you will find on the left hand column of each month; add this Right Ascension, the previous noon, to time of day for which the Figure is to be erected, and the sum will be the R.A. of the Xth house.

Remark, if the hours and minutes exceed 24 hours after addition is made, take the excess of 24 hours.

Rule 2. Find the longitude answered to this R.A. in the column of the Table of Houses, headed, "Time from Noon." This found, the number required in the next right hand column will be the degree occupying the Xth house. In a line with this is found the longitudes of the XIth, XIIth, Ist (Asc.), IId and IIId houses.

Houses opposite Houses		*Signs opposite Signs*	
Xth	IVth	♈	♎
XIth	Vth	♉	♍
XIIth	VIth	♊	♐

Houses opposite Houses		Signs opposite Signs	
Ist	VIIth	♋	♑
IId	VIIIth	♌	♒
IIId	IXth	♍	♓

What is the face of the heavens, November 27th, $4^h 34^m$ p.m. 1850?

	h	m	s
The Right Ascension of the Sun at Noon 27th	16	24	10
Add the time from noon	4	34	00
The Right Ascension of the Midheaven	20	58	10

The longitude nearly equal to this, casting away the odd seconds, is 12° ♒, which I place on the Xth house, and the same degree of the opposite sign ♌ on the IVth. In the IIId, next column, I find 9° ♓ which must be placed on the XIth house, and the same degree of the opposite sign, ♍ on the Vth. In the 4th column I find 26° ♈ ; place this on the XIIth and 26° of the opposite sign, ♎ on the VIth house. In the 5th column I find 20° ♊ 27' on the Ist, and 20° ♐ 27' on the VIIth house. In the 6th are 7° of ♋ which must be placed on the IId and 7° of ♑ on the VIIIth house. In the 7th column is 23° ♋ ; place this on the IIId house, and 23° of ♑ on the IXth. The figure now exhibits the signs of the zodiac at the aforementioned time of birth.

250. To Find the Planets' Places for any Hour or Minute between any Two Noons for which the Figure Is Erected—

Rule 1. Find in Simmonite's Ephemeris (we would now use American Astrology Ephemeris), the amount of longitude the planet moves from the preceding to the succeeding noon.

Rule 2. Then look in Simmonite's Astro-Tables, in Diurnal Logarithms, for the log, answering to that daily motion, and add the log of the time given, and the sum gives the log of longitude of that time. (We would now simply take the longitudinal motion for the interval from *Tables of Diurnal Planetary Motion* without using logarithms.)

Rule 3. Add the result to that planet's longitude, at the preceding noon; but if the planet be retrograde, then subtract the result from the planet's place at the preceding noon.

The student may generally equate by inspection all the planets' daily motion, except the Moon, Mercury, and Venus, without calculations, sufficiently near for Horary Profession.

Example: What is the Moon's place in the figure for 27th of November, 1850, at 34 minutes past 4, afternoon?

November 27, noon, the Moon in	17°	♍	38'
On the 28th, noon, the Moon moves to	1	♎	30
Moved in 24 hours	13		52
Add log of ☽'s long. in 24 hrs—13°52'	23		82
To time since noon, $4^h 35^m$	72		06
Moved in $4^h 34^m$ 2°38'	95		88
Moon on 27th	17	♍	38

73

Moon on 27th	17	♍	38
Add for $4^h 34^m$	2		38
Amount	20	♍	16

I place the ☽ 20° ♍ 16′ in the Vth house, because she has passed the cusp which occupies the 9th degree. The ☉ moves 61′ in the day, equal to 12′, which I add to the place at noon, 4 ♐ 56, add 12′, equals 5 ♐ 8, which I place in the VIth house, because Sol has not advanced so far in ♐ as the cusp of the VIIth. ♅ I place in the XIIth, in 27° ♈ retrograde; ♄ in 14 ♈ 31, in the XIth. ♃ 16 ♎ 00, in the Vth house. Mars is 5 ♐ 41, a little nearer the VIIth than the Sun, as he is a few minutes farther in ♐ . ♀ is 2 ♑ 03 in the VIIth house. ☿ is placed in the VIth just under the ☉ . We now place the Moon's Nodes in the figure; these nodes move in a retrograde motion, about 3′11″ per day, so they may easily be equated. On the 25th of the month, the Moon's node is 8 ☊ 47, and will have gone about seven minutes in 2 days, $4^h 34^m$, which node I place 8 ☊ 40 in the IIId house, and the South Node in 8 ☋ 40 in the IXth; for one node is always opposite to the other.

Mode of Equating the Planets

Rule. Divide the amount of longitude made in 24 hours, and also the time since noon, by 12; then multiply the quotients together, and the result is the answer in minutes of a degree, the last figure being a decimal.

Example. The ☉ made in 24 hours, 60′; divided by 12, gives 5; time since noon, 274 minutes, divided by 12, gives 23 one-twelfths; then 23 one-twelfths multiplied by 5, gives 11.6 or 11 minutes and 6 tenths of a minute, which may be called 12 minutes.

The figure is now completed excepting the Part of Fortune ⊕ .

To Find the Place of the Part of Fortune

Rule. Add the longitude of the Ascendant to the ☽'s longitude, from which sum, subtract the longitude of the ☉ ; the remainder is the longitude of the ⊕ .

Where is the ⊕ in the figure here given?

Right Ascension, $20^h 58^m 10^s$ M.C.

	Signs	°	′
The Asc. 20 ♊ 27 or	2	20	27
The ☽ 20 ♍ 16 or	5	20	16
	8	10	43
The ☉ 5 ♐ 08 or	8	05	08
	0	05	35

Place of ⊕ in the figure is 5 ♈ 35, in the XIth house.

I now recommend the student to gather out all the aspects that the planets are forming, or within orbs of application, which may be known by referring to article 14.

We shall now give rules for general judgment.

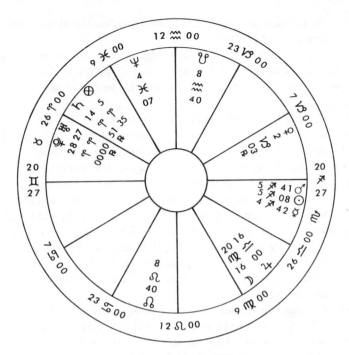

GENERAL JUDGMENT

FIRST HOUSE

251. (**Pluto**, *see* article 16.)

252. (**Neptune** ascending indicates the querent is confused, deceived or fretting much about matter quesited; much depends upon aspects; afflicted, there is much promise without fulfillment; difficult for the astrologer to make the querent accept interpretation as querent will not wish to believe the response. Some astrologers decline to interpret a horary chart with this position of Neptune.)

253. **Uranus** ascending, some strange, unexpected, and vexatious occurrences are about to take place; unsettled in mind, pursuing extraordinary and uncommon objects, especially such things as the house signifies of which he is lord. If well aspected, the sudden actions will be more advantageous. If afflicting the ☽ or ♀, unhappiness in courtship and unhappiness in marriage. The querent is partial to travelling, fond of novelty, and romantic in his ideas; fond of antique things.

254. **Saturn** herein gives heavy thoughts about the matter queried; pain in the teeth when young, and will have lost some front teeth. The querent will not be in good health; is subject to blows, bruises, falls, and given to shed tears. The disposition, thoughtless, reserved, fearful, firm in opinions, and not easily moved. (147-148).

255. **Jupiter** herein, unafflicted, denotes a good constitution; he is cheer-

ful, sincere; he is much respected, acts honourably, success attends him, and he is generally fortunate. (149-150)

256. Mars here is evil, subjecting the querent to burns, scalds, cuts, quarrels, uneasiness of mind, hot temper, scars or marks in the head or face; he is a liar, boaster, fond of disputation; and this according as ♂ is dignified. (151-152)

257. Mercury here, well dignified (157) the querent is a good speaker; he is restless, fond of travelling; has a busy, active mind; but if afflicted (158) or retrograde then a short memory and frequent disappointments, with a bad deliverence, or he has no elocution. ☿ □ ☽ , great disappointments; he is slandered, and has sorrow from that house from which the aspect is thrown, and of which they are rulers. If close to the Sun, the mind will be profound.

258. Venus here, free from affliction, good fortune; lives in credit; quiet, mild disposition, though given to pleasure, which will detriment his health. ♀ well aspected, gain by means of females; if ill aspected by ♂ the querent is unchaste; if by ♄ a rake; ascending, gives strength to the constitution, yet too fond of following after the animal inclinations; if in her debilities, fit for anything infamous. (155-156)

259. The Sun rising, gives a degree of pride, and if in good aspect with the ☽ , success in life unless ☉ be in ♎ or ♒ ; but if in ill aspect, rash and injurious; makes the native a boaster. If in aspect with ♂ the native is involved in love matters about the age of 19 years. In bad aspect of (♆), ♅ , ♄, or ♂ , then ill health and danger of accidents; if well aspected, long life and good health; fond of public employments. Sol's evil aspects denote death of relations, disgrace, loss of friends and honour.

260. The Moon in the Ist, fond of trudging about; if weak, the native is dissolute; if afflicted by aspect, then bad health, uneasiness of mind, and trouble according to the house she governs; given to drinking, gluttony, and debauchery; if strong and well aspected, healthful; afflicted by the ☉ , liable to injuries to the eyes; in good aspect to Sol, he marries respectably. In whatever sign she is will denote a mole or mark on that part of the body which that sign governs. (159-160)

261. The Part of Fortune herein, riches, and the native makes his own fortune, especially in good aspect of ♀ , ♃ , ☉ , or ☽ . The ☊ gives honesty, the ☋ , knavery; and the querent will attempt to deceive you, and will not deal fairly in his queries, therefore beware of him. He is in great anxiety of mind, he will very likely be pockmarked, or otherwise blemished in the face.

262. The Lord of the First, in his fall or detriment, the querent despairs of the matter; very likely has only one parent alive, ♂ of ☋ , injury to his character and health, and other damages according to the house in which they are placed.

SECOND HOUSE

263. The ruler hereof afflicted, retrograde, etc., loss of money lent, or a debt. Many planets here, great want of money, two or three planets ill dignified, much poverty. ♅, ♄, or ♂ herein, strong, and well aspected, denote the querent's substance to change from evil to good; but there, unfortunated, his substance is changing from good to evil. The ☽ herein, unafflicted gives wealth; but afflicted, the reverse. ♅ portends changes, and unsettledness in pecuniary procedure. The ☉, ♂, or ☋ here, a perpetual waste, with sometimes poverty. ♃ herein denotes success in money; so does also the ☉ unafflicted; ♀ according to her dignity or debility, gain or loss generally by means of females. ☿ gives a loss as he is situated, by learning, books, etc.

THIRD HOUSE

264. ♅ frequent warnings; disputes among relations or neighbours; ♄ here, the same, and loss by journeys, especially if they be peregrine. ♃, more success in short journeys, and favour among his family, according to the planet's dignities. ♂, spiteful neighbours; evil for journeys; danger of being robbed; want of money; the ☉, good from relatives and neighbours; ♀, good journeys, brethren and neighbours pious; ☿, crafty relations, swift journeys, according as he is dignified; the ☽ well aspected in ♈, ♋, ♎, or ♑, many short journeys, either for pleasure of health; ☊, good neighbours and relations; ☋, therein, the reverse; the ⊕, gain by journeys, brethren, or neighbours. A planet peregrine herein, or retrograde, the traveller meets with disappointment. The ☉ or ☽ afflicted portends trouble and anxiety to the parents, and probably death to them.

FOURTH HOUSE

265. (♆, there may be something mysterious concerning a parent, the conclusion or outcome of the matter inquired about may rest in mystery, and if afflicted, unsolved); ♅, the native has lost a parent and is in danger of losing property, or having disputes about inheritance; ♄, the native is often annoyed about money matters, connected as the right of his family; ♃ here, is more fortunate, and declares the querent is likely to have a legacy left him; ♂, the parents are in distress or dead, and the native is dissipated; the ☉ well placed here, declares the father to be noble minded, with honour in old age; ♀ gives the same; ☿, he gains by learning or by craft; the ☽, gain by travelling, and by emigrating, he possesses land; ☊, benefits; ☋ the reverse; ⊕ improves his property.

FIFTH HOUSE

266. ♅, ♄, ♂, or ☋ herein, untoward children; only small family, and disobedient offspring; great danger of miscarriage; ♃ or ♀, gives good children; fortune in speculations; the ☉, few children, but those high-minded and virtuous; ☿, ingenious issue; some annoyance from their untowardness; the ☽ gives children, and they well or ill disposed according to her aspects; a large family if ♋, ♏, or ♓ be on the cusp; the ☊ here is favourable for children, and they do well; the ⊕ causes the native to gain by his children, or by speculation, if unafflicted. Many planets herein, predict the querent is or will be given to pleasure (and particularly if Neptune is therein); or he may live dishonourably with some person, or he lives at a public place of resort. A planet here, exalted, denotes the inquirer to be fond of gaiety and pleasure. ♀, ruler of the fifth, in ♋ in the VIIIth, denotes, if the querent is a woman, that she will have chiefly female children, yet the majority of them will die.

SIXTH HOUSE

267. ♅ herein, indisposition of body, family sickness, cheatery by servants, loss of cattle, if any, also loss by servants; ruler of the VIth in the VIIIth, a death in the family shortly; ♄ herein, crosses and losses by small cattle; ♃, the reverse; ♂, danger of fever and destruction among cattle; ♀, profit in small cattle, servants, sickness by means of women, especially if afflicted by ♅, ♄, or ♂; the ☉, mental uneasiness; proud wasteful servants, and long sickness, unless assisted by the good aspects of ♃ or ♀; the ⊕ or ☊, good servants and profitable cattle; ☿ or ☋, knavish servants; unhappiness and nervousness. ♂, ruler of the VIth, afflicted by ♅ in ♈, declares the querent to suffer marasmus, or general waste of the body, low spirits, depressed appetite, and defect in the memory, more certainly if ☿ be ruler of the Ist. Many planets in this house, sickly at the time, many private enemies, especially if the ruler of the XIIth be therein. The rulers of the Ist and VIth, being in each other's houses, or afflicting each other, or if the lord of the Ist be the lord of the VIth, or in □ or ☍ of ♄ or ♂; or lord of the Ist combust, in the VIth, VIIth, or XIIth, the native will be sickly, and his servants dishonest. The native will have a mole signified by the sign on its cusp.

SEVENTH HOUSE

268. This is an important angle, and we are capable of predicting many things connected with affairs, merely from the position of the planets therein. (Neptune herein, the querent must guard carefully against deception from partners and associates, unless this planet is dignified or strongly well aspected; causes the querent to expect more through associates, including spouse, than can be realized.) ♅ herein, or afflicting the ☽, or lord of the VIIth, disappointment in courtship, disorder in domestic affairs, death of relations, disorder in wedlock, and long before the native marries; the wife or husband will be eccentric and difficult to please; ♄, long before he marries, and ill agreement in marriage, many enemies; if peregrine, as in ♉, ♊, ♍, ♎, ♐, or ♓, a poor husband or wife; if in □ or ☍ to the lord of the VIIth, an immodest person; just on the cusp shows much lingering illness, and liable to blows, bruises, and falls; ♃ here, a good husband or wife, unless he be in ♊ or ♍, the reverse, agreeable courtship; ♂, quarrels, law suits, public enemies, a bad wife or husband, disappointment in courtship, a lover given to change, and is unfaithful; if in □ of ☽; danger of being burnt to death. The ☉ here, indisposition, powerful enemies,

honourable marriage; ♀ here, a moderate wife, but careless, not many enemies; in ill aspect of ♂, unchaste husband or wife; ☿ here, setting, denotes removals, or ruler of the Xth, denotes changes in business affairs, a good wife, but quarrelsome; the ☽ setting, a change of residence, a good marriage, but infortunated an ill marriage; the ☊, fortunate marriage; the ☋, the reverse, and many foes; the ⊕, a wife or husband well off. Many planets in the VIIth, anxiety about lovers, husband or wife, many enemies. (In our experience the foregoing is only true if afflicted. The VIIth is not only the house of open enemies, but it is also the house of partnerships and relationships with others.) If in good aspect with ♀ or ☽, or with the lord of the Ist or VIIth, the native will marry more than once. If the lord of the Ist be stronger, or less afflicted than the lord of the VIIth, the querent will overcome his enemies; but if the lord of the VIIth be stronger, they will overpower him. Good aspects, reception, etc., between the lords of the Ist and VIIth, show harmony between a man and his wife.

EIGHTH HOUSE

269. The ruler hereof, herein, the querent has debts he will never get in; this lord in good aspect with the lord of the first, or to planets therein, the native will die a natural death; or if the cusp be ♈, ♏, or ♑, danger of a violent death; ♅ afflicting the ruler of the first and sixth, gives diseases in that part of the body signified by the sign possessed by ♅; ♄ here, doubtful legacies and destroys the wife's dowery, the poverty of enemies; the ☋, the same; ♃ gives hopes of a legacy and profit by marriage; the ☊ or ⊕ the same; ♂ shows a violent death, loss of substance, want of money, difference with lovers, or on account of legacy or money; ♀ here, a natural death, some gain by marriage; but ♀ or ♃ ruler hereof, in affliction, portends the querent will suffer by reputedly honest persons; the ☽ often shifting his or her residence.

NINTH HOUSE

270. ♅ herein a sectarian or enthusiast, fond of occult sciences, disposed to travel, and fond of seeing fresh sights; ♄ danger of drowning if he go on the sea, and losses thereon, he is atheistical, bad of all journeys; ♃ here unafflicted, a disposition mild and benevolent; ♂ journeys bad, and a religious bigot; ♀ afflicted, very immodest, inquisitive, but if unafflicted, kind and charitable; ☿ gives science, invention, fond of travelling, and ☿ weak, or in ☌ of ☉ the mind rather contracted and superficial, though he may be fit for plodding business; in ☌ ☽ here, he will travel; the ☽ here, especially in a moveable sign, much journeying, great insincerity in religion; the ⊕ or ☊, gain by journeys; the ☋ the same as ♄.

Lord of the IXth, just falling from its cusp, the querent is on a journey, and probably one of pleasure or visiting; also if the ☽ be passing through the VIIIth. The ruler of the IVth herein, and afflicted, the father of the querent is afflicted, and if ♅ afflict, the parent has suffered in his head, memory impaired, and his nervous system debilitated; his disease is called *atrophia.*

The rulers of the Ist and IXth in good aspect, the native will do well as a merchant, scholar or traveller.

TENTH HOUSE

271. This is a very important house, and predicts most weighty matter, therefore the planets there located must be intently studied. ♅ here, shows a person has more than one business, or he changes from one calling to another, with danger of sudden loss in trade (163); ♄ here, dishonour, short life to parents, danger of imprisonment, pain in the teeth, falls, trouble in business, and destroys the most hopeful things, all his affairs go wrong, and unless very strong aspects counteract this evil position, the querent is a child of misfortune; it denies honour to persons of rank; the ☋ here shows the same, with danger of discredit (147-148-164); ♃ here, success, prosperous trade, wealth and honour; ♃ ☌ ☉ here, lasting honour and respect, and his customers are respectable (149-150-165); ♂ here, fond of warlike proceedings and may gain by violence, but ♂ peregrine, scandal and dishonour, whether he deserves it or not, affliction or death to the querent's mother (151-152-166); ☉ here, honour and assistance from respectable persons, a rising fortune (153), but if afflicted the reverse (154); ♀ here, respectable, unless in ill aspect to ♄ , when the querent will be mean in his conduct. Whatever planet she aspects, she partakes much of the nature of that planet, and this must be particularly noticed; if well aspected, gain by means of females (155); if ill aspected by Mars, the native is unchaste; ☿ gives preferment, the querent is honoured by learning as 157, or if afflicted, a mere babbler (158-169); if afflicted by ♅ , of very shallow abilities; the ☽ here, unafflicted, profit and honour by trade, females, and by sea; preferment and gain, if ⊕ or ☊ be there, the reverse if ☋ be in the Xth.

The ruler of the Xth and the Ist in good aspect, and unafflicted by position, then success in business, he is honorable and persevering in his calling. But ♀ or any other planet ruler of the Xth, in ☌ or bad aspect of ♅ denotes the querent has a desire to change his occupation, difficulty in his employment, and discontented with his present situation.

ELEVENTH HOUSE

272. ♅ here, wavering friends and fidgety wishes; (Neptune here, deceptive friends or friends who promise without fulfillment); ♄ despair, false friends and death of children; ♃ friends true, riches, and happiness; ♂, false friends, ruin, and wicked children; the ☉ , good friends and happiness; ♀ , honourable and faithful friends, especially female; ☿ or the ☋ , inconstant and deceitful friends; the ☽ the friendship of women, if she be unafflicted; the ⊕ , gain by friendship.

The ruler of the XIth herein, unafflicted, good and sincere friends, in aspect with the first, friends will be permanent and advantageous.

TWELFTH HOUSE

273. ♅ here or near its cusp, clever in his business, changeable enemies, and they of a public character; ♄, anxiety, trouble persecution by false friends, more particularly if ♄ be ℞ or stationary, then ill luck if he keep cattle, and his enemies will be very undermining; but ♃ afflicted, many calamities, reproaches, damage from large cattle, adverse circumstances and bondage; if ♃ be unafflicted, few enemies and victory over them; ♂, bold and daring enemies, sorrow, trouble and danger of imprisonment, liable to accidents in the hands and feet; if weak, the enemies are unable to afflict him, loss by servants or by dealing in cattle, the ☋ is the same; the ☉ afflicted, many enemies, long and tedious diseases, extravagant and careless; ♀ gives profit by great cattle, private foes but unable to do any harm, consider well her condition, it often denotes the native to be vile, and if a female, infamous; ☿ gives knavish enemies, but this according to his condition which will make much difference; his enemies will be writers and different kinds of pettifoggers; and the ☽ makes the lower orders of persons foes, danger of losing by servants, especially if the ☽ be afflicted, great danger of being imprisoned; the ⊕ shows loss and frequent disasters. The ruler of the XIIth in the Ist or lord of the Ist in the XIIth, much anxiety of mind. If the lord of the Ist be in good aspect with the lord of the XIIth from the IVth, VIth, VIIIth, or XIIth, then enemies in the guise of friends.

274. Caution—The description of the houses as here laid down may be depended upon, but the lords of the different houses have no particular effect, although Gadbury says a great deal from pages 45 to 64 on the subject of **positions** in houses. The lord of Ist in the IId, says Gadbury, Lilly, Raphael, White, Salmon, and others, gives riches by the native's own industry, but this is not consistent with Horary Astronomy. For instance, the ☽, lady of the Ist located in the IId, afflicted by ♂, ♀, or the ☉, would denote the querent to be profligate, who instead of realizing fortune by his own industry would work his own ruin by extravagance, with the assistance of his dissolute connections and his own unsettled disposition, which would prevent him from adhering to anything good long enough to be serviceable. If posited in the Xth he would work his own downfall in the same manner, and if ♂ were in ☍ to the ☉ and ☽ his end would be violent, and if either ☉ or ☽ were in the Xth in evil aspect to its lord or to ♃ he would probably be transported. Thus the artist will see the indispensable necessity of adherence in answering questions proposed according to art. But **mark well**, the aspects of the planets have a powerful effective signification, for every planet is deemed a significator of something, therefore, the aspects he receives must be considered accordingly.

275. Of Moles, Marks or Scars on Persons—Notice the sign ascending shows a mole, mark or scar on the part ruled by that sign. The sign in which the ruler of the Ist is will give another mole or scar. The sign on the VIth will give another. The sign in which the ruler of the VIth is gives a mark. (In American experience, the foregoing must be considered with caution for the signs **alone** have no influence *per se*.) The sign in which the ☽ is denotes another. ♅, ♄ or

♂ in ill aspect will give a mark or scar according to their position. If the sign and planet be masculine the mark will be on the right side of the member, but if feminine on the left. (In our experience the former is true for males, but for females, it is the reverse.) If the sign and planet be above the earth, the mark will be before or frontal; but if under the earth, behind (or posterior). If the planets or cusp of Ist or VIth be in the first 10 degrees, the mark will be on the upper part of the member. If from 10 to 20 degrees, in the middle; if in the last ten degrees the mark will be in the lower part. The colours of the marks caused by the signs are in 229, the planets 227-228, the houses 230.

Example—If the Ist or VIth, or their lords, or ☽ be in ♈, the mole will be on the head; if in ♉, on the neck; if in ♊, on the shoulders, and so on according to the sign.

276. Signs and Houses Ruling Man's Body
House or Sign

House	Sign	Body Part
Ist	♈	All the Head and Face (We believe under jaw to a point just above ears to top of cerebrum, the base of the brain being under Taurus.)
IId	♉	Ears, Neck and Throat
IIId	♊	Arms, Hands and Shoulders (While this is overall rulership, specifically, ♊ rules the shoulders, ♋ Elbows, ♌ Wrists, ♍ Hands.)
IVth	♋	Breast, Epigastric and Stomach
Vth	♌	Heart, Sides and Back
VIth	♍	Bowels and Abdomen
VIIth	♎	Reins and Loins
VIIIth	♏	Secret Members
IXth	♐	Hips and Thighs
Xth	♑	Knees and Hams
XIth	♒	Legs and Ankles
XIIth	♓	Feet and Toes

A malevolent violently afflicting will sometimes give defects instead of moles or scars, as ♓ on the XIIth, and ♄ there gives weakness to the ankles, because the XIIth and ♓ rule the feet, and ♄ a malefic; witness Victoria. If the ☽ be exactly at new or full and in ill aspect of ♂, some blemish in or near the eyes, more especially if the ☉ and ☽ be in the angles.

277. General Remarks on the Moles of the Quesited—If you wish to know what moles the person enquired about has, the same rules apply as in 275, only be careful to take the right significator as directed in 240. If you enquire of a public enemy, a lover, or a thief, consider the VIIth their Ist; for the VIIth rules these parties, the XIIth their VIth, and there they will have a mole, etc., also in these parts ruled by the lords of the VIIth and XIIth, as well as those in which ♄ or ♂ is located. For a friend, take the signs on the XIth and IVth, and where their rulers are, for on those parts of the body they will have marks.

Remember, the XIth rules friends, and the IVth is the VIth from the XIth (225). For a master (employer) or your mother the Xth is the ascendant, and the sign thereon shows on what part of the body a mole may be expected, and the IIId is their VIth which will show another mole.

Example—Horoscope, page 75.

The querent would have a mark on the arms, as ♊ on the Ist denotes, also another on the reins and the loins, as ♎ signifies on the VIth, the ☽ in ♍, shows a mark on the upper part on the left side of the abdomen, also moles or scars in the head as ♄ and ♅ are in ♈, which sign rules the head.

Were the enquiry about a foe, that foe would have a mark or scar about the chin as the latter part of ♈ is on the XIIth, which is the ascendant of the enemy (we believe this would be just above the mouth as there is more recent strong evidence that Taurus has to do with the lower jaw); another mole on the belly, for the fifth is the sixth from the XIIth and ☿ ruler of the VIth in ♐. A masculine sign, and under the earth, shows a mole on the right thigh, towards the middle of it, on the back part, or that which is not visible. Mars, ruler of the XIIth, or ascendant of the foe in ♐, would give a reddish mark, or he might have a scar there, as the ☉, ♂ and ☿ are in ☌.

278. Of the Names of the Querent and Quesited—Many persons have reported it both far and wide that I can, do, and have told the name of both the querent and quesited. This certainly I have done very often, nevertheless I maintain it is not always possible to do so. However the following is my

Rule: Take that planet, whose name you wish to know, signifies; see if he be in aspect with another planet; if he be not, that planet whose house he is in is the planet that forms the name. ♃, ♂ and the ☉ denote short names, if they are angular, and if in the Xth the name begins with A or E. ♄ or ♀ gives longer names.

Significator		*Planets Joined*	*Probable Name*
☉	alone		Ann, Rodger, James, Joseph, Stephen
☉	with	♃	Lucy, Lawrence
☉	with	♄	Andrew, Mark
☉	with	♂	Robert, Peter
☉	with	☿	Benjamin, Edith, Margaret
☉	with	☽	Matilda
☉	with	♀	Alice, Maude, Matilda
☽	alone		Nell, Eleanor
☽	with	☿	Simon, Ann
☽	with	♄	Nicholas
☽	with	♂	Mary, James
☽	with	♂ & ☉	Mary, Mary Ann
☽	with	♀	Ellen

Significator	Planets Joined		Probable Names
☽ with	☉		Henry
☽ in	♒		Mary Ann
♄ alone			Jonathan
♄ with	☉		George, Elizabeth, Julian
♄ with	♀		William
♄ with	☽ & ♀		Joan, Harriet
♃ alone			Charles, Rachael
♃ with	☉		John, Richard
♃ with	♄		Thomas
♂ alone			Anthony
♂ with	☉		Robert, Peter
♂ with	☿		Catherine
♀ with	♄		Isabel, Eliza, Sarah
♀ with	☿		Agnes
♀ with	♂		Matthew
☿ with	☉		Clement
☿ with	♄		Edmund, Edwin, Edward
☿ with	♂ & ☉		Christian

279. Of Finding a Person at Home—The ruler of the VIIth is significator of the person inquired after, if that person be no relation. If a father, the lord of the IVth; if a mother, the ruler of the Xth; if a friend, the lord of the XIth; if a brother or sister or neighbour, the ruler of the IIId; if a child, the Vth; and so of the rest of the houses (240). If this said lord be angular from the house in question, or in the Ist, IVth, VIIth or Xth, from the house, the quesited is at home; if succeedent, not far off and easily found; if cadent, the person will not be found.

If the ruler of the Ist has good aspect with the planet signifying the quesited, or if there be a **translation** (238) between them, he may be met with, or be heard of by accident; the planet transferring such light will denote from its sex the person from whom the information will be received, whether male or female.

If more than one person be wanted, that person will be found who lives in the direction of the sign (234), containing the ruler of the house of the quesited and the querent, where that sign is posited. If the application be both to the lords of the exaltation house, **two** of them will be found; if also to the lord of triplicity, **three**.

Example—Horoscope, page 75.

Is the person at home? Jupiter ruling the VIIth, as the party inquired about is not a relation, and being in the Vth, indicates the person is not at home. Were it a friend the answer would be the same; because ♃ rules the XIth as well as the VIIth. Were it a sister, the ☽ ruling the IIId, and being cadent from her

84

own house, indicates the sister is far off.

280. Of Absent Brothers, Sisters, Cousins, Neighbours, Children of Friends, etc.—The Ist, its lord, and the ☽, are taken for the querent. The IIId and its ruler are taken to signify the lost one. Consider well the IIId, and the condition of the ruler of the IIId, as well as the ☽.

The ruler of the IIId in ☌ or bad aspect of (♆), ♅, ♄, ♂, or ☋, the condition of the brother is sorrowful; if in the IIId unafflicted, then he does well; but if the ruler of the IIId be therein afflicted, he may be in health, but is perplexed and in sorrow of mind.

The brother is sick or dead if the ☽ and ruler of the IIId are in ☍ of the ruler of the VIIIth, from the IId and VIIIth or from the VIth and XIIth houses. Also if the ruler of the IIId be afflicted in the XIIth by the ruler of the VIIIth and Xth, and if the ☽ be ruler in this case, and afflicted by ♅ (or ♆), then say the brother is drowned. Great danger of death if the ruler of the IIId be in the IVth, in □ of the ☽ in the VIIth. If you find the lord of the IIId and the ☽ combust in the natural IVth or VIIIth, or joined with the lord of the VIIIth, then the quesited is dead.

The ruler of the IIId in the Ist house, unafflicted, shows he is among friends, but there in ☌ of (♆), ♅, ♄, ♂ or ☋, then his friends are deceivers, and he has no hopes of success.

The lord of the IIId in the IId house, especially if retrograde or in his debilities, he is in great sorrow of mind, and will move from his present abode as soon as possible; but if his significator is much afflicted, he is then confined in prison (or an institution).

If in the IIId house, free from affliction, then say he is in health, but afflicted without mutual reception he is in distress, and wishes to move from his present place.

The ruler of the IIId in the IVth house, without aspects of the malefics, the quesited intends getting rich where he is, but being afflicted he will never gain much property.

In the Vth house, in ☌ of the lord of the Vth, it shows the absent brother to be in health and happily situated; but if the IIId be **void** of course, or in ☌ of any malefic, or other bad aspects of the infortunes, and those infortunes themselves impedited, the quesited is in poor condition and discontented.

When in the VIth house, afflicted any way, the quesited is sick; if he separate from the ruler of the VIth, he has been ill. He is sick if the lord of the VIth be in the IIId, unless well situated.

If you find his significator in the VIIth, unafflicted, he is in the same country he went to, and is well; if he be afflicted, then he has enemies, and fails in speculations.

In the VIIIth he fears death, and will die if he be in ☌ of the lord of the VIIIth; should he be herein afflicted, say death.

The ruler of the IIId in the IXth he has removed from where he first went, or is forming some clerical engagements, or is employed in traveling, and intends being married there, if already single.

The ruler of the IIId in the Xth, in good aspect of the fortunes, especially if the ☉ rules the Xth, or in mutual reception with ♃ or ♀ he is profitably employed; if combust and afflicted, danger of death.

The lord of the IIId in the XIth, in ☌ of the ruler of the XIth, he is among friends; a good aspect of the fortunes denotes him to be with friends, and that he still desires to stay; but if he be afflicted by any of the malefics, or be in his detriment or fall, then he is discontented and wishes to escape.

The lord of the IIId in the XIIth, and well aspected by the fortunes, and the fortunes themselves unafflicted, show he will deal in merchandise, by which he gains; but if he be infortunated in the XIIth, whether by aspects of the malefics or ruler of the VIIIth, then he is discontented, troubled, and not likely to see the land of his nativity again.

281. Will the Querent's Life Be Long?—The Ist, its lord, and the Moon are for the querent.

SIGNS OF LONG LIFE

The degree rising, the ☽ and the ☉ free from the P., ☌, ☐ or ☍ of the lord of the IVth, VIth, VIIIth or XIIth houses. The querent's significators in their dignities, in good houses, increasing in light and motion, and well aspected.

♃, ♀ and ☊, well fortified and rulers of good houses. Rulers of the Asc. in the Ist, or the fortunes in ✶, △ or ☌ of the degree ascending, or to the ☽, the ☉, or the lord of the Ist.

If all or most of these are reversed, short life is denoted or great danger.

SIGNS OF SHORT LIFE

Lord of the Ist R., or the ☽ peregrine, or combust in the VIIIth; ruler of the VIIIth afflicted in the Ist, or in ☐ or ☍ of the ☽, or ruler of the Ist. The ☋, ♅, ♄, or ♂ in the Ist, afflicting the Moon, or besieging the **Light of Time**, especially if these malefics rule the VIth or VIIIth; also **fixed stars** of the nature of ♅, ♄ or ♂; or ruler of the VIIIth, afflicting the cusp of the Ist, its ruler or the ☽.

When the significators are ill aspected from good houses, or the benevolent planets interpose their rays, the malevolence threatened will be mitigated, *et vice versa*.

282. How Long It Is Probable the Querent May Live—If the ruler of the Ist be going to ☌, ☐ or ☍ of ☉, or to either the lord of the VIIIth, VIth or IVth, see how many degrees he is distant and in what signs they are, and so judge according to 231. Death is approaching if the ☽, lady of the Ist, be afflicted by the lord of the VIIIth or ☽ afflicted therein.

See how many degrees the ☽ is from ♅, ♄, ☋ or ♂, or lord of the VIth or VIIIth, and so judge. If the malefics be in the Ist, mark the degrees distant between the **cusp** of the Ist or VIIth, and the aspect, so will it be years or months according to 231.

283. What Part Is Likely to Be Most Fortunate?—See in what part of the heavens ♃, ♀ or the lord of the Ist is, **if he be strong,** if not, reject him.

If ♃ or ♀ be in the Ist, XIIth or XIth, his younger days are most prosperous, or up to twenty-one years of age. If the Xth, IXth or VIIIth, most lucky from 21 to 35. If in the VIIth, VIth or Vth, from 35 to 50. If in the other parts, his latter days will be the best.

284. The Nature of Events Likely to Take Place—Observe the aspects which the ☽ has lately formed, and from what the lord of the Ist separates, of good or evil aspects; these will show what accidents have taken place, according to the houses in which they formed aspects, and of which they are rulers; their next application will show what they may expect, and judge according to our General Judgment; if ill aspects, judge evilly; if good aspects, judge fortunately.

285. When the Querent May Expect a Change—Erect a figure, and direct the significator to promittors, as in a nativity, if in a matter of great consequence. In ordinary cases, the number of degrees between the significators and promittors will point out the time sufficiently correct by taking a degree for a year. If violent fixed stars occupy the cusp of the Ist, Xth, or place of the ☽, some sudden mischief is near; but if their nature be good, it denotes some sudden benefits.

286. Of the Good or Evil Attending Life—This is taken from the figure generally. When ♃ or ♀, or the ☉ and ☽ possess good houses (230) and the malefics evil houses, then good may be anticipated generally. But when (♆), ♅, ♄, or ♂, or ☋ occupy the good houses, the querent will be subject to a troublesome life. If ♅ possess the Ist, the querent will act independently (146). If ♄ possess the important places, he will be melancholy and pensive (147 and 148). If ♂, he will be choleric and rash (151-152). If the ☋ be in the Ist, much scandal will attend him. Where a Nativity cannot be had, a horary question will answer all its purposes; and if asked with strong anxiety to know the result, a figure of this kind may be judged as a nativity.

287. What Part of the World Is Most Prosperous for the Querent?—When this question is asked in a general sense, it is proper to direct him to that part of the world where ♃, ♀, the ☽, or the ⊕ are posited; or if they be not together, where the strongest number of them are, but they must be strong and free from affliction, or nothing good will be done. It is better, therefore, to take the direction of that which is most dignified or fortified, than of two or three that are weak. The part of heaven will be found in 234, and the country in that part according to 203 to 214.

288. Which Way Must He Steer for Better Success?—If any particular purpose or pursuit be stated, he must follow the significator of such purpose. If health be the object, follow the lord of the Ist and the ☽; if riches be his object, the lord of the IId and the ⊕; if honour, business, or situation, let him follow in the direction of the lord of the Xth and the ☉. If they lie in different places, follow that which is strongest and well dignified. If neither of them be in good condition, or the malefics afflict them, then abandon the pursuit, or remain where he is. The places where the malefics are found are always to be avoided. The places of directions are 234.

Example: If the lord of the Ist were in ♈, in the IXth house, and fortunate, the querent would do well to travel South East; for ♈ is an eastern sign, and the IXth house is S.W. (*See* comment in 234) The journeys should be made to those countries subjected to ♈, and in the S.E. part of those countries.

289. Of the Welfare of an Absent Person—Generally, the absent person will be some relation of the querent. But if there be no relationship between them, then take the Ist, lord of the Ist, and the ☽ to signify the absent party. If he be applying to the ☌, or ill aspect of the lord of the real VIIIth, he is near death. If the aspects are past without the assistance of any benefic, he has ceased to exist for so many days, months, etc., as there are degrees between the significators.

If the ruler of the Ist be in the Vth, and the ☽ in □ to him, danger of death. The ☽ in ♈, lord of the Ist, in ☌ with the lord of the VIIIth in the VIIIth or IVth, he is dead, or if in the VIth, he will die. The lord of the Ist, or ☽ in the VIIIth or IVth, combust, the party is dead.

If the lord of the Ist, or the ☽, separate from the lord of the VIth or VIIIth, he has been in great danger; and if he apply to no aspect of the fortunes, he will long remain so; but if to good aspects of the fortunes, he will soon recover. If the lord of the Ist separate from a bad aspect of the XIIth, he has been confined, or in trouble.

In all other respects, his present, past, and future situation may be known by considering the figure according to the rules laid down in other departments of horary questions (240).

290. Of the Exchanging of Commodities—Would it be well to exchange the watch, ornament, dress or any other article?

The ruler of the Ist and ☽ are for the querent.

The Vth house, its ruler, ♃ and ♀, are the article (unless it is a working dress, when we would consider the VIth in place of Vth).

If the ☽ leave a bad aspect of the ruler of the Ist, Vth, ♃ or ♀, and apply to good aspects of the ruler of the Vth, ♀ or ♃, or to any **two** significators, then it is well to change, or purchase more.

BETTER NOT EXCHANGE

The ruler of the Vth afflicted, or the ☽, ♀ or ♃, badly situated, or ill aspected, let the exchange alone; for you will go from ill to worse.

291. Two Antagonists
   1. Will A or B win the foot race?
   2. Which will win the quoit match?
   3. Which will win the game at cards?
   4. Shall I be able to win the battle?
   5. Can I bargain to my advantage?

6. Shall I be successful in the raffle?
7. Shall I win this wager?
8. Shall I win or lose by purchasing these shares, etc.?

The lord of the ascendant and the ☽ are for the querent.
The Vth house, its ruler, and planets therein are for the gain or loss.
The VIIth house and its ruler signify the opponent.

RULES FOR WINNING

1. Rulers of the Ist and Vth, or the Ist and IId strong, or ♀ and ♃ therein, unafflicted and not retrograde.
2. The ☽ unafflicted, or the ruler of the Ist or IId or ☽ in ☌ or good aspect of the ⊕.
3. The ⊕ in the Ist, Xth or Vth, and not in bad aspect with the malefics, or the ruler of the Ist, Vth or VIIth.
4. ♃, ruler of **both** the Ist and IId or Vth, unafflicted.
5. The ruler of the Ist, or ☽ in the VIIth, or especially in ♉, in the Vth, or the ruler of the Vth in the Ist, in dignities, and not afflicted by aspect of (♆), ♅, ♄, ♂ or ☋.
6. The governor of the Ist in ☌, ✶ or △, to the lord of the Vth, especially if these significators are in reception.
7. The ruler of the IId a benevolent and powerfully posited.
8. A benevolent strong in the Vth or IId, and also in good aspect of the lord of the Ist, IId or Vth.
9. The ruler of the Vth better dignified than the ruler of the VIIth.
10. The rulers of the Vth and VIIIth separating from good with each other, and the lord of the Vth applying benevolently to either the ruler of the Ist, IId, or ⊕.
11. The ☊ in the Ist, IId, Vth, or Xth is a slight testimony.

LOSING TESTIMONIES

1. The lord of the Vth, IId or VIIth, an infortune, or R., or debilitated.
2. The ruler of the Ist or Vth, or the ☽, afflicted, or much debilitated.
3. The lord of the Vth in the VIIth, in reception of the ruler of the VIIth.
4. The lord of the Vth separating from the lord of the IId, and applying to ☌, ✶ or △, to the lord of the VIIIth, or ♅, ♄, or ☌, or ☋.
5. The ⊕ in the VIIth, or in good aspect to the ruler of the VIIth or VIIIth; or (♆), ♅, ♄ or ☌ in the Vth, and **not the ruler**.
6. The ☽ in □ of ♃ or ♀ will not detriment unless **she be debilitated**.
7. The ☋ in the Ist, IId, Vth or XIIth house.

If you find **equal** testimonies, judge the most powerful significators win; but if there happen to be more of the one than the other, always decide in all questions in favor of the greater number of reasons or testimonies.

Foot Race at Sheffield, July 9, 1849
Question: 2:30 p.m. July 9, 1849

Will Mosley Win Pinder this afternoon at Sheffield Hyde Park?

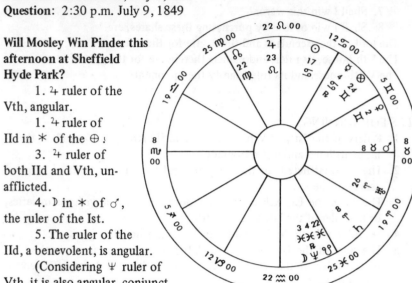

1. ♃ ruler of the Vth, angular.
1. ♃ ruler of IId in ✶ of the ⊕ ⸴
3. ♃ ruler of both IId and Vth, unafflicted.
4. ☽ in ✶ of ♂, the ruler of the Ist.
5. The ruler of the IId, a benevolent, is angular.
(Considering ♆ ruler of Vth, it is also angular, conjunct Moon, sextile to ♂ ruler of Ist, better dignified than the ruler of the VIIth.)
6. The ruler of the Vth, better dignified than the ruler of the VIIth.
7. The ☊ in the Xth house.
There are seven testimonies for winning (considering either ♃ or ♆ ruler of Vth.

FOR LOSING
1. ♄ posited in the Vth, and he is not its ruler.
2. ♂ ruler of the Ist, and in detriment.
3. These **two** testimonies are against him. (♆ is also conjunct South Node.) As there is a majority of 5 for winning, I said Mosley will win. **He did win, at six o'clock the same evening.**

292. Of Bills and Promissory Notes — The Ist house and the ☽ signify the querent.

The IId, the ⊕, and the ruler of the IId for the bill.

The VIIth and its lord denote the quesited, the VIIIth his money.

If the ruler of the VIIth or VIIIth afflict the ⊕, or the ruler of the IId, there is reason to fear the bill will not be honoured. The presence of (♆), ♅, ♄, ♂, ☿ or ☋, in the IId, unless the planets so located be well aspected by the ruler of the VIIth or VIIIth, or by the ⊕, ♀ or the ☽, from the VIIth, Xth or XIth, the bill will be dishonoured. If the ⊕ receive any evil aspect of the lord of the Ist it will not be paid.

If the Part of Fortune received a good aspect from the ruler of the Ist, VIIth or VIIIth, it will be paid.

Note: At the time of signing a bill, etc., take care that the ⊕ , ☿ or ♅ be not afflicted in the IId, VIIth or VIIIth, for this indicates fraud (♆ should also be included here). The ⊕ always denotes money, whether in cash or bills.

Your principal significators are the rulers of the Ist, IId, ⊕ , VIth, VIIIth and IVth. Then look to the planet which may afflict or assist your significators, unless affliction come from the VIIth, VIIIth, Vth or XIth house, it need not be feared. The ☋ in the IVth denotes evil to the firm in question. (♆), ♅ , ♄ or ♂ **unfortunate,** near the cusp of the IVth, shows the firm to be unfortunate, especially if the ruler of the IVth be unfortunate also. A fortunate planet in the IVth, well aspected by the ☉ , ☽ , or ruler of the VIIth or VIIIth, judge the firm will stand. In order to judge of the condition of the parties with whom you do business, look well to the planets aspecting the rulers of the VIIth and IVth. If many planets aspect and are well conditioned, the firm is doing well, and will be able to meet all demands. If planets of an adverse condition throw evil aspects to the rulers of the IVth, VIIth and VIIIth, judge the firm will suffer loss through the parties described by the planet afflicting. Yet if the rulers of the IVth, VIIth and VIIIth be in their dignities, it will not go to ruin a compromise. The evil aspects of (♆), ♅ and ☿ , to the significators are indicative of forgery or fraud.

293. Of Hopes and Wishes

> Hope that is seen is not hope; for what a man seeth, why doth he yet hope for? But if we hope for what we see not, *then* do we with *patience wait for it.*
>
> — Paul in Romans 8:24, 25

Query: Shall I Obtain My Wishes?—The XIth house, its ruler and planets therein, denote the hope or wish.

The Ist, its ruler, planets therein, and the Moon, signify the querent.

You May Expect it—If the ☽ be strong in ♉ , ♌ or ♒ , and she in good aspect of ♀ , ☉ or ♅ ; or if ☽ and these be in mutual reception; yet if the receiver of the ☽ be itself unfortunate, such as **detriment, fall** or other affliction, detriment is shown to befall the thing after obtaining it.

The rulers of the Ist and XIth in good aspect with each other, or with the ☽ , or in benevolent mutual reception; or governor of the Ist fortunate in the XIth, or the ruler of the XIth in good position in the ascendant, or the ruler of the XIth in an angle, strong, and received by the ruler of the Ist or in ✶ or △ to the lord of the Ist.

The receiver of the Moon and herself in mutual reception, and more especially if the ruler of the Ist be in mutual reception with the Moon, he shall receive his desire, so far as is feasible and practicable.

If the ☽ and the ruler of the Ascendant apply to ⊕ , ♀ or ♃ , not cadent, expect the thing desired. If the ruler of the XIth be a fortune and apply to the lord of the Ist by evil aspect, it will be obtained, but with difficulty.

The Thing Will Not Be Obtained—If the ☽ is not well connected with the ruler of the XIth or any benefic, or the ☊, in the XIth, **a failure**; also if the significators are in bad aspect, combust, retrograde, cadent, void of reception, or with bad fixed stars.

If the receiver of the ☽ be in ♈, ♋, ♎ or ♑, a promise of it, but eventually frustrated and disappointed.

N.B.—If the querent **name** the thing hoped for, then judge of it by its own proper house, and so on; as, if it be money, take the ⊕ or the IId house; if it be employment, take the Xth, and so vary your judgment according to the house to which it belongs (240).

294. Of a Ship at Sea and Its Voyage—The various parts of a ship are ruled much the same as the parts or members of man's body:

♈ the breast of the ship
♉ under the breast, towards the water
♊ the Rudder or Stern
♋ The bottom or floor of the ship
♌ The top of the ship above the water
♍ The belly of the ship
♎ The part above the breast in the water
♏ Where the Mariners abide
♐ The Mariners
♑ The End of the ship
♒ The Captain or Master
♓ The Oars in galleys, the wheels in steam vessels

The Ascendant and the Moon signify the vessel and cargo.

The lord of the Ascendant denotes those that sail in her.

When all these are fortunate, they signify that the ship is safe, and in prosperity; on the contrary, if they be impeded or afflicted, the vessel and all in her are in imminent danger, if not lost.

A malignant, which has dignities in the VIIIth, located in the Ist; or the lord of the ascendant in the VIIIth, in ill aspect with either the lord of the IVth, VIth, VIIIth or XIIth; or the ☽ combust, under the earth; all these are indications of loss to the ship. If the ascendant and the ☽ be unfortunate, and the lord of the Ist fortunate, the ship is lost, but the men saved.

On the contrary, when the ☽ is fortunate, and the ruler of Ist unfortunate, then the vessel will do well, or is safe; but that her crew are in danger of death by the ship-fever, or some epidemic or endemic disease.

These rules merely apply when she is on her voyage, and the querent is anxiously serious to know how the ship is or has fared. But to know the result of a voyage, we must investigate the figure as follows:

295. Will the Voyage Prove Prosperous?—If the fortunate planets and the ☽ be in the IXth, Xth, Ist, IVth or VIIth, and that at the same time afflicting the ☽, or the ruler of the Ist, well located, or the ruler of the Ist and IXth well situated, then the voyage will be good and safe.

But if ♅ , ♄ , ☋ or ♂ be in the above places, or in succeedent houses, the ship will meet with some misfortune in that part of the ship, or to those persons signified by the sign where the malefic is located; for which, see 294.

♄ afflicting the Ist and the ☽ , denotes sickness, shipwreck, enemies, or pirates; ♂ shows fire, fever and capture, if no good aspects of the fortunes intervene, the ☋ much the same as ♂. If the ruler of the Ist in this case be free from affliction, and strong, the crew will escape; if the lords of the angles be free from affliction, and the ruler of the Ist, most of the cargo and crew will be saved.

If the Xth house be afflicted by ♂ , and near violent fixed stars, ♂ being at the same time in ♊ , ♍ , or ♒ , the ship will be in danger of being burned by the enemy. But if ♂ be in the Xth, and not in the above humane signs, then the ship will be in danger of fire by lightning (more so if Uranus be involved), or accident.

If ♄ be in the Xth, it is very evil; danger of shipwreck, and the stronger the afflicting planet is the greater will be the danger.

Again, if a □ or ☍ exist between the ruler of the Ist and the disposer of the ☽ , without exception, there will then arise discord and contention among the seamen, or there will be so much dispute between the captain and his crew as often to cause an open mutiny. In this case, the strongest significator will overcome, that is, if the ruler of the Ist is better dignified than the disposer of the ☽ the men will overcome; but if the disposer of the ☽ is stronger than the lord of the Ist, then the captain will prevail and the mutineers be put down.

296. Will the Voyage Be Long or Short?—The ruler of the IXth, or a planet therein swift, or in a moveable sign and oriental, denotes the voyage to be short and quick; but if occidental, long and tedious; if in common signs, a reasonable time, and the ship may land at a different port from the one originally intended. The ruler of the IXth and the ☽ , and the ruler of the Ist in fixed signs, denote a long voyage; ♉ , ♍ or ♑ , on the ascendant, portends the ship to be a dull sailor.

If the ruler of the Ist be R., or either he or the ☽ apply to a R. planet, it signifies the person that goes on the voyage will return in a short time, or perhaps before he reaches the place intended. ♃ or ♀ in the Xth, denotes mirth; in the IXth, health.

297. Of the Issue of a Long Journey—If the querent's significator be fortunately situated, he will do well; also the same if the quesited's significator be well aspected and located, that is, when the query is made of a person absent. The significator in the Xth, success on the journey; if in the VIIth, at the place to which he goes; but if in the IVth, he will come home.

Whatever planet is significator, denotes the person or means by which he will be benefited or the contrary, according as that body is well or ill dignified. If it be ♅ , read 146 and 163 for the character and employment of the person benefiting the enquiry; if ♄ , it will be by old persons, or ancient matters, or farmers, as you will find in 147-148 and 164; if ♃ , benefits by clergy or magistrates, according to the querent's situation in life, which is found in 149 and 165; if ♂, those things and persons denoted in 151 and 166; if it be the ☉, by nobles or persons in power, as 153 and 167; if it be ♀, gain by women, or by dealing with those things connected with 155 and 168; if ☿, by writing or merchandise, letters of introductions, and such things as 157 and 169; and if the ☽, gain by such things as are denoted 159 and 170. Advise the parties to enter into those affairs, or avoid them, as the planet is good or evilly affected.

298. When Shall I Obtain a Situation?—See when the lords of the Xth and Ist form a good aspect with each other; if near an aspect, give for every degree a day or a week, according to their being angular or succeedent; or in moveable, fixed, or common signs; study well 232.

If the above do not apply satisfactorily, see when the ☉ and the ruler of the Ist gain a good aspect, or the time when the ☉ and the ruler of the Ist are favourably aspected, according to their Ephemeral motion; so long will the querent be before he or she obtains a situation. The day the aspect is completed will be the day when successful.

The quality of the situation will be judged by the dignity or otherwise of the ruler of the Xth; the ruler of the Xth and the ☉ portend the quality of the employer. The XIth and planets therein, and its ruler, indicate the wages, whether they be good or not.

299. Absconded Mother—Dead or Alive?—The Xth is her ascendant, the Vth her VIIIth, the IIId her VIth, and the XIIth her IIId. The ruler of the Vth in the natural VIIIth, and an infortune, she is dead. Danger of death if ♂ or ♄ be in the Xth or VIIIth. If it be ♄, she is drowned (this is more probably true if it were Neptune); if ♂, then violence; as cutting of throat, shooting, hanging, etc. Either the ruler of the Xth, Vth or VIIIth afflicted, danger of death. The lord of the Xth in the IVth, and in □ of the ☽, she is dead. The ☽, or the lord of the Xth in ☌ of the ruler of the VIth or VIIIth, in the Vth, VIIIth or IVth, dead. The ruler of the Xth, or ☽, combust in the Vth, VIth, VIIIth or IVth, she is dead.

These rules never fail if the querent fears self destruction. If the above rules, or the majority exist, say dead.

The student may erect a figure for February 11, 1850, 6:30 p.m. The querent's mother was found drowned; her mind at times was insane.

300. Questions

1. Will the querent obtain the money he has lent?
2. Shall I be able to obtain money from the club, etc.?
3. Shall I be able to obtain money for the goods sold and delivered?
4. Shall I get the good left in pawn, etc.?
5. Shall I be able to recover a certain debt?
6. Shall I be able to open a banking account with this bank?

The ruler of the Ist, planets therein, and the ☽, signify the querent.

The ruler of the IId denotes the substance of the querent.

The lord of the VIIth, represents the debtor, or the person of whom you intend asking the substance.

The VIIIth and its ruler show his means of paying it.

The Querent Will Obtain the Substance Demanded if the lord of the Ascendant or the ☽ out of its occidental debilities in good aspect of the ruler of the VIIIth, and the latter unafflicted either by aspect or position; or the lord of the Ist or ☽ be in ☌ of ♀ or ♃, and these too unafflicted, in an angle, in the VIIIth house; or the querent's significator in ☌ of ♀ or ♃, and these fortunes in their dignities in the sign ascending, or in the intercepted sign.

Even an infortune in the VIIIth, or ruler of the VIIIth, and that malefic receive either the ruler of the Ist unafflicted, or the ☽ ; but then all these must be in mutual reception, and in their dignities.

Lord of the VIIIth unafflicted, or he be in good aspect of ♃ or ♀ , in the Ist or IId, in reception, undebilitated, or these in application to each other by good aspect, or even they be in good familiarity of the ☽ or ruler of the Ist. All these denote the querent will be successful.

301. The Querent May Expect a Disappointment if the ruler of the Ist be retrograde, or refrain from good aspect of ruler of the VIIIth or VIIth, though the ruler of the VIIth or VIIIth should be ♃ or ♀, more especially if ♃ or ♀ be debilitated, although they may be angular; most bitterly the querent will feel it if the lord of the Ist should be ☿ retrograde.

The ☋, (♆), ♅, ♄ or ♂ in the VIIIth; or lord of the VIIIth, Ist, or VIIth in detriment, fall, peregrine, or retrograde; or a malefic joined to the ruler of the ascendant; or ruler of the Ist just set and debilitated.

Ruler of the VIIth or VIIIth posited in the Ist or IId and not mutually received by either Ist, IId or the ☽—the significators in □ or ☍ to each other —or ruler of VIIth or VIIIth apply by evil aspect to ruler of the Ist, IId, the ☽, or the ⊕, the quesited is a cheat, and has no good feeling to the querent.

It is said, a malefic interposing, or evil aspect, shows the cause or person from whom the impediment arises, by the house such planet rules, at the time of the question.

Instructions: Instead of taking the lord of the VIIth and VIIIth:

For the recovery of wages, take the lords of the Xth and XIth.

For asking of the father, take the lords of the IVth and Vth.

For asking of a brother, sister, or neighbour, take the rulers of the IIId and IVth.

For asking of a friend, take the lords of the XIth and XIIth.

By this means you may go round the heavens, only remember that the succeeding house signifies his substance to that which is his ascendant.

The following Map of the Heavens will show the indispensable necessity of taking the proper significators of the quesited.

The student must erect a figure for August 11, 1847, at 0:50 p.m., for an example.

302. Can I Be Successful in Borrwoing Money from a Club?—Mercury retrograde, ruler of the quesited money, out of all dignities, denotes the persons are unable to lend it.

Mars, ruler of the Ist, signifying the querent, out of dignities, just set, portends disappointment.

Venus in quincunx, the quesited significatrix to ♂ ruler of the querent, and received by ♀ , symbolically declares good feeling existing between the parties; yet the querent was disappointed, the quesited not having any cash at command, as I told the querent.

I directed the querent to try to borrow of a friend and he would be successful.

Here, ♀ ruler of the XIth for the friend, strong in her own house, on the cusp of the XIth, and ruler of the friend's IId as well as Ist, declares he would get it of a friend, and so he did within an hour's time.

303. Of Riches or Gain—The significators of riches are the IId house, its ruler, the planets therein, the ⊕ and its dispositor. The querent will be rich, as these are strongly dignified, free from affliction, well aspected by the fortunes, or in reception with them.

The Querent Will Gain Wealth if the rulers of the Ist and IId be in mutual reception, or in good aspect with each other, or the lord of the Ist is in the IId, or the lord of the IId in the Ist; this is strong in each other's houses.

If the ☽ apply to the ruler of the IId, either by ☌ or good aspect from good houses in the figure; or ☽ in her dignities in the IId, in ☌ , ⚹ , or △ of ♃ or ♀ or the ⊕. The ☽ or any other planet transferring the light of the lord of the IId to the ruler of the Ist, then he will live in esteem.

The ⊕ in the Ist, gain by his own industry. The disposer of the ⊕ well aspected and free from affliction are signs of riches, especially in the Ist or Xth.

The best sign of riches is the lords of the Ist and IId, and ♃ joined together in the IId, Ist, Xth, VIIth, IVth or XIth. The next best testimony is their application to ⚹ or △ , with reception. All the planets angular, swift in motion, is good. All of them direct, in good houses, and each having some accidental dignity.

♃ , who naturally signifies riches, or ♀ , or ☊ , free from bad aspects of (♆), ♄ , ♂ , or ♅ , and posited in the IId, denotes riches; and if this happens in fixed signs, so much the better.

The luminaries in ⚹ or △ , from good houses, is a symbol of riches and honour, especially if they be essentially dignified.

SYMBOLICAL TESTIMONIES OF POVERTY

♅ , ♄ , ♂ or ☋ in the IId peregrine, R., or afflicting the ruler of the IId, ♃ , ♀ , or ⊕, either by body or aspect, is a sign of poverty.

Many planets ill dignified in the IId, is a sign of poverty. The ☉, ♂ or ☋ , in the IId, wasting the estate already possessed. The ☉ in bad aspect of ♃, denotes also extravagance.

When the significators of substance apply to each other by □ or ☍, if they are in mutual reception, may show the acquiring of riches, but it will be with great difficulty; neither will he take good care of the substance he may then possess.

304. By What Means Will the Querent Obtain Riches?—If you have found that the querent will obtain wealth, you may know whence and by what means by the following:

The ruler of the IId in the Ist, especially if well aspected by ♅, gain without much labour. If the ruler of the IId or ☽ promises substance, by mutual aspect, observe from what house the aspect is, or what house the ☽ rules; if neither of these is the promiser of substance, see in what house the ⊕ and its depositor are in.

If the planet assisting be in the Ist, the querent will gain by his own industry; or if a poor man, he will thrive by labour, or by care, or invention. But if the assisting planet be not lord of the IId, he will gain by well managing his own affairs, etc., or by such things as are of the nature of that planet, the sign he is in being also considered.

The lord of the IId in the IIId, or in good aspect with each other, well aspected, shows that his wealth will be derived from his neighbours, or kindred, or by inland journeys.

The ruler of the IId in the IVth, fortunately placed in good aspect of the lord of the IVth, and not afflicted as aforesaid, the querent will attain riches by his father, or by lands, or houses purchased, or by money lent by his relations.

The ruler of the IId in the Vth, and in good aspect of the lord of the Vth, portends gain by cards, racing, gaming, or other amusements, keeping alehouses, or places of recreation, or connected with theatres, and such things as the Vth house denotes (stock market).

The lord of the VIth gives gains by workmen, servants, dealing in small cattle, physic, stewardships, and things denoted by the VIth house.

The ruler of the VIIth denotes gain by women, wives, bargains, lawsuits, war, or commerce.

The lord of the VIIIth casting the aspect, denotes legacies, or a wife's portion, or gain by traveling to some country where he will settle and become rich unexpectedly, especially if the planet should be ♅.

The ruler of the IXth indicates riches by voyages, wife's relations, by some lawyer, or clergyman, or by religious profession, or learning. If ♋ or ♓ be on the IXth, he may gain by a voyage; but if ♉, ♍ or ♑ be on the IXth, he should remove to those places denoted by those signs, and by dealing in such commodities as that country produces.

The ruler of the Xth promises gain by holding office under some king or great man, or by any mechanical profession. If the querent be young, he should learn those businesses that may be shown by the sign and planet in the Xth, or its ruler if not in the Xth.

The XIth and its lord portend unexpected benefits by recommendations of friends, great men, and unexpected good fortune. The fortunate aspect cast from the XIIth increases the querent's substance by horses or great cattle; or if the sign be ♊ or ♒, by means of prisons, by thieftaking; as a jailor, sheriff's officer; if the sign be ♈, ♉ or ♑, by cattle, horseracing; if ♍, by corn.

N.B.—The student must be careful in observing to answer this query by the same figure with which he answered the first question; that is, whether the querent would be rich or poor. Also be careful to keep in mind his rules at the head of these enquiries, namely, the lords of these houses or planets therein casting a good aspect to the lords of the Ist or IId, or ☽ or ⊕.

305. The Cause of Poverty or Hindrance of Gain—If the figure deny riches, the evil arises from the planet or planets afflicting the lord of the Ist, IId, the ☽, or ⊕, or its depositor. If the lord of the Ist afflict, the querent is his own ruin; if the lord of the IId, he is poor and cannot help it; if the ruler of the IIId, he will be kept poor by frequent removals, poor relations, or by some neighbour underselling him. And so judge by the significators of the houses as in the last series of causes (241).

Wherever the ☋ is will always show the cause of loss or poverty, according to the house it occupies. Also ♃ or ♀ may be struck by being afflicted, for every planet must denote the work for which he is by Providence assigned.

306. The Time when the Querent May Attain Riches—Mark well the application of the ☽, or ruler of the Ist, has to the planet or planets signifying the substance of the querent. See how many degrees they are distant from each other, and so judge of weeks, months, or years, as they are angular, etc., fixed, etc., as directed in paragraphs 231 and 232.

307. Will a Ticket in a Lottery Be a Blank or a Prize?—The ⊕ well aspected and its depositor in a good aspect, and the ruler of the Ist and the ☽ well dignified and aspected, there is no doubts of the ticket being a prize.

The ⊕ in the Xth, or many planets dignified in angles, and the ☽ at the same time unafflicted and in good aspect to the ☉—these portend a chance of success.

If the ruler of the Ist or IId and ⊕ and ☽, be in affliction in any way, then loss; and you may safely foretell of the ticket being drawn a blank. I more generally take the Vth house for these things, the same as in horse racing, etc.

308. Will the Querent Obtain the Money Lent, Good Forwarded, Sold, and Delivered?—This question may be answered by the rules given in 300 and 301, but we will here give some specific tokens for these questions. As usual, the lord of the Ist, planets therein, and the ☽, signify the querent. The IId and planets therein, the substance of the querent.

The ruler of the VIIth or planets therein, represent the quesited, and the VIIIth and its ruler denote the substance of the quesited.

The Querent Will Obtain the Substance Demanded—The ruler of the Ist or the ☽, in good aspect of the lord of the VIIIth, and he unafflicted; or in ☌

of ♃, or ♃ in the VIIIth, and ♃ and ♀ unafflicted, or these latter have dignities in the Ist; lord of the VIIIth in the Ist or IId, in reception by house of the lord of the IId; ruler of the VIIIth receiving the lord of the Ist or the ☽; the ☽ in ☌ of ♃ or ♀ in the Xth or XIth, and they unafflicted.

The Querent Will Be Disappointed—The significators in ☐ or ☍ without reception; (♆), ♅, ♄, ♂ or ☋ in the VIIIth; lord of the VIIth or VIIIth R., or in detriment or fall; lord of the VIIth or VIIIth in the Ist or IId, and not received by either the lord of the Ist or the Moon.

309. Will the Querent Receive His Wages or Salary?—Look well to the lord of the Ist and the ☽ for the querent; the Xth and XIth to signify the person and salary quesited. The foregoing rules will answer this, only remember that instead of taking the rulers of the VIIth and VIIIth, you take the rulers of the Xth and XIth for the quesited.

The rulers of the Ist and Xth, XIth and IId, in good aspect with each other, the salary will be gained. The lord of the Ist or ☽ joined to the lord of the XIth in the XIth; lord of the Ist in good aspect with the ruler of the XIth; the ☽ in good aspect with either the lord of the Xth or XIth, all these show easily gained.

But if the ☽, or ruler of the Ist, be in good aspect of the infortunes, and the unfortunate planet receive them, by house, then the querent will gain after long waiting, and with many solicitations. If there be no reception, it will not be obtained.

If the infortunes interpose the friendly signs, see in which house that malevolent is, and that denotes the person or thing that will be the hindrance.

The time of receiving will be marked by the number of degrees between the lord of the Ist and the ☽, and the lord of the XIth, as in 231.

310. Of Agreement Between Brethren or Neighbours—The ☽ and ruler of the Ist are for the querent. The IIId and its ruler denote the quesited.

Generally Good Agreement—The lord of the IIId a benevolent, and in the Ist or IIId; the ☽ in good aspect with a planet in the IIId, or its ruler; the Ist and IIId either in good aspect or mutual reception; ♃ or ♀ or ☊ well situated in the IIId. Those persons whose significators do not apply are most impervious, and apt to disagree; but those whose significators apply are flexible, willing, and yielding, and desirous of agreement.

Not any General Agreement—If the rulers of the Ist and IIId, or Ist and the ☽ be in ill aspect of each other; or if the ☋ be in the IIId or in ill aspect of the lord of the Ist. Any bad aspect of (♆), ♅, ♄, or ♂, to the ☽, or ruler of the Ist from the IIId or Ist. If the ill fortunes be in the ascendant, then the querent is stupid, or most to blame; but if the IIId, the quesited is the irreconcilable party. If (♆), ♅, ♄, ☋ or ♂ are R., peregrine, or combust, the malice and mischief they threaten will be the more mischievous.

Is the Advice Good or Bad?—If you desire to know when in difficulty or embarrassed circumstances whether the advice is to your benefit which you have asked of a friend, erect your figure, and judge from the following rules:

The Xth house, its lord, and the Moon signify the counsel.

If the ☉, ♃, ♀ or ☊, be in the Xth, or if ☽ apply by body or aspect to the ruler of the Ist, the advice, counsel, or persuasion is good. Or either of the fortunes in the Xth, and applying by ✶ or △ to the ruler of the Ist, the same.

If (♆), ♅, ♄, ♂ or ☋ be in the Xth, peregrine, R., or otherwise debilitated, or afflicting the ☽, or ruler of the Ist, then conclude that the pretended friend is knavish and only pretending friendship. Also the sign ascending being moveable, and the ☽ and ruler of the Ist in moveable signs, justify you in giving the same judgment.

311. On Short Journeys—The Ist, its lord, and the ☽, are for the querent. The IIId and its lord signify the journey.

Is It Well to Go My Short Journey?—The lord of the IIId, Ist, and Moon direct, swift and well dignified, or in ☌, ✶ or △ of each other; or the ☽ in the IIId in ✶ or △ to the Ist or its lord; lord of the IIId in the IIId, and in ✶ or △ to the Ist, or its lord; lord of the Ist well dignified in the IIId—sure to go.

An Agreeable Journey—If the ruler of the Ist or the ☽ apply to good aspect of a planet fortunately posited in the IIId; lord of the IIId in good aspect to a fortunate planet in the Ist; ♃, ♀ or ☊ in the IIId, a profitable journey, especially if the fortune apply by ✶ or △ to the cusp of the Ist.

Not Very Successful—Lord of the Ist stationary, slow, or R., he makes tardy progress, and meets with incidental impediments and disappointments.

(♆), ♅, ♄, ♂ or ☋, in the IIId, or afflicting the lord of the IIId, or the ☽; ♅ there denotes the peregrinator to meet with accidents and extraordinary or unexpected hindrances; ♄ there shows him melancholy concerning such things as that house signifies of which ♄ is the lord; ♂ or ☋ in the IIId, danger of being robbed, and if in ♈, ♌ or ♐, accidents or lameness.

Lord of the VIth afflicting lord of the Ist, IIId or ☽; or the lord of the VIth with ☋, he will be sick.

If the lord of the Ist, IIId or the ☽ be afflicted by ♇, ♅, ♄ or ♂, from angles, danger of death; or the lord of the Ist or IIId going to combustion, or evilly aspected by the lord of the VIIIth, especially if he be (♆), ♅, ♄ or ♂.

Lord of the XIIth afflicting lord of the Ist or IIId, or the ☽, he meets with private enemies; if lord of the VIIth afflict, then public enemies.

Whatever planet afflicts the ruler of the IIId, judge of the nature of the evil to be expected; and the house over which the planet rules will show the nature of the evil.

312. Of Anonymous Letters—Sometimes persons receive letters of a friendly, sometimes of an unfriendly and degrading character, and the receiver knows not whence and from whom they come. In order to discover the appearance and intention of the sender, take:

    1. The IIId house and ☿ to denote the letter.

    2. The ruler of the IIId portends the description of the sender. The house in which he or she is posited indicates the relation or otherwise of

the sender, as if in the Ist, or in ♂, or good aspect with the ruler of the Ist, it is a person with whom the querent has frequent conversation or intercourse. In the IId, a person with whom the querent has had pecuniary transactions. And thus go round the heavens, judging according to the signification of the 12 houses (and signs) in paragraphs 15 to 143.

If the ruler of the IIId be in bad aspect with the lord of the Ist, then the sender is malignant and ill disposed towards the querent. But if the ruler of the IIId be debilitated, then the sender cannot hurt the querent; if powerful, judge the contrary.

313. Of Purchasing Property

1. The Ist, its lord, and the ☽, signify the querent or buyer.
2. The VIIth, its lord, and planets therein, signify the seller.
3. The IVth, its lord, and planets therein, signify the property.
4. The Xth, its lord, and planets therein, denote the price.

Query 1. Is it Well to Purchase the Property? Yes: Purchase if any of the following rules are in.

1st. ♀, ♃ or ☊ on the Ist, or ⊕ unafflicted in the first.

2d. Lord of IId in the Ist, or in ✳ or △ to the degree on the Ist or IVth, and not afflicted.

3d. ♀, ♃ or ☊, in the IVth, or beholding the cusp favourably, it is well to purchase.

Query 2. Shall I Purchase, etc., the Property?
You May if You Think Proper:

1st. If the lord of Ist, or ☽, be unafflicted in the IVth, or lord of IVth in Ist.

2d. Lord of the Ist, or the ☽, in ♂ with the lord of IVth.

3d. Lord of the Ist, or the ☽, in ✳ or △ with reception of the lord of the IVth.

4th. If lord of IVth, VIIth, or the ☽, apply to good aspect of lord of the Ist.

5th. You will easily agree if lord of VIIth join lord of the Ist by reception.

6th. Lord of VIIth apply or translate its light by reception in □ or ☍, you agree, but with difficulty.

7th. If the ☽ translate the light of one significator to the other, you agree by a third person's interference.

8th. Lord of the VIIth in the VIIth, or casting a good aspect to its cusp, or ♀, ♃, ⊕ or ☊ be therein, the querent profits least by the bargain.

You Will Not Agree

1st. (♆), ♅, ♄, ♂ or ☋ in the Xth, or they afflicting either lord of Ist or Xth; and if it be land they differ about the timber, etc., or buildings; if a house, about repairs.

2d. (♆), ♅, ♄, ♂ or ☋, afflicted in the IVth; or lord of IVth be in □ or ☍ to the cusp of the IVth.

3d. If there be no application, reception, or translation of light between the lords of the IVth, Ist, or ☽ with each other, it will be very difficult to bargain.

Query 3. What Is the Quality of the Property?

1st. This is chiefly judged by the lord of the IVth house. (♆), ♅, ♄, ♂ or ☋, in the IVth, either impotent or peregrine, the property is not good, the buyer will waste it.

2d. Lord of IVth R., or in its detriment, the property is bad, and will not stay long with the buyer.

3d. ♃, ♀ or ☊, in the Xth direct, the timber will be profitable, and the property let well; if R., the contrary.

4th. If ♅, ♄, ♂ or ☋, be in the Xth, few trees, and the house will not let well; if he be R., the buyer loses rents, etc.

5th. If there be no planet in the Xth, take its lord and judge of the results as he is weak, afflicted, etc.

6th. ♈, ♌ or ♐, on the IVth, or its lord in these signs, the estate is hilly, dry and hard.

7th. ♉, ♍ or ♑, on the IVth, or its lord therein, the ground is of a mixed nature, partly hilly, etc.

8th. ♋, ♏ or ♓, on the IVth, or its lord therein, the soil is watery, and there are rivulets, etc.

9th. If (♆), ♅, ♄, ♂ or ☋ be R., in the IVth, it will partake greatly of the nature of that misfortune, and will not be profitable. ♏, on the IVth, and ♄ therein, the land is marshy and boggy, and the house damp (same if ♆ is in this position).

10th. ♄ or ♅, on the IVth, in ♈, ♌ or ♐, the land is barren and dry; and if they be afflicted, it is strong and worthless.

11th. ♄ or ♅, on the IVth in ♊, ♎ or ♒, the property is not of a good quality; and if they be afflicted in ♊, there has been bad management, etc.

12th. ♄ or ♅, in ♉, ♍ or ♑, the soil is clay and heavy; and if they be afflicted, it is not manageable.

Query 4. Will the Property Be Dear or Cheap?

1st. This is known by the lord of the Xth. Lord of the Xth angular and strong, the price will be high, and the seller stick up to his terms.

2d. Lord of the Xth weak, cadent or afflicted, the price will be low, and the seller want money.

3d. If (♆), ♅, ♄ or ♂ be in the VIIth, and not lord thereof, care must be taken concerning the writings, agreements, etc.; for the seller is for his own ends, etc.

4th. A fortune in the Xth, they agree, and the parties will be satisfied.

To everything there is a season, and a time to every purpose under the heaven; a time to be born, and a time to die; a time to get and a time to lose; a time to keep and a time to cast away.

— Ecclesiastes 3: 1-8

314. On Removals—The following rules will answer questions on removals of situations, residence, house, tenements, etc.

Query 1. Is It Well to Remove from One House, Place, etc., to Another?

The Ist house, its lord and ☽, signify the querent.

The VIIth house and its lord signify the place to which he would go.

The IVth house and its lord signify the substance of the querent.

The Xth house and its lord signify the profit of the removal.

It Is Better to Remain, if any Two Rules Are Found

1. ☽, ♃, ♀, ☿ or ☊, unafflicted in the IVth or Ist.
2. Lord of the Ist or IVth in the VIIth, or the lord of the IVth and VIIth, fortunate planets, swift, or powerfully posited.
3. Lord of the IVth or Ist in ☌ of ♃, ♀, ☿ or ☊.
4. Lords of the Ist and VIIth in good aspect.
5. Lord of the Ist stronger than the lord of the VIIth.
6. Lord of the IVth in the VIIth, and he, ♃, ♀ or ☽ separating from ♃ or ♀. The ☋, (♆), ♅, ♄ or ♂ in VIIth.
7. (♆), ♅, ♄, ♂, ☋ or ☿, afflicted, even then better remain.

Evil planets in the VIIIth, or afflicting its lord, the property would be affected whither the querent would go.

Query 2. It Is Better for the Querent to Remove

1. Lord of the VIIth in good aspect with a good planet; and the lord of the Ist or IVth with evil planets.
2. (♆), ♅, ♄, ♂ or ☋ in the IVth or Ist; lord of the IId weak.
3. Lords of the Ist and IVth, or Ist and VIIth afflicted by the malefics.
4. The ⊕ in the VIIIth, XIIth or VIth; or ♅, ♄, ♂ or ☋ approaching to aspects of ♃, ♀ or ☊.
5. Lord of the Ist or ☽ separating from the malefics.
6. Lord of the VIIth stronger than the lord of the Ist.
7. ♃, ☊ or ♀ in the VIIth.

Query 3. What Afflicts in My Present Place, etc.?—See what planet afflicts the lord of the Ist or the ☽.

1. If lord of VIth be in the Ist, or afflicts lord of the Ist, or the ☽, ill health; or ill luck by means of servants.
2. If the lord of the XIIth afflicted, ill disposed neighbours, etc.
3. If ☽ be in the VIth, VIIIth or XIIth, or lord of the IId in ill aspect to the lord of the Ist, adverse fortune, etc.
4. Lord of the Ist peregrine in the IId; or he the afflicting planet, poverty where he is; also if the lord of the IId be afflicted.
5. If the lord of the VIIIth, afflict, he suffers by deaths, etc.
6. If the lord of IXth afflict, he suffers from wife's kindred.
7. If lord of Xth afflict, loss of trade or of credit. etc.
8. If lord of XIth, false friends, etc.
9. If lord of IVth, injury by repairing the house, etc.

10. If lord of VIIth, injury by an opposite neighbour who undersells him, etc.
11. If lord of Vth, children oppose, bad speculation, gambling, etc.

Query 4. About What Time Shall I Remove?
1. The depositor of the lord of the Ist, VIIth or the ☽, by any planet in an angle, but the IVth and that planet slow, a removal when the disposer comes in ☌ of lord of VIIth, or turns R., or leaves the sign he possessed.
2. See also when the lord of the Ist or VIIth, or a planet in the VIIth leaves the sign in which he is then posited, and about that time the querent removes. The cusp of the VIIth movable, sure to go.

Query 5. What Would Afflict whither I Would Remove?
1. If lord of VIIIth afflict lord of VIIth, money matters would be very fluctuating and afflicted; some losses.
2. If lord of IXth afflict lord of VIIth, harm by means of relations, neighbours, as IIId house signifies.
3. If lord of VIIth is afflicted by lord of Xth, the querent's father will injure by means of property, as IVth house.
4. If lord of XIth afflict, children oppose, as Vth house.
5. If lord of XIIth afflict, sickness, servants, as VIth house.
6. If lord of Ist afflict, wife opposes, lawsuits, enemies, as VIIth.
7. If lord of IId afflict, suffers by death, as VIIIth house.
8. If lord of IIId afflict, losses by means of wife, as IXth house.
9. If lord of IVth afflict, loss of honour, credit, trade, as Xth.
10. If lord of Vth afflict, false friends, rebellious sons, as XIth.
11. If lord of VIth afflict, secret enemies, persecutions, as XIIth house denotes.

Query 6. Which Way Must I Steer for Better Success?—See what planet is strongest in the figure, and has the best aspect to the lord of the Ist or IId; and according to the quarter of heaven and places that sign rules which the promising planet possesses; and thither better remove.

Astrological Judgments on Removals

Question: Removal February 12, 1842; 4:30 p.m.

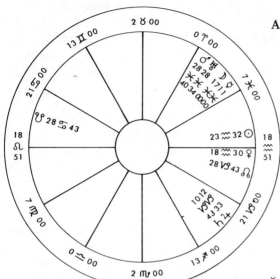

A lady interrogated the following questions:

I. **Is it Well for Me to Remove?**

1. The ☉ in ♒ exactly describes the querent.
2. ♄, lord of the VIIth and sign ♒, indicates the place to which she wishes to remove.
3. ♂, lord of the IVth and ♍, signify her substance.
4. ♀, lady of the Xth and ♉, signify the profit of the removal.
5. Lord of Ist, ☉ in his detriment in the VIIth, angular; and ♄ lord of the VIIth strong in his own house, are testimonies of better to remove. ♀, lord of IId weak, as being in his detriment, and in his fall; ☉ separating from ✶ of ♄, and applying to a ☌ of ♅; and ☌ and ♅ evil planets in the VIIIth, are all indications that it would be better to remove.

II. **What Afflicts in My Present Place?**

Mercury, lord of the IId in his detriment and fall, indicates the querent to be in poverty, and loss of money. (This the querent confessed.)

Lord of the Ist, ☉ in his detriment and in S □ of   lord of the VIth, indicates ill health. (This was true.)

III. **When Shall I Remove?**

The ☉ is lord of the Ist posited in the VIIth, and he leaves the sign on February 19th, and about that time you remove. (Reader, she removed on the very day!)

315. Of Succeeding to Property — The Ist, its lord, and the Moon, signify the querent; the house and its ruler belonging to the person leaving the property by will or otherwise must be taken as their significators; as the IVth for the father; the Xth for the mother, master or mistress; the IIId for brother, sister, cousin; the XIth for a friend, etc. The houses succeeding them denotes the property; because they are their seconds, as the Vth for a father, the XIth for mother, master or mistress, the VIIIth for lover, husband, or wife; the IVth for sister, cousin, brother or neighbour, the XIIth for a friend, etc.

If the lords of the querent and quesited's seconds be in each other's reception by house, or applying by good aspect, the querent will inherit the expected property. If the lords of both their seconds be the same planet; or lord of the quesited's IId dispose of the querent's ⊕ in the natural Ist or IId; or if the rulers of the querent's Ist and IId dispose of the quesited's lord of the IId, or the quesited's ⊕, which may be calculated for that purpose; or if a benefic be in the IId of the quesited, in good aspect of the ruler of the Ist, or the ☽, or the querent's IId cusp or its lord, or if there be translation of light between the lord of the querent's IId and the querent's respective lords—all these are signs that the querent will inherit, and vice versa.

And if the lord of the querent's IId be combust, or R., the property will not do him much good; and if the lord of the quesited's IId be so situated, there is not much property, if any. If the two seconds' lords apply to each other by evil aspect, provided there are other good testimonies that the property will be obtained, then it will be had, but not without difficulty. If there be separation from good aspect, it is to be feared the legacy will be left elsewhere, or that the querent's hopes are ill founded.

Will the Querent Enjoy the Estate of His Father?—As the above said, the IVth denotes the father, and the Vth being his IId, denotes the property.

It Will Be Obtained—The lords of the IId and Vth in mutual reception. The ruler of the IId in the Vth, or ruler of the Vth in the IId. The lord of the Vth disposing of the ⊕ in Ist or IId. The ruler of the Ist or IId disposing of the lord of the Vth. The ☽ separating from the Vth by ✶ or △, and applying to the ruler of the Ist or IId, ♃ or ♀ in the Vth, beholding the ruler of the IId, or a planet in the IId.

When Received—Lords of the IId and Vth applying by good aspect, or by retrogradation, the querent will receive some of the property shortly, or in his father's lifetime; but if the lord of the IVth be in aspect with (♆), ♅, ♄, ♂, or ☋, or with these in the IVth, denotes the father will not part with it during his lifetime.

Doubtful Testimonies—The ruler of the Vth, R., or afflicted by a malevolent planet, presages that the estate which the querent's father intended will be wasted or otherwise disposed of. If there be any good aspect, reception, etc., between the rulers of the IVth and any other planet, stronger than there is between the lord of the IVth and lord of the Ist, the father regards the party signified by that other planet better than the querent; if it be the lord of the IIId, or any planet in the IIId, then it is one of the querent's brothers, etc.

316. Of a Thing Mislaid—**How and Where to Find It**—Consider to whom the thing hidden or mislaid belongs; if to the querent, take the lord of the IId, and I should advise the artist not to answer any but the person who has lost the goods or articles.

If the ruler of the IId be in any of the four angles, say it is at home or where the querent suspects, particularly if the dispositor of the ⊕ cast a good aspect to the lord of the IId in the angles. A fortune ascending having dignities in the IId; the ☽ in the IId in good aspect to the lord of the Ist, or in the Xth in trine to a planet in the IId, or in the IId in △ to its lord, or to the lord of the Ist; the lord of the Ist in the IId; the luminaries in △ to each other or to the cusp of the IId; the lord of the IId in the XIth or IVth; the lord of the VIIIth in the Ist or joined to its lord; ♃, ♀ or ☊ in the XIth or IId; the lord of the IVth in good aspect of the lord of the Ist or IId, or in the IVth well dignified, are all signs of its being found again, and has been merely lost.

(All of the foregoing holds true in American experience also IF the mislaid article is not identified or made known to the astrologer. However, if the querent makes known just what the article is, then in lieu of the IId determine what house precisely rules such an article and apply the foregoing principles. For instance, an article of jewelry is ruled by the Vth; a letter, communication or written papers, by the IIId; a book by the IXth, etc., etc.)

The Nature of the Thing Stolen or Missing—This is judged by the ruler of the IId or planets therein. ♀ signifies cats, engines, water-closets (sic!), baths, new coin; ♄ shows lead, iron, tin, instruments, dark articles, shoes, umbrellas, wool, earthy materials, agricultural implements, carts, cows; ♃ denotes oil (this now is assigned to Neptune), money, silk, honey, poultry, paint, men's clothes, merchandise, horses; ♃ and ♅, paper money; ♂ portends silver (we would assign this to the Moon), arms, grass, red cloths, sharp instruments (we would assign "iron" to Mars instead of to Saturn); ☉ declares gold, yellow cloths, diamonds, keys, and valuable articles; ♀ denotes women's attire, pawn tickets, rings, brooches, especially if ♂ and ♀ be in aspect, ear-rings, and white cloth; ☿ shows paper money, books, paper, pictures, ornaments, scientific instruments, writing apparatus; the ☽, all common commodities, crockery, with ruler of the VIIIth, funeral attirements; ♀ and ☿, joint rulers of the IId, pawn tickets, especially if they be in VIIth.

The Place where the Thing May Be Lost—The ruler of the IId in the Xth, then it is in his hall, shop, dining-room; if in the Ist, where he most frequents or where he put it; if in the VIIth, where the maid or wife most frequents, or in their rooms; and if in the IVth, where his father or old person most frequents, or in the oldest part of the house.

The Kind of Place where the Things Are—The ruler of the IId, ☽, or ⊕, or any two of these which will give the testimony stronger, be in ♈, ♌ or ♐, the things lost are near the chimneys, or where iron is laid, in the eaves, or near a wall or upper part of a room; if in ♊, ♎ or ♒, hanging upon a line or trees, or upon high shelves above the ground; if in ♋, ♏ or ♓, it is in or near some dairy, water-closet, pump, wash-house, moist place, or near water; if in ♉, ♍ or ♑, near some pavement or floor, laid on the ground, or under the earth, as in the cellar.

If the significator be going out of one sign into another, the article is behind something, or fallen between two rooms or places, as wainscoting, or niches of boards, or at the joining of two rooms. Notice also the quarter of the house by the sign in which the significators are, according to the points of the compass found in 234.

The Article or Thing Will Not Be Found—The luminaries under the earth, even in good aspect, will give a slight hope, but if ever found it will be long first; also if the lord of the IId be afflicted.

317. Of Treasure, Mines, whether Recoverable or Not—To discover mines, hidden treasure, and other things supposed to be concealed in the earth, you must observe whether there be any planet strong in the IVth, or if ♃ or ♀ be in the IVth, there is treasure; the lords of the Ist and IVth joined in any of the angles; the ⊕ in the Ist, and the luminaries or the benefics in good aspect, there is treasure. Any planet dignified in the IVth in good aspect with the ruler of the VIIth, then there is treasure; as if ♄ be lord of the VIth, there is coal or other minerals; ♃ strong and ruler of the VIIth, in good aspect of the lord of the IVth, there is silver, or cloths, etc. hidden; if ♀, women's ornaments; if ☿, money, writings, medals, books, or such like; if ☉, gold or jewels; if the ☽, silver, and common articles; if ♅, new invented articles; (if ♆, oil).

There Is No Treasure, etc.—If the ☉ or ☽, or the ⊕ be cadent, or form no aspect among themselves. If (♆), ♅, ♄ or ♂ be afflicted in the IVth, or the ☉ or ☽ weak in the IVth. The ruler of the IVth, or ☽ separating from good planets denote there has been treasure hid, but is removed. But if they separate from ill aspect, then say there never was treasure hid.

318. Of Illegitimate Children—In giving general judgment on figures, it is sometimes necessary to give the querent confidence in the ability of yourself, and in the truth of Astrology, from some important past event; and to do so, take the following rules to show—

A Dishonoured Courtship—Lords of the Ist and Vth afflicting the lord of the XIth; ruler of the Vth and ☽ in the Vth, in detriment or fall; lords of the Ist and Xth afflicting the lord of the Vth; (♆), ♅, ♄ or ♂ afflicting ♀, or ruler of the Vth from the XIth and Vth, or those malefics rulers of the VIIth in the Vth afflicting the lord of the Ist. Lords of the Ist and Xth afflicted at one and the same time by the ruler of the Vth. ♂ in ☌, □ or ☍ of the ☽ from the Vth. ♀ afflicted by ♄ or ♂, an immodest person, especially if ♂ or ♀ be in ♋ or ♑, or the ☽ in ☍ of ♀ and in □ to the ☉. ♂ and ♀ being rulers of the Ist and Vth, VIIth and XIth, all at one time. These rules never fail. The Ist, the Vth, and the rulers thereof moveable, or in moveable signs; a fruitful sign on the Vth, or ♀ in the Vth, evilly aspected by (♆), ♅, ♄, ♂ or ☋, show she is unchaste.

The Female Is Chaste—If you find the Ist, the Vth, and their rulers in fixed signs unafflicted. Many planets angular, or the ruler of the Ist or Vth with the ☉. The ☉ in the VIIth, or ruler of the VIIth in the Ist, a good testimony. ☿ and ♃ in their own houses; though if (♆), ♅, ♄, ♂ or ☋ be in the Vth, and not badly situated, she then had many temptations.

319. Of Absconded Children—The ruler of the Ist and the ☽, denote the father and mother. The ruler of the Vth and ☿ portend the runaway or lost child.

The Absent One Will Return—Rulers of the Ist and Vth, or lord of the Vth or ☿ retrograde, or lord of the Vth applying to good aspect of the ruler of the Ist or a planet therein; the ☽, ☿, or lord of the Vth separating from ♃ or ♀; the ☽ in ✶ or △ to the cusp of her own house. If the ☽ transfer the light of the lord of the Vth or ☿ to the lord of the Ist.

If the ☽ separate from the lord of the Ist and be joined immediately to the ruler of the Vth, news will be brought of the runaway.

Lord of the Vth or ☿ in ☌ of the ☉, he will be found against his inclinations.

Ruler of the Vth, the ☽ or ☿, afflicted in the Xth, especially by ♅, ♄, ♂ or ☋, or R. planet in affliction.

Lord of the Vth or ☿ in the IVth or XIIth afflicted by the malefics from the Vth, found in prison.

The Lost One Not Found—Lord of the Vth in the VIIth, IIId or IXth and very swift, or lord of the Ist and Vth in □ or ☍, or separating from each other.

320. Of Offspring Generally

The Woman Will Have Children—If the lord of the Ist be in the Vth, or the ruler of the Vth or ☽ in the Ist unafflicted; the ruler of the Ist, ♀ or ♃ in ☌ of the ☽ in the Vth; a fortunate planet in the Ist, IIId, Vth, XIth and IXth houses. The cusp of the Vth possessed by ♋, ♏ or ♓, and the lord of the Vth, Ist, or the ☽ in these signs. Translation of light between the lords of the Ist and Vth, particularly if made by the ☽.

The Number of Children—I would advise the student to be very mindful how he answers this question; for it is extremely difficult to say, unless the Natus be cast for life. However, I generally find the number of offspring by the number of good aspects between the ruler of the Vth and other benefic planets.

It is said that ♀ being lady of the Ist, and in the Vth in ♋ or ♏ gives three children, and if this sign be ♓, there will be six children; should the ☽ be with ♀, there will be nine children. A fortune in △ to good planets gives an additional three, or if in ✶, two.

Testimonies of Barrenness—The ruler of the Ist, Vth, or the ☽, in ♊, ♌ or ♍. ♀ in ☌ of ☉, or in bad aspect with (♆), ♅, ♄, ♂, ☋, or any of these in the Vth, or if the ruler of the Vth is affected by the above. If children should be born under these influences, they will not live long.

A Woman Enquiring—She Is Enciente—The ruler of the Ist or ☽ applying to the lord of the Vth, by ☌, ✶ or △, from good houses, or the ☽ or ruler of the Ist in the Vth; the lord of the Vth with his dispositor.

The significators applying to good aspect in fruitful signs or houses; as the Vth, VIIth or XIth, or ♃ be there.

♃ and ♀ swift in angles, free from bad aspects of the malefics, or in the Ist in ♉, ♌, ♏ or ♒. ☽ in the VIIth, and aspecting its lord in the XIth; or the ☽ in the XIth beholding the lord of the VIIth in the VIIth.

Lords of the Ist and Vth in ♋, ♏ or ♓, in the Vth, VIIth, or XIth.

Lords of the Ist, Vth, or the ☉ in reception with a planet in an angle.

She Is Not Enciente—Lords of the Ist and Vth afflicted in ♊, ♌ or ♍. The malefics or ☋ in the Vth, or angular and afflicting the ☽. ♀ and the ☽ afflicting each other. If there is a majority of testimonies for enciente, then the contrary, and these are found in the Vth, then say abortion or miscarriage.

If a Man Ask Unknown to a Woman

She is Pregnant—Lord of the Vth beholding a planet by good aspect in the Ist, IVth, VIIth or Xth with reception. If lords of the Ist, Vth or VIIth be ♃, ♀, ☉ or ☽, or the ☊, or any of the foregoing in the Vth. Lord of the Vth in the VIIth, or the lord of the VIIth fortunate in the Vth. ☿ in aspect to a malefic and not in aspect to a benefic, cannot be relied upon.

She Is Not Enciente—♃ and ♀ afflicted, or ♀ joined to ♅, ♄ or ♂, or be in ☌ of the ☉, R. or stationary, especially in ♌, ♍ or ♑. The malefics in the Vth in □ or ☍ to the lord of the Vth. Lord of the Ist in ☌ or reception of a R. planet. Lords of the Ist and Vth in no aspect.

Will the Child Be Male or Female?—A BOY—Lords of the Ist and Vth, and the ☽ and the signs of the Ist and Vth in ♈, ♊, ♌, ♎, ♐ or ♒. Disposer of the ☽ or Jupiter in the seventh house. If the lord of the Ist be ♅, ♄, ♃, ♂ or the ☉, and the lady of the Vth be ♀, or the ☽, take the strongest testimonies; consider well the ☽, and if she apply mostly to masculine signs, judge accordingly. If the foregoing testimonies be in female signs, the child will be a FEMALE. ☿, must also observe, is convertible, and is either gender, according to the planets with which he is connected by aspect.

Whether the Child Will Live—The child will die in infancy: Lord of the Vth R., or in ☌ of the ☉, or in the IIId, VIth, IXth or XIIth, or in his detriment or fall, or weak, afflicted by either of the rulers of the VIIIth or XIIth. Lord of the Vth, weak in the XIIth or VIIIth, or lord of the Ist and Vth afflicted, or ♅, ♄, ♂ or ☋ in the Vth, and retrograde.

There Will Be Twins—If ♊, ♐ or ♓ be on the cusp of the Ist or Vth, and ♃, ♀, ☉, ☽ and rulers of the Ist and Vth be also therein. But unless all these concur, it is not safe to say twins.

The receiver of the ☽ by house with the ☊ or ♃, or ♀. Fixed or moveable signs on the Ist or Vth, and the ☉ or ☽ located therein, there will be but one.

The Length of Time She Has Been Pregnant—See the rulers of the Ist and Vth, or lord of the Ist and the ☽, and which are nearer past aspect. If they separate from a ☌ or S⚹, she is in her first month; if from a ⚹, her second or sixth month; if from a △, her third or fifth month; if from a □, her fourth; and if from an ☍, her seventh month.

It is said, if the receiver of the ☽ be angular, or ♂ in the VIIth, the party has just conceived. If ♄ be in the VIIth, she is quickened.

Time When the Birth Will Take Place—Observe when the ☉ or ♂ is in ☌ of the lord of the Vth, or there be a ☌ of the Ist and Vth in the Vth, these show the time.

Notice when the lord of the Ist goes out of one sign into another, or transits the place of ☽, ♃ or ♀, especially in the Ist, Vth or XIth—that is the probable time.

See how far the ruler of the Vth is from the cusp of the Vth, and for every sign give one month; also how far the lord of the Vth is from passing the Ist, and at that time a delivery. Together with this, you must take notice how long she has been pregnant by the foregoing rules, and then consider the tokens of delivery which may take place about that period.

The Time When She May Become Enciente—Having before found the possibility of issue, in what time it may be—Some say if the ruler of the Vth be in the Ist, it will be in the first year; in the IId, the second year; in the Xth, the third year; in the VIIth, the fourth year; in the IVth, the fifth year; and so on according to the pre-eminence of the houses.

Others, with more propriety, measure the time by the application of the ruler of the Ist, or the ☽ to the lord of the Vth, ♃ or ♀, reckoning by degrees, according to the nature of the sign the applying planet is in, as before.

The Querent Has Just Conceived—If translation of light has passed between the lords of the Ist and Vth, or if the ☽ be just separated from the ruler of the Vth in a fruitful sign, or in the Vth, VIIth or XIth houses; also if the lords of the Ist and Vth, or the ☽ be in reception with a planet that is angular; or if the ☽ and the lord of that triplicity she is in be both in fruitful signs; or if ♃ or ♀ be both angular and free from affliction.

321. Of a Messenger Sent on Important Business—The Ist and its lord denotes the sender, the lord of the Vth, the messenger, the ☽ is the message, and the VIIth and its ruler the person and place to whom it is sent.

What Business Is Effected?—When the ruler of the Vth separates from the lord of the VIIth, and applies to good aspect of the lord of the Ist. If he separates from the lord of the IId or VIIIth by any aspect, he brings money with him. If the ☽ separates from fortunes, the business has succeeded well, but if from malefics, not very well. If the ruler of the Vth or ☿ translates the light of the lord of the VIIth to the lord of the Ist, he has succeeded.

What Takes Place on the Journey?—A fortune in the IIId or IXth denotes traveling, but if an infortune, there shows the contrary. ♄ causes privations and disappointments, ♂ or ☋ danger of robbers, losses and insults. Where there is reason to apprehend danger, the lord of the Vth in ☍ to an infortune, or either of the luminaries in same situation, are very bad symbols. If the ☽ alone be afflicted, the messengers meet with bad reception. If slow, there will be delay.

If the ruler of the Vth apply to (♆), ♅, ♄ or ♂ by □ or ☍, before he can separate from the ruler of the VIIth, gives impediment to the party to whom it was sent. But if the ruler of the Vth go to a □ or ☍ of the infortunes, after he has separated from the lord of the VIIth, he will receive disappointments on his way home.

The Time of the Messenger's Return—When the lord of the Vth comes to a ∗ , △ or ☌ of the lord of the Ist. When the ☽ separates from the lord of the Vth and applies to the lord of the Ist, the querent will have intelligence of his messenger. The application of the significator to a ponderous planet denotes the day. The ruler of the Vth R., he returns when the planet becomes direct, or according to the number of degrees he wants of being direct (232).

The Character of the Messenger—Mark well the ruler of the Vth, what planet he is, and whether he be dignified or debilitated, and so judge according to 144 to 160.

If the rulers of the Vth and Ist are in mutual reception, or in good aspect from good houses in the figure, the messenger is faithful and honest. But if there be no reception or aspect, and the configuration be in the dignities of an infortune, the contrary may be expected. Also if the ruler of the Vth be combust or retrograde, then doubt his integrity or ability to perform the business.

322. **Of Servants and Lodgers Generally**—When this question is put by the master or mistress, take the Ist, its lord and the ☽ to signify the querent; the VIth house and its ruler to denote the servant or lodger.

The Servant, Apprentice, or Lodger Will Be Honest—If the ruler of the VIth be in good aspect of the lord of the Ist, or the ☽ , or to a good planet in the Ist. The ruler of the VIth in the dignities of Jupiter or Venus, unless their ruler be detrimented in ♉ , ♎ , ♐ , or ♓ , as ♂ and ♀ are, then the servant will be honest. If the ☽ transfer the light of the lord of the VIth, by good aspect, to the ruler of the Ist.

Do Not Engage the Servant, Apprentice, etc.—Wasteful—whether it be washerwoman, servant, workman or worker-woman, apprentice, etc. Sol afflicted in the VIth, or in ♎ or ♒ on the VIth; or the lord of the VIth afflicted in the IId. The ☽ in the VIth in □ to the ruler of the VIth in the IId, the servant is a knave. The principal significators void of aspect or reception.

Dishonest, if the ☋ be in the VIth or afflicting the ruler of the VIth, and the latter being in the IId especially. Also, the ruler of the VIth in ☌ or ill familiarity to the Ist or its ruler; bad if the ☽ be in ♏ in the VIth. If the ☽ transfer the light of the lord of the VIth to the ruler of the Ist by bad aspect. ☿ ruler of the VIth R., or combust, or in ☌ of the ☽ , or ill aspected to (♆), ♅ , ♄ or ♂, the servant's intellect will be shallow, and his principles or disposition not good. Also if the ruler of the VIth be in the VIIIth or XIIth, or in □ or ☍ to the cusp of the Ist.

When Is the Best Time for Engaging Servants?—The best time, when the rulers of the Ist and VIth, or the ☽ and ruler of the VIth are in good aspect with each other, and especially in mutual reception; this will be best seen by *Simmonite's Aspectarian.* Let the ☽ be in ♉ , ♋ or ♓ , for women servants. For men servants, let the ☽ be unafflicted in ♊ , ♍ , ♐ or ♒ . If the ☽ be afflicted in ♓ when you engage a servant, he will prove unfaithful. If the ☽ be in ♑ , he will be idle, run away, but return in a day or two, but he will go again.

Is this Servant, Workman, etc., Faithful?—The ruler of the VIth well dignified, unafflicted, or well aspected either by the rulers of the Ist, IId or the ☽ . The VIth or VIIth possessed by ♃ , ♀ or ☊, then the servant is faithful.

But if the ruler of the VIth afflict the rulers of the Ist, IId or the ☽ , or the VIth be possessed by ♄ , ♂ or ☋ , and they not dignified, or be in ill aspect to a planet in the VIth, then he or she is not to be trusted.

323. On Removal of Tenants

1. The Ist, its lord, and the ☽ are for the querent.
2. The VIth house and its lord are for the tenant.
3. The VIIth and its lord signify the substance of the querent.
4. The lord of the XIIth and its position in sign show whether the tenant will go.

Judgment

1st. The lords of the VIth and XIIth in good aspect or mutual reception declare they will agree.

2d. The cusps of the VIth and XIIth moveable, or their lords in moveable signs or near the end of a sign, denote the tenant will leave.

3d. They remove when the lord of the VIth or XIIth, or a planet in the XIIth leaves the sign, and probably when he turns R.

4th. Lord of the VIth or XIIth and the Xth afflicting each other, the rent is too high; also if the lord of the VIth or XIIth is afflicted in the VIIth or Ist.

5th. Lord of the VIth or XIIth afflicted by the lord of the VIIIth, or in the VIIIth, a neighbour injures him. And so judge who afflicts the lord of the VIth or XIIth, considering the VIth is the tenant's last, etc. (The author undoubtedly means "considering the VIth is the tenant's *first*, etc.")

324. Of Small Cattle and Dogs—By small cattle is meant sheep, pigs, calves, and small animals, as dogs, cats, and so on.

If the rulers of the Ist and VIth be in ☌ , ✶ or △ of each other, the querent will thrive by dealing in the above. The ruler of the VIth in ☌ , ✶ or △ of the ⊕.

It Will Be Evil to Deal in Them—An ill fortune or ☋ in the VIth, or a malefic afflicting either the lord of the VIth or a planet therein. The ruler of the VIth in bad aspect either with the ruler of the Ist, IId, ☽ , ☋ or ⊕ , or its dispositor. The lord of the VIth retrograde, combust, cadent or peregrine. ♄ in the VIth, they die of murrain or epidemics; ♂ there, they will happen accidents, bad bargains or be robbed of them, or lose them by their own carelessness.

When Is the Best Time to Buy?—When it is found by any figure or the Natus that it is well to deal in cattle, then notice when the ruler of the VIth is strong by house or joy, and in good aspect with the ruler of the Ist. If you wish to buy cheap let the ☽ be passing through ♉ , ♋ , ♍ or ♓ , separating from ☌ or ill aspect of (♆), ♅ , ♄ , ♂ or ☋ , and applying to good aspect of ♀ , ♃ , ⊕ or the ruler of the ascendant.

An Evil Time to Buy—An evil time to buy when the ☽ or ruler of the VIth separates from good planets and applies to the ☋ or to the malefics. Also when the ruler of the VIth is either debilitated by position or afflicted by ill aspects of the malefics, or the lord of the Ist.

325. **Of Strayed Small Cattle, or Servants**—As usual, the ruler of the VIth denotes small cattle, hired servants, lodgers, workmen, apprentices, clerks, and so on.

The Strayed One Will Be Found—If there be a good aspect between the Ist and VIth, or a slight testimony if between the VIth and the ☽. Ruler of the VIth retrograde. If the Moon translate light from the lord of the VIth to the Ist. Lord of the VIth fortunate in the IId, Vth or XIth, in good aspect with ☉, ♃ or ♀. Also if lord of VIth be rising in the ascendant.

He Is Not Disposed to Return—Ruler of the VIth swift and in the IIId, IXth, or falling into the Vth. If there be no good aspect, reception or translation between the rulers of the VIth and Ist, or if the ruler of the IXth be in the VIIIth or XIIth, or joined to an infortune. Ruler of the VIth in □ or ☍ of the ruler of the Ist or the ☽, or with the ☋, or combust. These rules denote neither the finding nor the returning of lost cattle or runaways.

Which Way Is the Servant or Cattle Strayed?—The ruler of the VIth must be considered, and the house in which he is located must be taken for the direction according to 234. In ♋, ♏ or ♓, near water or a seaport, if a person, or if cattle, on or near marshy ground, as meadows and such like places. In earthy signs, ♉, ♍ or ♑, on good ground or dry localities. In ♈, ♌ or ♐, near woods, plantations and shrubberies.

326. **Of Women's Marriages**—In women's marriages, the ruler of the Ist and the ☉ must be investigated, and how they are connected with the ruler of the VIIth and ♂.

Will the Man or Woman Marry?—In this it matters not whether the querent be male or female, for the general rules following will answer for both, provided the party be sincere in the inquiry.

The Querent Will Marry—The luminaries in good aspect with ♃, ♀, ♂ or the ruler of the VIIth. Ruler of the VIIth or Ist in the VIIth, Vth, Xth or XIth, and especially in good aspect with the lord of the ascendant. The ruler of the Ist, the ☽, ♀ or ♂ in the VIIth, especially in dignities, and the ruler of the VIIth in the Ist. Lord of the VIIth, ☉ and ♂, in ♋, ♏ or ♓. Rulers of the VIIth and Ist in good configuration.

Lord of the Ist in or near the cusp of the VIIth, in its debilities, declares the party to be almost melancholy to be married. (♆), ♄, ♅ or ♂, lord of the VIIth in the Ist indicates uneasiness about their lover. The ☽ for the man, or the ☉ for the woman, or the ruler of the Ist for either in its fall, the querent despairs of the matter and is careless about it.

The Woman Will Not Marry—At birth, if the ☉ has left or apply to bad aspect of ♅ or ♄, or the ☉ to one and the ☽ to the other malefic, while these two planets are in ill aspect to each other, or the ☽ afflicted by them at the same time the ☉ may be. This will apply in Horary figures, the age of the querent at the time being duly considered.

The ☉, ♂ and ruler of the Ist in ♊, ♌ or ♍, especially in □ or ☍ to each other, or the ruler of the VIIth; ♂ afflicted or weak, late before marriage. The ☉, ♂ and the lord of the Ist, or any two of them in their fall, she either cares nothing abou it or despairs of being married.

She Will Marry this Lover—Lord of the Ist in ☌ of the ☉, or either of them in ☌ of the lord of the VIIth, in the Ist, Xth or XIth; also lord of the Ist in the VIIth fortunate. Lord of the Ist and the ☉ in ⚹ or △ formed from the Ist and XIth, VIIth and IXth, or out of the VIIth and Vth; or lord of Ist and VIIth in ☌ or any good aspect.

The Expected Marriage Falls Away—The rulers of the Ist and VIIth refraining from aspect, or the ☉ and ruler of the VIIth separating from good aspect. If the rulers of the Ist and VIIth, or the ☉ and ♂ in □ or ☍; the ☽ applying to a planet in its fall; the ☽ separating from ill aspect of (♆), ♅, ♄ or ♂ declares some evil has happened. If (♆), ♅ or ♄ receive the light of the ruler of the Ist and VIIth, and should have a □ or ☍ at the same time of a malefic. An ill aspect between the luminaries. All these denote a breaking off.

Prevention of Marriage and Its Cause—If the significators of marriage are applying to friendly aspect, and an evil planet interpose, the marriage will be obstructed; observe of what house he is ruler; and where posited. If the IId lord, it will be want of money, or other want of means. The lord of the IIId denotes that it will be caused by the querent's kindred or neighbours, or by means of some short journey.

The lord of the IVth shows that her father will not agree, or it may, especially if a feminine planet, be the mother of the quesited, or by means of some settlement of house or land, etc.

The lord of the Vth causes obstacles by means of children, or by the querent being a character for loose living, etc.

The VIth denotes sickness in the querent, or opposition by some relative of his father, or by means of servants, or private enemy of the quesited, or the querent has a bastard, or child by another husband.

The lord of the VIIth, or a planet therein, denotes a public enemy of the querent, a lawsuit, or a rival.

The VIIIth denotes a lack of money on the part of the quesited; or, if other testimonies concur, it may be that the querent's death may intervene to prevent the match.

The IXth in like manner shows opposition by the relations of the quesited, or the interference of some lawyer, priest, or that the querent may go on a long journey or voyage, and so the match be hindered.

The Xth and its lord show the father of the quesited, or the mother of the querent, or some person having authority over the querent.

Or, if it be the XIth house or its lord, then the friends of both the parties dislike the match; or those who first introduced the parties or endeavoured to bring it about, will now try to dissolve the connection.

If it be by the lord of the XIIth, or by a planet therein, there is some underhand dealing or secret enmity to the querent. The affair shall be much retarded, but the querent shall never know by whom; or some private scandal will do harm, and break off the matter.

Husband Described—

1. Observe in the Nativity the planet to which the ☉ first applies, and that planet describes the future husband; also observe in what sign that planet is, and co-mix them, as is given in the description of persons, from paragraphs 15 to 140.

2. If the birth cannot be had, describe the man by that planet to which the ruler of the ascendant applies by good aspect, especially if it be in the VIIth, or more particularly if it be the ruler of the VIIth.

3. If these do not answer your purpose, then notice the planet to which the ☉ first applies by good aspect in the Horary figure.

4. Let her avoid the description of the man to which the ☉ approaches by ill aspect. For bad aspects always show disagreement and unhappy marriage.

Of the Time of Marriage—The degrees of distance between the rulers of the Ist and VIIth by ☌, ✶ or △, or the lord of the VIIth from the cusp of the Ist by ☌. Lord of the VIIth or ☽ to ♀ or ☉, or the ☉ to good aspect of ♂. A □ or ☍ of the lords of the Ist and VIIth, if in mutual reception. The time must be judged according to the degrees of distance of the significators according to the Measure of Time in paragraphs 231 and 232.

Has He Another Lover?—He has another if the ruler of the VIIth be in ☌ of any planet, except the Ist be also in the VIIth. Or several planets in the VIIth, and not any of them the ruler of the VIIth (cusp). The ☽ besieged between two planets, and neither of them the ruler of the Ist or VIIth.

But if none of these occur, then say he is not addressing any other female that he cares at all for.

Of the Circumstances of the Husband or Wife—

Able to Provide a Good Living—If the lord of the VIIIth be in good condition and free from affliction the querent will be a person able to obtain a good livelihood; and it is a good sign if ♃, ♀ or the ☊ be in the VIIIth. Lord of the VIIIth and IId in each other's houses and in good aspect. A fortune, ruler of the VIIIth and disposing of the ⊕ in the VIIIth.

No Great Gains by Marriage—If (♆), ♅, ♄, ♂ and ☋, or any two of them be in the VIIIth. Lord of the VIIth afflicting the ☽ or the ⊕. Lord of the VIIIth or IId in his debilities.

Persons and Means Hindering Property—See what planet afflicts the lord of the VIIIth, and of what house he is ruler, and that will describe the person; the house in which they are located will indicate by what means, which may be discovered in the "Prevention of Marriage and Its Cause," page 115.

☿, ruler of the VIIIth, in the IXth, in □ or ☍ of the ⊕ indicates by means of lawsuits respecting the future partner's property. If ♄ be lord of the VIIIth, in the IXth, afflicting the ⊕, it may be a farmer or kinsman that hinders. Mark the signification of each house over which the afflictor rules.

How the Parties Will Agree in Marriage—

Good Agreement—Lord of the Ist or ☽ in ☌, ✶ or △, if lord of the VIIth or ♀. The ☽ in ☌ of ♃ or ♀, they are industrious. ♃ or ♀ well posited in the VIIth; or even the lord of the VIIth in □ of the Ist, but they must be in mutual reception. The ☽ in good aspect to her disposer by house or exaltation.

Contention and Its Cause—Lord of the Ist and VIIth in □ or ☍, or ☽ afflicted, beholding the Ist by ill aspect; (♆), ♅, ♄, ♂ or ☋, in the VIIth; or these malefics in the Ist, the querent is to blame, or is loose, according to the sign ascending. Pity the man who marries a woman who has ♄ in her Ist; she is sure to turn out a harlot, and she is likely to elope. I would recommend every man to avoid marrying a woman who has ♄ rising. The ☽ in her fall, or in □ or ☍ of the malefics, or any R. planet the man is blameable. The ☉ in his fall, or in □ or ☍ of the malefics, the woman is blameable.

Lord of the VIIth angular, and more weighty than the ruler of the Ist, the quesited strives for mastery. ♀ afflicted by (♆), ♅, ♄, ♂, ☋; or R., or in fall, worse for the man. The ☽ afflicted, they both suffer. ♅, ♄, ♂ or ☋, afflicted in the Xth or IVth, continual brawls, or separation by means of parents.

Any planet afflicting the ruler of the Ist or VIIth, in the IIId, injuries by means of neighbours or relations. In the IVth or Xth, by parents; if in the Vth, by looseness of offspring; if in the VIth, by servants, or persons visiting or lodging; if in the VIIth, by open enemies; if in the IId or VIIIth, by money difficulties; if in the IXth, the quesited's relations; ♀ and ♄ in ☌, beholding ♂, jealousy. The ☽, void of course, and in conjunction of the ruler of the VIIIth, or in the XIIth with ♅, ♄, ♂ or ☋, one of them will soon die, or have some misfortune.

Will Wife or Husband Be a Stranger?—

A Near Resident—Ruler of the VIIth in the VIIth, or on the Ist, or both these significators in one house. If the sign of the VIIth and ruler of the VIIth disagree in the quarter, mix them, preferring the sign.

A Stranger—Lord of the VIIth in the IIId, IXth or peregrine. If the ruler of the VIIth and IXth be one and the same planet.

Which of the Two Is Best Connected?—Judge whether the lord of the Ist and the querent's significator, or the lord of the VIIth, the quesited's, is best affected, and so judge.

The Querent Is Best Connected—If the Lord of the Ist be in the Xth, Ist, VIIth, or IVth, and the lord of the VIIth in the IId, Vth, XIth or VIIIth. But a more sure way is by observing which of the two significators is the most powerful in dignities.

The Quesited Is the Best—Lord of the VIIth in the Ist, Xth, VIIth or IVth, and the lord of the Ist in the IId, Vth, VIIIth or IXth.

Will the Querent Marry More than Once?—If the querent's significators be in double bodied signs, they will marry more than once; and the same if they are joined with, or apply to, many planets, particularly from the Vth, VIIth or IXth houses. Many planets in the VIIth, or in good aspect with the ruler of the Ist or the luminaries, are all signs of repeated marriage.

If the significators are in fixed signs, or in aspect to only one planet, the querent will marry but once. In this case, prefer the ☽ for the man and the ☉ for the woman, to the ruler of the Ist. If the luminaries have no application, or but one, the querent will never marry, or but once, let the lord of the Ist be situated how he may.

Whether Man or Wife Dies First—The ruler of the Ist and the ☽ signify the querent, and the lord of the VIIIth portends his death, etc.

Ruler of the VII denotes the quesited, and the lord of the IId portends his or her death.

See which significators; that is, the lord of the Ist and VIIIth, or VIIth and IId, are first in ☌ with ☉, that will die first; in ♈, ♋, ♎ or ♑, death shortly; in ♊, ♍, ♐ or ♓, longer before death; ♉, ♌, ♏ or ♒, many years before death.

Whose significators are angular, or strong in dignities, free from affliction or combustion, or free from the lord of the VIIIth, that party will live longest, more especially if in good aspect with ♃ or ♀, he or she will outlive the other by several years, except the parties are both very aged, then the survivor's health will be good.

The Querent Dies First—If the ruler of the Ist or VIIIth first hastens to the ☌ of ○; or if R., or in his fall; or if the ruler of the Ist be in the Ist, or ♃ in ☌, □ or ☍ to either lord; or if the ruler of the VIth or XIIth be ♅, ♄ or ♂, et contra.

The Quesited Dies First—If the ruler of the IId or VIIth is in the above situation; but if the ruler of the Ist or VIIIth be in the above condition, then the querent dies first.

Has the Lady another Lover?—

She Has Another—If her significator is in ☌, ✶ or △ of any planet than that which signifies the querent; or if several planets be in the VIIth; or the ☉ in aspect to many planets, or he be joined to ♂. If the ☉ or the lord of the VIIth be in ☌ of ♂ or ♃, and ☊ be there. The ☋ in the VIIth denotes at least discreditable desires.

The lord of the VIIth with ♄, she loves an elderly person; if with ♅, a mechanic, engineer or author; if with ♃, a pretended religionist, or a professional man; if with ☿, a clerk, writer or bookseller.

She Has Not Another—The ruler of the VIIth void of course, or with ☊, or if no planet be in the VIIth. The lord of the VIIth aspecting only the ruler of the Ist. ♂ in the VIIth, unless he be in his own house. The description of the person may be described by the planet signifying the party, considering at the same time the sign in which that planet is located.

Has the Gentleman Another Lover?—(see page 116)

He Has Another—When any planet is in the VIIth and not the ruler thereof. Lord of the VIIth or the ☽ with ♀, and she is very giddy; if in ✱ or △, the lady is fond of him; but if the ☽ or lord of the VIIth does not dispose of ♀, she cares not for him. Either the ruler of the VIIth or the ☽ in ☌ of the triplicity ascending, and the separating from the lord of the Ist.

Lord of the VIIth or ☽ separating from 1 to 3 degrees from any planet except the ruler of the Ist. Lord of the VIIth or ☽ in ☌ of ☊ or ☋, or any other planet be with them. Lord of the VIIth and ♀ in ☌ in ♏, especially in the VIIth. If the ☽ or lord of the VIIth be in ☌ of ♂, ♃ or ☿, he has one described by that planet, and her age may be known by the number of degrees he is advanced in the sign. If with ☿, a teacher or youth, if with ♄ he loves an elderly person; if they separate, he is leaving her; if with the ☉, a person of consequence; if ♅, changeable, also with ♀ or ☉.

Will the Absconded Husband or Wife Return?—

A Return—Ruler of the VIIth or IXth R., either in the Ist or applying to the ruler of the Ist. Lord of the Ist in the VIIth unafflicted. A translation of light between the lords of the Ist and VIIth. The ☽ quick or in good aspect to the ruler of the Ist, especially if from the Ist. The ☽ separating from ♃, ♀ or ☊, and applying to aspect of ♅, ♄, ♂ or ☋. Lord of the VIIth combust. Ruler of the Ist beholding the infortune, which afflicts the fugitive, will be found against his or her will.

Lord of the VIIth with a stationary planet in an angle or succeedent, he or she knows not which way to go. The ☽ separating from the lord of the Ist, and going to ☌ of the lord of the VIIth, the fugitive will be heard of. The ☽ aspecting her own house with a ✱ or △, he or she returns, or will be heard of in two or three days. The lord of the VIIth or ☿ combust in the XIIth, danger of imprisonment. The lord of the VIIth applying to the ☉ or to the lord of the Ist.

A Woman Leaving Her Husband—The ☉ under the earth; ♀ between the IVth and Ist and R.; also lord of the Ist, the ☽, and the lord of the VIIth in △, she returns.

Lord of the Ist, ☽, and lord of the VIIth in □ or ☍ without reception, she does not return.

♀ in an angle, disposing of the ☽ at the same time, the ruler of the Ist also in ♈, ♋, ♎ or ♑, content to separate.

What Distance Is the Fugitive?—See where the ruler of the VIIth is and judge according to paragraph 235.

To know which way they are gone, take notice where the ruler of the VIIth is; in what house and sign, according to paragraph 234.

To know the time of returning, see when the rulers of the Ist and VIIth are in good aspect with each other, as directed in 232.

327. On Letting Property—The Ascendant, its rulers, and the ☽ are taken for the querent.

The VIth house, its lord and planets therein are for the tenant.

The house, premises or property will let if the ruler of the Ist and VIth are in good aspect of each other.

The ☽ in good aspect of the lord of the VIth, or a planet therein, is a promising testimony of letting.

If the property should let under a bad aspect, the tenant will not pay his rent well, and the owner will have trouble from him.

The time of letting will be when the rulers of the Ist and VIth are in good aspect with each other, which time will be pointed out by the regular way of measuring events. Read well the directions given in paragraphs 231 and 232, page 65. See also when the ruler of the Ist and VIth are in good aspect with each other, by ephemeral motion, and about that time the property will let.

328. On Making Purchases or Sales—If the ☽ be joined with the ruler of the VIIth, the querent may make the purchase, unless she be in ♍. The lighter planet of the Ist or VIIth will be the occasion of the sale. ♅, ♄, ♂ or ☋ in the Ist, there will be great labour in the bargain.

If the infortunes possess the VIIth, beware of the seller; he will try to trap the buyer. The IVth house shows the result; if the ☽ be void of course, there will be many meetings, but never any agreeable bargain concluded.

329. When to Sell Large Cattle—The ruler of the ascendant denotes the seller. The XIIth and its ruler portend the horse, cow, etc. The VIIth and its ruler signify the buyer.

Sell when the ruler of the VIIth and XIIth, or the VIIth and ascendant are in good aspect with each other, and these may always be known by the Astronomical Ephemeris published yearly.

A good price may be obtained when the rulers of the XIIth and IId or Ist and VIIth are in mutual reception and good aspect with each other, and especially if they be in their accidental fortitudes. The cattle is defective if the ☋ be in the XIIth; and if it be in the VIIth, the purchaser will deceive the seller; if in the Ist, the contrary.

330. Of Theft Questions Generally—The ascendant and its ruler are for the querent. The ascendant also denotes the kind of place whence the money or good were taken.

The VIIth, its lord, or a peregrine planet therein, or in any angle, or in the IId house, may also signify the thief. (American experience indicates planets in the VIIth and the ruler of the VIIth indicate the thief or thieves.)

The IId house, its ruler and the ☽, denote the things stolen. (American experience indicates this is true when specific house rulership cannot be shown for the articles stolen, or if the astrologer does not know what has been stolen.)

The IVth and its lord show the place whither the articles are taken and then are. (While this is true, the house in which the ruler of the VIIth is posited frequently indicates the direction in which the thief has gone.)

Query 1. Who Is the Thief?

One of the Family—Lord of the VIIth in the VIIth, or the significator of the thief in the Ist or the VIIth. ☉ or ☽ in the Ist, or in their own house, or in △ or ✶, if they be in mutual reception in the Ist or VIIth. The lord of the Ist and thief's significator in one house, or joined together; if in the IId or IVth, one of the household; if in the Vth, a son or daughter; if in the IVth or VIth, a servant or a lodger. Lord of the VIth in the IId, a servant or lodger.

The Thief Is a Stranger—The significator of the thief in the IIId or IXth of the figure, or from its own house, or in the VIIIth or XIIth.

Query 2. Whether the Thief Be a Domestic is known thus:
☉ signifies father, master, son's wife; if setting, a neighbour (167).
☽ signifies mother, mistress, daughter's husband (170).
(♅ signifies persons who may not be discovered; secret enemies, etc. – 162.)
♅ signifies friends who may be on a visit, or go occasionally (163).
♄ signifies servant, grandfather, lodger, stranger (164).
♃ signifies professors of religion or professional men (165).
♂ a relation, brother, cousin, or neighbour (166).
♀ a woman, wife, housekeeper, or waiter (168).
☿ a young person connected with the family (169). ♂ and ☿ combined, they are common thieves and are villainously disposed.

Query 3. Is the Suspected Party the Thief?
Your Suspicion is Correct—If the ☽ or ruler of the Ist behold the ruler of the VIIth by any bad aspect, or she be in ♂ with the significator of the thief. The ☽ in conjunction with any planet in an angle. The ruler of the Ist in an angle beholding a planet in a cadent house by ill aspect; or lately separated from an infortune. But if the ruler of the VIIth be a peregrine planet in an angle, and in no aspect to either the ☉ or the ☽, or to the ruler of the Ist, then judge the contrary.

Query 4. What Marks, Scars, or other Tokens Has the Thief?—Consider the face of the VIIth and the position of the ruler of the VIIth, and the place of the ☽, and then judge the thief has a mark, mole or scar upon that part of the body ruled by those signs (275 and 277).

If the significator of the thief apply to ill aspect of (♆), ♅, ♄ or ♂, out of angles, some punishment will soon befall the thief; as if the ill fortune be ruler of the VIth, danger of imprisonment; if of the IIId, danger of death; if of the IVth, he will soon be brought to justice; if of the Xth, an unfortunate end.

Query 5. General Signification of the Thief—The lord of the VIIth in the Ist, it is one of the family, or there is cause to suspect the owner himself; if it is in the IId, it is his wife, sweetheart, or maid-servant. In the IIId, a brother, sister, cousin, companion, messenger or favourite servant. In the IVth, his father, or some old man, or a father's relation, lodger or inmate, or an agricultural servant of the querent, or labourer in agriculture, mines or buildings. In the Vth, a child of his or of his cousin, or nephew, his kept mistress or a companion, or one frequenting a tavern. In the VIth, a servant, lodger or some servant or labourer, or some sickly or melancholy person. In the VIIth, an enemy who owes him a spite, or a vile prostitute. In the VIIIth, some person in the habit of coming to the house occasionally to labour, kill cattle, nurse, char, or one to whom the querent has been a friend. In the IXth, some vagrant, or one pretending to religion, some needy author, sailor, or man of learning reduced to distress. In the Xth, some great person of consequence, who is now necessitated to turn thief. In the XIth, some friend or person in trust, or one that has done the querent a service. In the XIIth, some rascally vagabond, beggar, or miserable wretch, some envious person, or one who lives by theft.

Query 6. Of the Bodily Description of the Thief—Whenever you have described the significator of the thief, notice in what sign he or she is posited, and then describe as the planet is in that sign according to the descriptions given on pages 13 to 52, paragraphs 15 to 143. The disposition of the party, according as the planet is well or ill dignified, pages 52 to 54, paragraphs 144 to 160.

Query 7. Of the Thief's Business—This is known by the planet who is either ruler of the IVth or is found in the IVth, and so judge according to the dignity or otherwise, as the planet may happen to be. This is known by referring to paragraphs under the head "Employments," pages 54 to 56, paragraphs 161 to 170.

Query 8. Of the Age and Sex of the Thief—The usual method of judging the sex is to consider the gender of the significator of the thief. Thus ♅, ♄ (sic!), ♂, ♃ and the ☉, denote the thief to be male. If ♅ or ♄ be significator, it is a man, and very old, except he be at the beginning of a sign, which shows him to be about 40. If ♃, ♂ or the ☉, it is a man about the age of 30. And if ♀ or ☿, the thief is very young. ♀ and the ☽ show a female; and ☿ as he is most in familiarity with male or female planets. If the ☽ be in her Ist quarter and significatrix, the thief is young; if in her 2d quarter, between 20 and 30; if after the full, between 30 and 45; and if past her last quarter, between 45 and 60.

Query 9. Is there One Thief or More than One?—If the angles of the figure are in fixed signs, or the significator of the thief in a fixed sign, in no aspect with any planet in the IId, only one is concerned.

More than One Thief—Many planets afflicting the ruler of the IId, the ⊕, or its dispositor. The significator in double bodied signs, or in ✱ or △ with other planets; also the ☉ and the ☽ in angles in □ aspect; if the significators be in ♋, ♏ or ♓; or the angles being moveable; the ☽ in a double bodied sign and in the Ist.

Query 10. Which Way and What Distance Is the Thief?—The significator of the thief in the different houses will show the direction from the querent's home where the thief then is; as 234. Mix the house and the sign and then judge, as 233.

The distance is known by the position of the ruler of the VIIth being angular, or otherwise according to the directions in 235. But to be a little more particular, if the thief be in the end of a sign, or separating from combustion, or applying to a planet in the IXth or IIId, he is making off with the property; also if the ☽ and ruler of the Ist be in different quadrants. If the thief be in a fixed sign, take three miles for every house he is distant from the lord of the Ist. If in a common sign, one mile; if in a moveable sign, he is so many doors distant. If the ☽ be angular, he is at home; if succeedent, about home; cadent, a good way off. The lord of the VIIth in the Ist, the thief lives near the querent. The lord of the VIIth in the VIIth, he is hid at home.

Query 11. Description of the Thief's Door—The thief's door is said to be described by the position of the ☽ ; as if she be in a fixed sign, there is but one door; in a moveable sign, the door has a step or two to go up; if ♅ aspect the ☽ , it is an oldish door with glass over the top; if ♄ aspect the ☽ , it is a mended or very old door; if the ☽ aspect ♂, it is old and iron is seen outside of it; if both ♄ and ♂ aspect the ☽ , the door is iron or very strong; if the ☽ is but three or four days old, or three or four days from the change, it is a back door, or the house is in a yard; if the ☽ be afflicted, it is a broken door; in common signs, there is more than one door.

Query 12. The Stolen Goods Will Be Recovered—Notice the aspect the luminaries bear to each other, and the disposer of the ☽ , and the ☽'s application to each other will show recovery. The ☽ , ruler of the VIIth in △ to the lord of the VIIth or Ist. ♀ or lady of the IId in the Ist. ♃ direct, and in the IId. The ☽ in the Xth or IId, and in △ to a planet in the Xth or IId. The luminaries in △ and in △ to the cusp of the IId. Lord of the IId in the XIth, IVth or Ist. The ☽ in ☌ of ♃ or ♀ in the IId. Lord of the Ist or IId in ☌ of the ruler of the Ist with reception. The disposer of the ⊕ in the Ist or IId. Lord of the Ist in the VIIth with the ⊕ , found after much search. ♃, ♀ or ☊ in the XIth, gives hopes. The lord of the VIIth in combustion. The luminaries, both in the Xth, sudden recovery. The lord of the IId in his exaltation. Lord of the Ist and IId ☌ . Lord of the VIIth in the Ist, he brings them. The ☽ in the IXth in ☌ , □ or ☍ , of ♅ , ♄ or ♂ , and the aspected planet R., the thief brings them back. If the significator of the thief be afflicted in the VIth, he will be transported or imprisoned.

Query 13. The Stolen Goods Will Not Be Recovered—The ☋ , (♆), ♅ , ♄ or ♂ , out of their essential dignities in the IId (or the house actually ruling the stolen article). The lord of the IId in combustion or in the VIIIth. The lord of the IId in □ or ☍ with the lord of the VIIIth. The lord of the VIIth and VIIIth in ☌ ; or if the lord of the IId behold neither the Ist house nor its lord; or the ☉ and ☽ not aspecting each other, nor the ⊕ ; or if both the luminaries be under the earth. The significator of the thief stronger than the lord of the Ist or IId, or in evil aspect to the ☽ .

Query 14. Are the Goods Missing Stolen or Not?—

The Goods Are Not Stolen—If the Moon be in the IId, or she lady thereof, going to ☌ of ruler of VIIth, they are mislaid. The ☽ lady of the Ist in the IVth, and lord of the IId therein, or in the IId, and especially these and the ☽ in ✶ or △ to lord of the VIIth, taken in jest. The ☽ , lady of the Vth in conjunction with ruler of VIIth, mislaid through thoughtlessness. The ruler of the

VIIth in the Ist, or disposing of the ☽ , or lord of the Ist, or the ☽ disposing of the ruler of the VIIth. ♅ or ♂ in ♋ , in cadent houses. If neither the disposer of the ☽ nor ruler of IId have not lately separated from the VIth, then the articles are misplaced.

The Goods Are Stolen–If the ☽ or lord of the Ist or IId, or the ⊕ be in conjunction or evil aspect to the significator of the thief. Any ill aspect of an evil planet, or the lord of the VIIth to the Ist or the ☽ denotes the thing is stolen. ♅, ♄ or ♂ in the Ist or IId; or lord of the Ist peregrine. The significator of the thief in ill aspect to the disposer of the ☽. If neither the lord of the ascendant nor ruler of the IId, nor the disposer of the ⊕, nor the ☽ separate from other planets, but other planets separate from them.

Query 15. Will the Article Be Stolen?–The thing will be stolen if the Moon rule the VIIth, or any planet therein, and at the same time dispose of a planet in the IId, Vth or XIth, and herself or the planet in no good aspect to the cusp of those houses. The lord of the Xth in ☌ , □ or ☍ with the significator of the thief, then the thing will be stolen.

Query 16. The Thief Will Be Taken–Lord of the VIIth and VIIIth in the Ist or in ☌ in the Ist. The ☽ in the Ist or in △ to the ruler of the Ist. ☉ or ☽ in aspect of the lord of the VIIth. Lord of the Ist in the Ist. The ☽ in the VIth, VIIIth or XIIth. The ☽ in the VIIth, going to ☌ of the lord of the VIIIth. ☽ in the VIIIth in ☌ of ♂. Lords of the VIIth and VIIIth in ☌ of Ist. The ☽ or lord of the VIIth joined to ♅ , ♄ , ♂ or ☋, in an angle. Lord of VIIth in ☌ of ☉, he will soon die. The ☽ joined with a R. or stationary planet, he returns. The ☽ separating in aspect and aspecting the thief's significator. The ☽ in the VIIth, and applying to the □ of ♂ , ☉ or ☿ . The ☽ separating from the □ of ♅ , ♄ or ☿ , and applying to □ of ☉ , or the ☽ separating from the ☌ of ♅ or ♄ , and applying to a □ of ☿ . The ruler of the Ist and VIIth together in the Ist.

Query 17. The Thief Will Not Be Taken–The lord of the VIIth in good aspect with ♃ or ♀ in the XIth, by means of friends; in the IIId, by strangers; in the IXth, by his kindred; in the Ist, by other thieves; and by those who may have received the goods or one who has received stolen goods from the thief. If in the Xth, he hides himself; if in the XIIth, by means of the domestics; if in the IId, by means of his wife (sic!).

Query 18. In what Direction Does the Thief Live?–Observe in what sign and house the significator of the thief is, and then judge according to 233 and 234. In a fiery sign, bear eastward; in a watery, bear towards the lowlands, northwards; in an airy sign, go upwards, or to hilly grounds, westward; and in earthy signs, go among quarries, woods, farm houses, dunghills, or clay localities, southward.

Querry 19. Whether the Thief Holds the Goods–If the significator of the thief is in good aspect of any benevolent, and at the same time disposed of another planet, which is a fortune, they are then in the hands of the thief. But if otherwise situated or affected, then they are sold or divided, or otherwise disposed of.

Query 20. Of the Time the Thing Will Be Recovered—Observe the two planets signifying recovery and notice the degrees distant between their body or aspect, and turn the distance into time, according to the directions given in paragraphs 231 and 232.

When both luminaries behold the first, a speedy recovery. The significators increasing in light and motion and located in fortunate parts of the figure, presage a sudden recovery.

Query 21. Of the Dress of the Thief—Observe what sign and house the significator of the thief is in, and the colour that significator denotes, and so judge and comix according to the paragraphs 227 to 230.

331. Partnerships—N.B. Most of these questions will be similar to those on marriage.

Query 1. May I Enter into Partnership or Society?—The ruler of the Ist and the ☽ denote the querent, and the IId and its ruler, his money matters.

The ruler of the VIIIth signifies the quesited, and the VIIIth shows his pecuniary affairs.

The Xth house portends the honour, credit, benefit, and so on, by the partnership.

The IVth house and its ruler denote the extent of Partnership, whether to good or ill.

Query 2. Partnership Will Do Well—The lords of the Ist and VIIth in good aspect, mutual reception, or the lords of the Ist or VIIth not applying to each other, but in mutual reception.

Query 3. How Shall We Agree?—If the rulers are in ♉, ♌, ♍ or ♒, more especially if there is mutual reception, you will agree, and the partnership or society endure long. If in ♈, ♋, ♎ or ♑, without reception, you will have many contentions and disagreements; at other times agree well; yet you will mistrust each other, and no great gains will accrue from the firm. The significators in ♊, ♍, ♐ or ♓ are a symbol of good.

Query 4. What Will Be the Cause of Disagreement?—See what house the afflicting planet is ruler of; as if it be the lord of the VIth, evil servants defraud or make strife between you; if rulers of the IId or VIIIth, money matters are bad; and so judge according to the signification of the house over which the afflictor rules. An evil planet in the Xth, or ruler thereof afflicted, want of trade, a tardiness in disposing of the commodities.

Query 5. Shall We Succeed Well in Business?—The ruler of the Xth strong and he a fortunate planet, unafflicted, good success. The ☽ applying to good aspect of the fortunes or to the ruler of the Xth, and he not vitiated. Good planets in the Xth portend prosperity.

Not Very Good Success—If the ☋ is in the Xth; if ill planets behold the lord of the VIIth and Ist; if the ruler of the Xth is unfortunately situated or aspected.

Query 6. Which Will Be the Best Affected?—If the ruler of the Ist be more ponderable than the lord of the VIIth, and better dignified, it denotes the querent will be the most benefitted by the partnership; but if the ruler of the VIIth is most ponderous, the quesited gains most.

♂ or ☿ being lord of the IId, or ☋ therein, and afflict the ruler of the VIIIth, the querent will defraud; but if ♂ or ☿ is ruler of the VIIIth, or ☋ therein, and afflict the IId's lord, the quesited will cheat. That significator which afflicts the ⊕ will waste the common stock. An evil planet in the Ist, the querent is false; but being in the VIIth, the quesited is not to be trusted, and he is in poor circumstances.

He whose significators are the strongest will prosper and be the most fortunate; and he whose significators are the weakest will be injured, if such significators are posited in evil places in the figure.

If the ☽ separate from a good planet and apply to an evil one, although a good beginning, it will nevertheless end in debate and strife; if the ☽ separate from one evil planet and apply to another, it signifies a bad beginning and a worse ending.

A good planet in the IVth, or the ruler of the IVth in good aspect to the ruler of the Ist, IId, VIIth, VIIIth or the ⊕ denotes a good end. See in the IVth house for the rest of this judgment (218).

Retrograde or peregrine planets are evil. If the ruler of the VIIth or VIIIth is R., the quesited's affairs are desperate and he wishes to retrieve them; if in the VIth, peregrine, have nothing to do with him, except there is application between him and ♃. In the same condition is the querent if his Ist or IId is so situated.

332. Lawsuits

> Brother goeth to law against brother; there is utterly a fault among you, because ye go to law one with another. Why do ye not rather take wrong? Why do ye not rather suffer yourselves to be defrauded? Nay, ye do wrong, and defraud, and that your brother.
>
> –I Cor. 6:5-8

Observe:

1. Lord of Ist, Sun and Moon signify the querent.
2. The VIIth house and its lord signify the adversary.
3. The lord of the Xth denotes the lawyer, etc.

The lord of the IVth, and ☽'s application show the result.

Query 1. Shall I Have a Lawsuit?

No, You May Prevent it and Be Reconciled:

1. If the lord of the Ist or the ☽ be unafflicted, and in good aspect with the lord of the VIIth; with mutual reception, you will agree.
2. If lord of the VIIth dispose of lord of Ist; or lord of Ist dispose of lord of VIIth, you will agree by means of some person's interposition.
3. If the lord of Ist and VIIth aspect one planet.
4. If ♈, ♋, ♎ or ♑ be on the VIIth, you may be reconciled by your own prudence.

5. If the ☽ or any planet leave an aspect of lord of the Ist or VIIth and apply to either lord of VIIth or Ist, you will be reconciled by a third person described by the applying planet and the sign it is in.
6. If lord of Ist be the applying planet, the querent will seek to be reconciled.
7. If lord of IId be applying planet, by means of money, friends or assistants, as the IId house portends.
8. If lord of IIId apply, by means of brothers, neighbours; as IIId house signifies.
9. If lord of IVth, by means of fathers; as IVth signifies.
10. If lord of Vth, by amusements, gaming; as Vth house signifies.
11. If lord of VIth, by uncles, aunts, etc.; as VIth house.
12. If lord of VIIth, by means of the querent's wife; as the VIIth house.
13. If lord of VIIIth, by adversary's friends; as VIIIth house.
14. If lord of IXth, by wife's kindred; as IXth house signifies.
15. If lord of Xth, by mothers, masters; as Xth house.
16. If lord of XIth, by friends; as XIth house signifies.
17. If lord of XIIth, by money of friends; as XIIth house.

If none of the foregoing rules are found, then say the querent will have law; also, if the VIIth house have two or three evil planets therein. If the cusp of the Ist or VIIth be possessed by ♄, ♅, ♆ or ♂.

Query 2. Who Will Be Most Ready to Agree?
1. If the lord of VIIth apply to lord of Ist, ☉ or ☽; or lord of VIIth R., the adversary.
2. If lord of Ist apply to lord of VIIth; or lord of Ist R., the querent wishes to agree.
3. That party will be most ready to agree whose significator is disposed of by the other.
4. If they compound, the first attempt thereto will be made by the significated, by the lighter planet.
5. If the lord of Ist and VIIth hasten to mutual aspect, and the lord of the IId interpose an ill aspect, they will dispute by means of money matters; as IId house.
6. If lord of IIId interpose, disputes by neighbours; as IIId house.
7. If lord of IVth, as it signifies, and so of the rest of the houses.
8. If lord of IXth, Xth or ☿, they dispute by means of the lawyer, judge, or the person who is to decide.

Query 3. Who Conquers in Lawsuits?—Observe whether the lord of the Ist or VIIth be best aspected, most powerful, and that one shall gain the day. The adversary gains if any of the following are found:
1. Lord of Ist afflicted by aspect or position, as R., fall, etc.
2. Lord of the Ist in the VIIth; or lord of VIIth in the VIIth or aspects the ☉ or ☽, in favour of the adversary.
3. If both the lords of Ist and VIIth be afflicted, neither party will

conquer, but both will be detrimented.

4. Both lords of Ist and VIIth in equal dignities and in angles, neither party will submit, and probably both are ruined.
5. Lord of IVth afflicting the lord of Ist or IId; or lord of Ist or IId afflicting lord of IVth, the adversary conquers.
6. If the ☽ apply to good aspect of lord of VIIth or VIIIth, and to ill aspect of lord of Ist or IId, the adversary overcomes, through craft or quibbling.

Query 4. The Querent Overcomes if:

1. Lord of VIIth be afflicted by aspect or position.
2. Lord of Ist better fortified than lord of VIIth.
3. Lord of the VIIth in the Ist.
4. If ☽ or ☉ be in the Ist, or aspect lord of Ist, or the ☉ or ☽ be received by lord of Ist, good for the querent.
5. ☽ apply to good aspect of lord of Ist and to ill aspect of lord of VIIth, the querent conquers.
6. Lord of IVth in ill aspect of lord of VIIth or VIIIth, the adversary loses money.

Query 5. Will the Judge, Lawyers, etc. Proceed Fairly?—If the lord of Xth be ♅ or ♄, he will not decide aught.

1. Lord of the Xth R., he will not act fairly, nor strive to terminate the cause. If ♅ or ♄ be lord of Xth, and ♀, ☉, ☿ or ☽ be in any respect but an opposition, there will be an ill report against the judge, etc.; but if it be opposition, the case will be protracted by the judge. If ♂ opposition ♅ or ♄, the judge will have a bad character; also if ☉ □ ♅ or ♄, he may be disgraced. If a planet be in Xth and have no dignities there, nor received by lord of Xth, the parties will not be satisfied. If ♊, ♍ or ♓ be on the Ist or VIIth, the cause will be moved out of that court. If lord of Xth have an ill aspect to either significator, the judge will be against that party.

2. Lord of Xth direct, or in his own house, except it be ♅ or ♄. Lord of Xth in his triplicity or joy. If the lord of Xth receive both significators, the judge will settle the matter before it comes to a full trial.

333. On Warlike Expeditions: Shall I Return Safe from War?—The Ist, its lord, and the ☽ are significators of the querent; the VIIth and its lord, of the enemy. If the figure be erected for a relation, the house of such relative may be taken, as before decided, for the ascendant, and the opposite house, which is the VIIth, for the enemy; or it may be erected at the will of the querent for a relation, as for any other person, by giving them the real ascendant. If ♂ be weak in the figure, the querent will be fearful and probalby be disgraced; and the same if ♅ or ♄ be in the ascendant or Xth. The ☋ in the Ist or Xth is said to have a similar effect. The lord of the Ist combust, retrograde, peregrine, or cadent are all disastrous tokens.

♄ in conjunction with the lord of the ascendant shows fear and great misfortune. The □ or ☌ of infortunes denotes much evil; ♄ shows defeat, and

♂ wounds; and if he oppose either of the luminaries, there is danger of a violent death, and if it be by application and nearly partile, he will be killed on the spot. ♅ gives burstings up of magazines and guns. ♂ on the ascendant, particularly if ill dignified, shows he will be dangerously wounded, and if he be in □ or ☍ to the ☽, it is certain death. The lord of the VIIth stronger than the lord of the Ist and in ☍ to him or the ☽ shows defeat, and if he be an infortune, denotes great danger. The lord of the ascendant or the ☽ separating from the infortunes, denotes great danger. The lord of the ascendant or the ☽, separating from the infortunes and applying to the fortunes is an undoubted sign of victory and safety. ♂ well dignified in the Xth, or in △ to the lord of the ascendant or the ☽ denotes victory; and if he □ or ☍ the ☉ or ☽, there is great danger. The lord of the Ist joined to the ☊ denotes courage and strength; in all aspects between the lord of the VIIth and Ist, that which is the strongest will be most victorious. If the lord of the Ist and the ☽ be wholly free from affliction, the querent will return safely. Evil planets in the VIIIth are fears of death. An evil planet lord of the Ist, and a good one in the ascendant, then he is wounded, but not killed.

334. Of Besieged Places—When it is required to be known whether a place besieged will be compelled to surrender, the IVth house must be the significator of the place besieged, the lord of the IVth is the governor, and the Vth its means of defence in every respect.

If the lord of the Ist be stronger than the lord of the IVth, and joined with him in the Ist or Xth, or in reception with the ☽, or in own house and disposing of the lord of the IVth, and he be combust, retrograde, or in no aspect to the IVth except he be well dignified in the Vth, it will be taken.

The lord of the IVth in reception with the lord of the Ist, the governor is treacherous and will surrender it.

If the lord of the IVth be stronger than the lord of the Ist, free from the malefics, etc., supported by benefics, angular, in good aspect with ♂ or the ☉ well dignified, or if the lord of the ascendant be unfortunate, afflicted, combust, retrograde in the IVth house, cadent or peregrine, it will not be taken. ♄ in the Ist or Xth will defeat and disgrace the besiegers, and if in □ or ☍ to either of the luminaries, or to the lord of the Ist, the commander of the expedition, or the querent, if he be one of the besiegers, will be killed or desperately wounded.

Whether Two Armies Will Fight or Not—Observe the ascendant, its lord, the ☽ and the lord of the VIIth. If they be in conjunction in any angle, they will fight. If the lords of the Ist and VIIth be not in conjunction but are in □ or ☍ from angles, they will engage; or if there be any planet which transfers the light of one to the other by □ or ☍, there will be a fight if there be no reception between them. But if there be none of these and the heavier planet receive the lighter, there will be no serious engagement.

325. Of Public Enemies

Query 1. Has the Querent Public Enemies?—The ruler of the Ist or the ☽ afflicted by aspect of the lord of the VIIth. The lord of the Ist in □ or ☍ to many planets, many public foes; the same if many planets be in the VIIth

(268). And their relation, condition and quality are known by the house they rule. If the ill aspects are applying, the enmity will increase; but if separating, it will decrease.

Query 2. Will the Enemies Overcome?—The querent overcomes: this must be judged as in a lawsuit (332).

The enemy overcomes if the ruler of the VIIth be the best affected by position or aspect, according to Query No. 3 of 332.

Query 3. Description of Enemies—The number of adversaries is known by the number of planets afflicting the ruler of the Ist; their appearance by the planets situated in the signs at the time of the question. Investigate the persons described by the twelve signs.

The number of foes will be described by observing all the planets which afflict the ruler of the Ist and the ☽, as well as any planet which may happen to be in the ascendant.

Their power to do evil may be known by the malignancy of the planet or its aspect, exaltation, joy; or the contrary, by its debility, fall and so on.

336. Shall I Be Able to Pass the Insolvent Court?—Ruler of the Ist and the ☽ signify the querent. The VIIth, its lord and planets therein denote the opponents or creditors.

This is judged much the same as lawsuits. If the ruler of the Ist, or the ☽ be well situated or unafflicted, or the ☽ and lord of the Ist are in good aspect with the ruler of the Xth or IVth, or ♀, or with the ☉, then the querent passes.

But if the ruler of the VIIth be unafflicted or in good aspect with the ruler of the IVth, Xth, or with ♀ or ♃, or the ☉, the creditors or opponents overcome.

He whose significator is most afflicted will be the greatest loser.

If the ruler of the Ist be the strongest in every way, and should at the same time be R., shows the querent is put back for a third or fourth hearing, but will pass when that significator becomes direct or elevated or in good aspect with the ruler of the IVth or Xth house.

If ☿ be ruler of the IVth or IXth, then the lawyer has not made out the case sufficiently clear, or the balance sheet is defective.

337. What Kind of Death the Querent Will Die—Ruler of the VIIIth unafflicted in the VIIIth, a natural death. If ♃ or ♀ be unafflicted in the VIIIth or aspect the cusp by ✶ or △, a natural death. ♅ in the VIIIth or afflicting the ruler of the VIIIth, portends death by drowning (this should be indicated by ♆, not ♅) or machinery. ♄ denotes death by agues, dropsies, consumption; ♂ by fevers, epidemics, falls, wounds, etc.; the ☉ by pleurisy or some obstruction in the viscera; ☿ by phthisis, lethargy or phrenzy; and the ☽ by watery diseases, colic, drowning; the ☋ with the significator of death is evil. The lords of the Ist and VIIIth the same planet, denotes the querent brings on his own death by imprudence.

The time of death is only known by directing the *hyleg* to the *anareta*; and this can only be done where the time of birth is known.

338. Whether the Querent Will Suffer from what He Fears

He Will Suffer—If the ruler of the Ist or ☽ be unfortunate and falling from an angle, especially if in the XIIth, or the ☽ be afflicted by the ruler of the XIIth; and he will be accused of much of which he is not guilty. The ruler of the Ist applying to an infortune, the thing threatened is true; but if applying to a fortune, it is false or ungrounded.

Of No Important Consequence—if the ruler of the Ist ascends in the XIth or Xth, or be joined to a fortune. The ☽ cadent and applying to a cadent planet, the supposed danger will be nothing. The ☽ in △ to the ☉ discovers all suddenly.

339. On the Recovery of Debts—The Ist, its lord, and the ☽ signify the querent. The VIIth and its lord denote the debtor. The VIIIth, which is the debtor's IId, and its lord, his means of paying it (308).

The Debt Will Be Paid—If the ruler of the Ist be a fortune, or the ☽ be in ☌ or good aspect of the lord of the VIIIth, or with a planet in the VIIIth. If the lord of the VIIIth be a fortune and in the Ist or IId, applying to good aspect of the Ist or the ☽. A fortune having dignities by house or exaltation in the Ist, and also joined to the ruler of the Ist or the ☽. The ruler of the Ist or the ☽ joined to ♃ or ♀ in the Ist, Xth or VIIth.

The Debt Will Not Be Obtained—♅, ♄ or ♂ ruling the VIIIth, VIth or IId, and afflicting the ☽, or lord of the Ist. Lord of the VIIIth a malefic and in no reception of the lord of the Ist or IId, the money will be lost. Lord of the VIIth in the VIIIth without mutual reception. The ⊕ afflicted in the Ist, IId, VIIth or VIIIth, he is not able to pay the debt. A malefic in the VIIIth without mutual reception.

Frustrating Rules—The lord of the VIIth or VIIIth R., combust or peregrine, with no good familiarity with the fortunes, shows the debtor to be a cheat or a dishonourable wretch, from whom little good can be expected, particularly if he be ♂ or ☿, ill dignified. If the ruler of the VIIth or VIIIth apply to the lord of the IId or to the ⊕ or its dispositor, his design is to defraud; and if the evil application be to the lord of the Ist or the ☽, he owes the creditor ill will, and is determined if possible not to pay (241).

It is said a malefic interposing an evil ray shows the cause or person from whom the impediment arises, by the house over which the planet rules (240).

Useful Observations—If you receive a bill of exchange or promissory note, the figure at that time will show whether it will be paid or not, according to the above rules of debts. If the ⊕ receive a good aspect of the lord of the Ist, it will be paid; but if the ⊕ receive an evil aspect of the lord of the Ist, it will not be paid (292).

The ⊕ always denotes money, whether in cash or bills; but property, whether in goods or lands, houses, etc., is always shown by the ruler of the IId, or a planet therein.

340. Will It Be Safe to Cash the Person the Bill?

Safe to Cash It—If the ruler of the Ist, IId or ⊕ be unafflicted, especially by the ruler of the VIIth, VIIIth, or the disposer of ⊕.

Not Well to Cash the Bill—If the ruler of the VIIth, VIIIth, Ist, IId, or ⊕ be afflicted, or badly situated by position in the figure or in the zodiac, or if the rulers of the Ist or IId should happen to be the lords of the VIIth or VIIIth at the same time (292).

341. Shall We Have Deaths in the Family Soon? — ♅ or ♃ passing through the VIIIth, you will that year. The ruler of the VIIIth, IIId, Xth, or IVth heavily afflicted, then death is approaching the family. But if none of these occur, then death is not likely to enter the family soon. The malefics coming from the IXth to the cusp of the VIIIth, then say death after many months.

342. Am I Likely to Stop at Home with Parents?

Removal from Home—All the angles or cadent houses possessed by the moveable signs. The ruler of the Ist setting or in a cadent house with moveable cusp. The ruler of the Ist leaving a sign in the VIIth, IIId or IXth. The ruler of the Ist afflicted by the lord of the IVth or Xth.

But No Removal—If the ruler of the Ist be in any of the fixed signs, unless he be leaving that sign and not cadent.

343. Of Legacies

Query 1. What Will Be the End of the Sick Person's Will? —The answer to this question would be most rationally given from the position of the heavens at the time the invalid performs the last act of execution; i.e., when he places his fingers on the seal. The rules are as follows:

The ☽ or lord of the Ist or VIIIth in a moveable sign denotes mutability, and that after a short time the will shall be re-made, but regard must be here had as to whether the testator will recover from his indisposition or not; for if you observe in the same figure the ☽, the ascendant, and its lord, to be afflicted, it denotes the speedy death of the party, and thus the will shall stand, especially if ♂ be not in the ascendant or aspect it, but is joined by body to the ☽, yet though it is kept, in a short time it shall be lost or stolen; if ♄ afflict the ascendant the will shall be altered (if Neptune afflict the ascendant, the querent will be deceived). If ♅ or ♄ be in ☌ of the ☽ or lord of the Ist and in no aspect to the ascendant, it signifies that the sick person shall yet live, and the will then made shall not be revoked, but continue in force after his death. ♃ and ♀ so posited intimates that the testator shall recover, and some time after he shall destroy the former will and make another.

Query 2. Will the Wife or Husband's Portion Be Obtained?

It Will Be Obtained—If the lord of the VIIIth be not impeded or afflicted by the unfortunate planets. ♃, ♀ or the ☊ on the cusp of the VIIIth or in the VIIIth. The ⊕ in the VIIIth, in the dignities of ♃ or ♀, and these casting a ✶ or △ to these planets in the VIIIth. A friendly aspect between the rulers of the IId and VIIIth, with reception. The lords of the VIIIth and IId in each other's houses and not afflicting one another.

It Will Not Be Obtained—If there be a □ or ☍ of the Ist or IId and ruler of the VIIIth. The lord of the VIIIth combust or R., ♄, ♅ or ♂ in the

VIIIth, and peregrine, very little may be obtained. And if the chief significators are afflicted, there is no portion of consequence to be expected.

Query 3. Will the Husband or Wife Be Well Off? — The quesited will be better than the querent. Observe the ruler of the VIIIth and planets therein. If the lord of the VIIIth be well aspected by the ☽, ♃, ♀, ☉ or ⊕, or they be unafflicted in the VIIIth. Lord of the VIIIth or ☊ in the VIIIth. Lord of the VIIIth and IId in each other's houses well aspected. Lord of the VIIIth disposing of the ⊕ in the VIIIth, in good aspect to ♀ or ♃. The ⊕ in the VIIIth, and in ♌ or ♒, or ☿ in ♐, or ♃ and ♀ in good aspect of the ⊕. The disposer of the ⊕ in good aspect of ♃ or ♀. The lord of the IVth or Xth in good aspect with the lord of the VIIIth, from angles.

Query 4. Persons and Means Hindering the Property — Sometimes it happens that persons have a claim to property, or expect it, knowing that there is wealth or estate, but are wronged out of it. In this case we are to observe planets afflicted, the rulers of the VIIIth and Ist, and the sign and house they are in will describe the person and show the cause of the querent not receiving his or her right.

♀ lord of the VIIIth in the IXth, in □ or ☍ of the ⊕ indicates a lawsuit respecting the wife's (or husband's) property.

If ♄, ♅ or ♂ be lord of the VIIIth, in the IXth, afflicting the ⊕, it may be a farmer or kinsman that hinders. And thus go through the heavens and signs, by whatever afflicts the VIIIth or ⊕; as in the "Prevention of Marriage."

It Can Never Be Obtained — If ♅, ♄, ♂ and ☋, or any two of them be in the VIIIth, or if the lord of the VIIIth or IId be in its debilities.

Query 5. Will the Querent Obtain the Expected Legacy? — In judging this question we cannot too greatly impress on the student's mind the absolute necessity of directing his attention to the proper house.

If the querent expects a legacy from his own mother, then the Xth house of the figure signifies her, and consequently the XIth, her substance, property, etc. If it be the querent's wife's mother, then the student must consider the IVth house of the figure, which, being the Xth from the VIIth (his wife's house), constitutes the ascendant of his wife's mother, and so forth.

If the ascendant, its lord, and the ☽, which are the querent's significators, be strong in their own houses, unafflicted by body or aspect of ♅, ♄, ♂ or ☋, and if the lord of the quesited be friendly with ☽, or lord of the ascendant, and aspect her or him by ✶ or △, or join with her or him in ☌, it shows that the legacy will be left as desired.

The lord of the VIIIth debilitated, and ill planets in the VIIIth, or ruler of the Ist afflicted in the VIIIth, all are testimonies of gain by legacy.

The lord of the VIIIth house, being in the ascendant, or in good aspect with the ☉, ♃ or lord of the ascendant, unafflicted, many good planets posited in the VIIIth, denotes gain by legacy.

Yet you must also observe whether the querent's second house, its lord, or the ⊕ be afflicted, and then, collecting the testimony, judge accordingly.

The VIIIth and IId houses, their lords, and the ⊕ being afflicted, and the querent and quesited's lords being enemies by nature, shows that the enquirer will not obtain the hoped for legacy, and the student will be able to say what will be the hindrance in this matter by consulting other aspects and parts of the figure, for which purpose the rules immediately preceding these will, we hope, be found of some use.

344. Shall I Be Able to Effect an Insurance?

You Will Not—If the ruler of the IXth and the Ist or the ☽ are in bad aspect; also, if the ruler of the VIIth is in bad aspect of the ruler of the Ist or VIIth house. If the rulers of the VIIth and IXth are ill fortunes, there is not much hope. The company or their managers or agents are indifferent about pushing the execution of the affair.

Expect to Succeed—If none of the foregoing testimonies are powerful and the rulers of the IXth, VIIth, Ist and IId houses are in good familiarity.

Money Can Be Advanced—When you find the benevolents ♃ or ♀, or ⊕ in the VIIth or IXth houses.

But Otherwise—The malefics in the IId, VIIth or IXth, and no reception between the rulers of the Ist and IXth, or between the lord of the IId, Ist and the disposer of the ⊕, by mutual reception.

This question may be answered generally by the same rules as borrowing money from a club, bank, etc. (302), only the IXth house more particularly portends insurance companies.

345. Of the Success of a Book, etc.—This question may be answered either by setting a figure to the time when the writing of the book was commenced, its publication, or when the author felt an ardent desire to know its fate.

The production is signified by the IId house, its lord, and planets therein posited.

If ☿ and the Part of Fortune be in the IXth, or ☿ is lord thereof, well dignified and unafflicted by evil planets or by the lord of the IVth, VIIIth or XIIth house, or if ☿ be in his own house or dignities, and at the same time cazimi of the ☉, in good aspect to the lord of the IXth house, then fear nothing — the work will prosper.

A Good Prognostic—When good planets are in the IXth △ to ☿, in the Ist house; or ☿ in the IXth, well aspected by good planets in the ascendant.

No Good Success—If ☿, or ruler of the IXth be in the VIth or XIIth house, or if ♄ or ♂ be in the IXth, or most of the planets under the earth, afflicting the IXth house or its lord, there is then a dreary time, and the publishers will not exert themselves to push the work.

The planets denoting this, and particularly the one afflicting ☿ and the ruler of the IXth, will discover the cause of the calamity.

346. Will the Querent Profit by the Science?

Both Profit and Delight in the Science—When the lords of the Ist and IXth are in ☌, ✶ or △, with each other from angles or succeedent houses, or ♃, ♀

or ☊ in the IXth, in their own dignities and in good aspect of the ruler of the ascendant.

The ☽ in the IId in ⚹ to the ruler of the IXth, in the XIth, especially if ♒ be on the IXth, and ♅ be in good aspect to the cusp of the Ist, Xth or IXth house.

Not Much Gain—If none of these astro-symbols happen, but on the contrary there should be a □ or ☍ between the rulers of the Ist and IXth. When the planets ♄ or ♂, or the ☋ should be in the Ist or IXth, or afflicting their lords, or the ☽; or if ♄ or ♂ happens to rule the IXth, and be located in a bad place of the figure.

A good judgment may be gathered, answering this question, by investigating the "General Judgment of the Houses (270).

347. Will Husband, Wife or Lover Return from Abroad?—The ruler of the Ist and ☽, as usual, denote the querent. The ruler of the VIIth and planets therein portend the absent husband, wife, lover, partner, thief, and other persons denoted by the VIIth house.

The following rules will also answer for servants, lodgers, workmen, and so on, by taking the ruler of the VIth in the same way you consider the ruler of the VIIth. But this we have more minutely explained in 280.

For mother (299), master, father-in-law, kings, nobles, magistrates, and so on, by taking the ruler of the Xth instead of the VIIth, and thus proceed round the houses.

Rules: The ruler of the VIIth in the IVth or Xth, and especially in fixed signs, he is not thinking of returning, also the disposer of the ☽ afflicted.

New Will Be Heard of the Party—☿ or the ☽ in the Ist or Xth; if they separate from a fortune, the news will be good, but if from an infortune, the contrary; if from ♅, the querent is eccentric in his or her mind and does not know which way to proceed for the best; if from ♄, sickness or poor employment.

The State of the Absent Person—The planet from which the quesited's significator last separated is the significator of the state and condition in which he or she lately was; the significator separating from the ill fortunes, some evil has befallen him. The planet to which the quesited's significator applies prognosticates the state in which he now is or shortly will be, according to the degrees of distance between the significators.

The quesited in combustion shows evil, such as imprisonment; and if it be in the house of death, which is the VIIIth from the quesited's, or the ☉ be lord of the house of death, it generally portends death before the quesited can return.

Intends Returning—The ruler of the quesited in the IIId or IXth, applying to a planet in the Ist, he is on his journey homeward. If the quesited or ☽ apply to a R. planet or the quesited be himself R.; but if his significator be afflicted, portends some impediment has taken place, which prohibits his arrival for some time.

348. Will the Benefice Be Obtained? —Ruler of the Ist and ☽ astrally signify the clergyman; and the IXth house portends the living, or any other ecclesiastical preferment sought for.

It Will Be Obtained—If the ☽ or ruler of the Ist be in good aspect with the lord of the IXth. If the ☽ or lord of the Ist be in the IXth, or ruler of the IXth in the Ist, in mutual reception. The lord of the Ist or ☽, in good aspect to the ☉ or ♃, in the Ist or IXth. If the principal significators be in ✶ or △, with reception; if they be in ☐ and at the same time in reception, then gain after much labour and delay. If the ruler of the Ist separate from good aspect immediately of the lord of the IXth, then gain by the means of a person denoted by the translator.

Not Obtained—The ruler of the Ist R. or combust, or he or the ☽ in evil aspect with the infortune, it will come to nothing. If in the XIIth, IIId or VIth, in evil aspect with the lord of the IXth, very doubtful. If an infortune be in the IXth, or its lord be R., then continual uneasiness. Malefics in the Ist or IXth, afflicting the lord of the Ist or IXth, or the ☽, trouble and disappointment.

The Cause of Hindrance—Observe the planet which casts a ☐ or ☍ either to the lord of the Ist or ☽, and take notice over which house he rules, which will furnish you with the cause of his rejection.

The afflicting planet being lord of the IIId, it is through a relation or neighbour. If of the XIth, a pretended friend plays the knave with him, it may be a parson, for they will deceive each other when filthy lucre is in the mess, or some fat living to be enjoyed. If lord of XIIth, some secret enemy. If lord of the Xth, his patron dislikes him. If of the IXth, his interest is not strong enough, or the parishioners or the bishop dislikes him on account of some article of his dogma or creed. If of the VIIth or Vth, he is thought contentious, immoral, or some way improper. If of the IId, he either wants generosity or the means. If of the VIth, he will lose it through ill health, want of activity, or some unforeseen misfortune.

349. Of the Most Appropriate Business—This should always be judged more particularly from the Horoscope at Birth, and judge according to the perspicuous and concise rules in the "Arcana."

But when a querent is desirous of knowing what trade is best to follow in order to be providentially fortunate and happy in his calling, take the ruler of the Ist and the ☽ to denote the querent, and the ruler of the Xth and Vth, as well as planets in the Xth, for the trade. (Simmonite undoubtedly means VIth instead of Vth.)

If the greater part of these be in watery signs, they will do best as publicans, druggists, brewers, distillers, medical botanists, or any trade that makes or deals in liquids, herbs, or drugs.

If in fiery signs, he will do best as a chemist, apothecary, surgeon, physician, smith, cutler, glass-blower, steel melter, or any trade that works by fire.

If in airy signs, a lawyer, accountant, surveyor, clerk, astronomer, astrologer, meteorologist, painter, miller, draper, printer, bookseller, or any light, clean business, not too sedentary, and chiefly in the retail way.

If earthly signs, a gardener, grazier, coachmaker, carpenter, bricklayer, mason, agriculturist, or any calling connected with the earth or substances produced from it.

350. Shall I Prosper in Business?

You Will Prosper—If the trade is going on and the ☽ and the lords of the Ist and Xth are in good familiarity with each other, and with the luminaries and fortunes, the querent will be a good workman. If the Xth is possessed by the ⊕ , ♃ , ♀ or ☊ . The lords of the Xth, XIth and Ist are in good aspect with each other, then gain by his business.

Not Very Prosperous—If the rulers of the Ist, Xth, the ☉ and the ☽ are in bad familiarity, he will be dull, unpromising and unfortunate. Losses and pecuniary vexations if the ☋ or ♄ , ♂ or ♅ be afflicted, or afflicting the XIth or its ruler.

351. If the Calling Be a Profession or Art

—Take the ruler of the IXth, ☿ , and the ☽ instead of the lord of the Xth. If these and the lord of the Ist be in good aspect in angles, or in good aspect of ♃ or ♀ in the Ist or IXth, or the lord of the Ist and IXth in the XIth, and above all if ☿ be joined to, or in good aspect with the ☽ and free from affliction or combustion, good progress in his art. If ☿ and the ☽ be in bad aspect with the lord of the Xth or IXth, or they be combust of the ☉ or R., it is an evil symptom. The ☋ in the Ist or IXth, or the lord of the IXth be an ill fortune, are bad omens. If the ☉ has no good aspect with these significators, it is a poor astro-symbol for the querent.

352. Whether a Petition to Parliament, or any Person, Will Have Success

—The Ist and its lord signify the Petitioner; the Vth, its lord, and the ☽ signify the petition. The Xth, its lord, the ☉ , denote the person to whom the petition is directed, or with whom entrusted.

Successful—Lord of the Ist, ☽ , and the Ascendant, unafflicted, or aspected by the fortunes. If to a king, etc., let the lord and cusp of the Xth be unafflicted.

Ruler of the Vth or ☽ in Xth or Ist, dignified and unafflicted or in good aspect of lord of Xth, and he a fortune or the ☉ , or if he be an infortune but well dignified. The fortunes angular and the infortunes cadent, or the ☽ in Xth strong or in good aspect to the ☉ , or the lord of the Xth, or in good aspect to a planet in the Xth.

Not Successful—Ruler of the Ist, Vth or ☽ afflicted by the lord of the IVth, VIIIth, Xth or XIIth, or if the lord of the Vth afflict, the petition was not ably advocated; or the ☽ afflict, the petition is not made well in some of its clauses.

353. Shall I Obtain the Situation Desired?

Situation Gained—The Ist, its lord, and the ☽ are for the querent. The Xth, its lord, and the ☉ signify the honour, place, etc.

Lord of the Ist or ☽ fortunate in the Xth. Lord of the Xth or ☉ strong in the Ist house. The ☽ and the lord of the Ist in their dignities, free from affliction. Lord of Xth fortunate in the Xth, or well aspected. Lord of the Ist or Xth in ☌, ℙ, or good aspect to the ☊, ☉, ♃ or ♀, in the Xth or Ist. Lord of the Xth receiving lord of the Ist or ☽ by reception. The ☽ is parallel, or good aspect to a planet which has its exaltation in the Ist house.

The ☽, ♃ or ♀, separating from the lord of the Xth and applying to the lord of the Ist. The ☽ in parallel or good aspect to the ☉, or to the lord of the Xth. Lord of the Ist or the ☽ in good aspect to the lord of the Xth. Any planet in parallel or good aspect to the lord of the Xth or the ☉, let the querent make application to such persons as the applying planet describes. Lords of the Ist and Xth, fortunes in ☌, and the ☽ applying to them.

Lord of the Ist in ☌, ℙ, or good aspect to the lord of the IVth, or lord of the IVth in ☌, ℙ or good aspect of the lord of the Xth, you may by hard labour. ♃, ♀, ☿, ☊ or ☽ in ☌, ℙ or good aspect of the lord of Xth, and having dignities in the ascendant. If ♅, ♄ or ♂ are strong in the Ist and in ☌, ℙ or good aspect of the lord of the Xth, it may be gained after much delay. A translation of light from the ☉, or lord of the Xth to the lord of Xth or the lord of the Ist. If the promissor be in an angle, easily obtained; in succeedent, but slowly; in cadent, with difficulty.

Not Obtained–If not more than two of the above rules are found, expect a disappointment; also if any three of the following are found:

♅, ♄, ♂ or ☋ in the Xth or they afflict the lords of the Ist, Xth, or the ☽, the querent is hindered by the person who is to solicit.

Lord of the Xth in □, ℙ or ☍ to the ☉, ☽, or to lord of the Ist, without reception.

♅, ♄, ♂ or ☋ in evil aspect to the lords of the Ist and Xth, great perplexity and anxiety; also, if ♂ or lord of the Xth be in his detriment or fall.

♅, ♄ or ♂ strong in the Ist, in their own house or exaltation, and in good aspect to the lord of the Xth, a probable gain by some person who intercedes.

354. Shall I Continue in My Present Situation?

You Will Not Be Removed–If the lords of the Ist and Xth be in ☌ or good aspect; and if the most ponderable planet of the two be in any angle but the IVth. The ☽ in ☌ of the lord of the Xth in the Xth house; or if the lord of the Ist or the ☽ be in good aspect of the Xth or its lord. Lord of the Ist in good aspect of ♃, ♀ or ☊, in the Xth, and no evil aspect is found by (♆), ♅, ♄, ♂ or ☋, long ere he leaves. Lord of the Ist in the Xth, or lord of the Xth in the Ist, the same.

355. Shall I Leave My Situation? –When a person is in any employment, office or trust, and is afraid of being turned out of the same, observe the following rules, for if more than two occur, he is sure to leave.

If the ☽ or lord of the Ist be in evil aspect of the lord of the Xth, or the ☉ without reception, in danger of losing office. The lord of the Ist or ☽ separating from the lord of the Xth and applying to (♆), ♅, ♄, ♂ or ☋, sure to go. If the lords of the Xth and Ist be in evil aspect, and the most ponderable in the IVth, or approaching it from the Vth. The ☽ in conjunction with any planet not in his own dignities, though with reception (unless it be ♃ or ♀ by ✶ or △), he will leave. Either the ☽ or lord of the IVth in ♈, ♋, ♎ or ♑ in the IVth. The ☽ in ♑ and afflicted, or void of course, and lord of the Ist afflicted.

356. When Shall I Leave My Situation? —The disposer of the lord of the Ist, Xth, or the ☽, with any planet in any angle but the IVth, and the planet slow, you will be removed when the disposer comes in ☌ of the ☉ or turns R., or leaves the sign he possesses. See when the lord of the Xth or a planet in the Xth leaves the sign in which he is then posited; for about that time he leaves.

357. What Will Be the Cause of My Leaving? —The lord of the Ist or the ☽ in evil aspect with any planet, and that planet in ☌ or good aspect with either the lord of the Xth or the ☉, he receives harm from such persons as are described by the planets which are in good aspect of the ☉ or lord of the Xth. The lord of the Ist R. and in ☌ of the ☉, you have incurred the displeasure of your master, or the person under whom you are.

358. Shall I Be Restored to My Situation? —The following rules will answer the question of the re-election of any member of parliament, for any place he has formerly represented; as well as any clergyman, minister, banished officer, or dethroned monarch to power, etc., or the return of an individual to any office or employment.

Restored—If the lords of the Ist and Xth are in mutual reception; and returned speedily with honour. If the lord of the Ist be joined to a planet in the IIId or IXth, and after separation, the lord of the Ist join any planet in the Ist, Xth, or VIIth. If the lord of the Ist join the lord of the Xth, and the heavier planet behold the Xth by good aspect. If the ☽ be in ♈, ♋, ♎ or ♑, unafflicted. If the ☽ be strong and in ☌ of a planet in the Ist. Lord of the Xth in ☌ to a planet, except it be the ☉. Lord of the Xth a lighter planet than lord of the IVth, and separating from the lord of the IVth. If the lord of the Xth be lighter than the Ist, and he in ☌ of the lord of the Xth.

Never Restored—Lords of the Ist and Xth separating from each other. Lord of the Ist aspected and not received. The ☽ in ☌ of ♅, ♄, ♂ or ☋ in the IXth, he removes far off. The ☽ or lord of the Xth afflicted in the Ist, Xth, VIIth or IVth.

359. Shall I Get My Wages Advanced?

Yes, an Advance—Lord of the IId in good aspect of the ruler of the Xth, and especially if in mutual reception. Ruler of the IId strong in the Xth, or the ruler of the Xth strong in the IId, or the ⊕ in the Xth or in good aspect with its ruler, or with the ruler of the XIth. The rulers of the XIth and IId in good aspect or mutual reception. The luminaries in good aspect (309). But if none of these testimonies occur, then say the querent will not have an advance, and the employer cannot afford it if the ♄ be in the XIth house.

360. Will It Be Well to Engage this Work?

Well to Engage—If the ☉ or ruler of the Xth, XIth, Ist or IId, are in good aspect with each other or well situated themselves. ♃, ♀ or the ☊ in the Xth. The ruler of the Ist or IId exalted in the Xth or XIth. The ⊕ unafflicted in the Ist, IId, Xth or XIth (248).

Decline It—If the above significators are not so situated, or if the IId or Xth or their lords be afflicted. The ☽ or ⊕ afflicted in the IId or XIth.

361. Will It Be Well to Leave the Situation?

Remain as You Are—If the ruler of the Xth be in its detriment, fall, or any other debility, or if the ruler of the Xth is hastening into affliction, especially if a fixed sign be on the Xth. If the planet or aspect be a fortune, to which the ☉ next applies. The ruler of the XIth a fortune, or fortunately situated in the Ist, IId or Xth. But if none of these appear, then say better to remove away.

362. Whether an Exile Will be Restored

—The ascendant and its ruler are for the officer, nobleman, gentleman, etc.

He Will Be Restored—If the ruler of the Ist be in ☌, except it be the ☉, with the lord of the Xth, and the most ponderable planet behold the cusp of the Xth.

If the lord of the Ist should not happen to behold the cusp, if the ☽ be joined to any fortunate planet in the Ist or Xth. If the lord of the Xth be joined to a planet in the Xth, except it be the ☉. The lord of the Xth a lighter planet than the ruler of the IVth and separating from him. If the ☽ be in ♈, ♋ or ♎, easily returns. If the ruler of the Xth be a lighter planet than the lord of the Ist, so also if the ☽ be joined to the lord of the Xth, and behold the Xth, unless disposed of by a peregrine planet under the earth.

The ☽ joined to ♃ or ♀ in its dignities but not restored if ♀ or ♃ be not in its dignities. The lord of the Ist in dignities, in ✶ or △ to a planet, mutually received, restored.

The Government, Office, etc., Not Restored—If the ☽ be afflicted in the IIId or IXth house, but if she be well situated and well aspected in the IIId and IXth house, then he tries to gain office and popularity in another place.

The Time of Restoration—Observe when the promissors come in powerful good aspect with each other, according to their degrees of distance, or if more likely, by their ephemeral motion.

These rules may be further corroborated by those given (358) for discovering whether a querent will be restored to a former situation or office.

363. Of Friends Generally

Query 1. What Kind of Person Ought I to Trust as a Friend? —See if there be any good planets in the XIth and, if so, describe the friend or friends according to the number of planets therein, observing the sign in which they are placed, for those will give a description of persons, either male or female, most to be trusted.

Never trust a person who has once made a breach of friendship.

Also take notice what planets are received by the lord of the Ist, or in good familiarity with the ruler of the ascendant, either at birth or in the horary figure, and the sign in which they are, and they will describe their friends, and this latter especially if there be no planet favourably situated in the XIth.

Query 2. Is the Quesited a Friend to Me? —The ascendant and its lord are for the querent, and the XIth house and its ruler denote the quesited.

The Friend Is Sincere—If there be a benevolent aspect between the ruler of the Ist and the XIth, or a friendly reception between them, or between the disposer of the lord of the Ist and XIth. The ☽ in friendly aspect to the ruler of the XIth; good planets or ☊ in the XIth; as if this cast a good aspect to the cusp of the IId house, its lord, or to the ⊕, gain thereby.

Not a Faithful Friend—If the ☋ be in the XIth, much deceit; the lord of the Ist or the ☽ in ill aspect of the ruler of the XIth, or of ♅, ♄ or ♂. If ♃ or ♀ be afflicted by the ruler of the XIth. The lord of the XIth in the XIIth, secret enmity. ☿ in the XIth, perfidious.

Fortunes and infortunes make much difference in this question; malefics always cause that which is disagreeable, however well posited; and benefics, however ill disposed, never denote a very great degree of malignity. Application signifies reconciliation if the aspect is good, or a renewing of enmity if evil. Separation shows a falling off in attachment if the aspect is good; or if it had been evil it denotes contempt or indifference, and if no good aspect follow with a benefic, the connexion will be dissolved forever.

364. Of Private Enemies—When persons know or suspect they have private enemies and fear the effects of their malice, in wanton mischief and so on, we take the ruler of the Ist and the ☽ to signify the querent or the injured party; the ruler of the XIIth, or planets afflicting therein to portend the enemy. The afflictor of the ☽ or ruler of the Ist will describe the general appearance of the enemy, as well as if the lord of the XIIth afflicted the ruler of the Ist.

Query 1. What Is the Description of this Foe? —Observe the ruler of the XIIth if he be ♅, ♄, ♂ or ☿ in bad aspect of the Ist or of the luminaries denote a foe or foes and are described by that planet and by the sign in which it or they happen to be. The foe's dress is portended by the sign on the XIIth and its ruler combined with the sign in which the lord of the XIIth is posited (227-229). The house in which the afflictor is placed will manifest in part the cause and quality of the enmity, as well as other peculiarities concomitant with the affair.

Many ill planets in the XIIth or VIIth denote many foes; also if the lord of the Ist be evilly affected in the VIIth or XIIth, or either of their lords in the Ist, there are enemies. If the lord of the XIIth behold the ruler of the Ist, from the VIth, VIIIth or XIIth, or from the IVth, VIIth or Xth, he has malicious wishes; also enemies there are if the lord of any other house besides the XIIth be in □ or ☍ to the lord of the Ist, or to the ☽ from the IVth, VIth, VIIIth or XIIth house.

Query 2. The State and Quality of the Foes—If the lord of the XIIth afflict the lord of the Ist or the ☽ from the IIId, they are kinsmen or neighbours, especially if the lord of the IIId afflict likewise. If the IVth, it is the father; if in the Vth, his children, or some visitor or companion; if he be in

VIth or joined to its lord, it is his servant or very probably his uncle who is also afflicted with some secret malady; if the ruler of the VIth be in the XIIth, he is sickly. If the lord of the XIIth afflict the Ist out of the VIIth, it is his wife, patron or partners. If the lord of the XIIth be in the Xth or with its lord, he is in favor with some respectable person; and if he be strong it will not be well to interfere with him. The lord of the XIIth in the XIth, a foe in the guise of friendship. He may also expect evil from that part where the ☋ is posited, especially if its dispositor be in evil aspect with either the lord of the Ist or the ☽

Query 3. The Power of Their Enmity—If the lord of the XIIth be a superior planet or dignified, they are more powerful and consequently dangerous. If the lord of the Ist be more angular or better dignified, or better supported by the benefics than the lord of the XIIth, he will overcome his enemies, and vice versa.

If the lord of the XIIth be also lord of the Ist and in evil aspect with the ☽ , the querent is chiefly the cause of the evil by his own indiscretion, and if an evil planet be in the XIIth he has formed an ill connection, and will reap discontent as the fruit of his own folly.

Query 4. He Has No Private Enemies—If the ruler of the Ist or ☽ is unafflicted or ♃ or ♀ be in the XIIth unafflicted. If the Ist house, its ruler and the ☽ be well posited in the figure with no evil rays of the malefics, he has no private enemies. Many planets in mutual reception indicate no particular enemies. If the lord of the XIth be stronger than the lord of the VIIth or XIIth, friends will be more powerful than enemies.

If the planets signifying enemies are peregrine, retrograde, or combust, they are mean, rascally characters.

365. Is the Absconded Child Dead or Alive?—This enquiry particularly belongs to the XIIth house, as it is the VIIIth from the Vth; and the VIIIth signifies death.

Fear the Child Is Dead—If the ruler of the Vth be afflicted by position or aspect in the Xth or XIIth. The Xth or VIIIth lord heavily afflicted; if it be ♄, drowned; if ♂, other kinds of violence. The lord of the Vth in the IVth and in □ of the ☽ , dead. The ruler of the Vth or ☽ combust in the Vth, VIth, VIIIth, XIIth or IVth, dead.

Judge this question exactly as you do for absent brothers, sisters, etc., only remembering to take the ruler of the Vth in every case the same as you do the ruler of the IIId in paragraph 280.

Of Imprisonment or Banishment—The XIIth house is that from which we astro-symbolically prognosticate, concerning persons imprisoned, banished, transported, or in any other way exiled.

The ruler of the Ist and the ☽ denote the querent, be it parent, relation or neighbour.

Freedom Is Denoted—By the ruler of the Ist or ☽ being swift and unafflicted, especially if the lord of the XIIth is in a moveable sign, and at the same time in good aspect to a fortunate planet; also if the lord of the XIIth be stronger than the ruler of the VIIth, IIId or IXth. If the lord of the Ist or the ☽ separate from the lord of the IVth and immediately apply to a fortune.

A Long Confinement—If the ruler of the Ist or the ☽ be in fixed signs in the cadent houses. If the lord of the Ist be in the IVth, VIth, VIIIth or XIIth, in combustion or retrogradation. The ruler of the Ist afflicted by ♅, ♄ or ♂, or the lord of the Ist under the ☉'s beams, then the querent fears long confinement, which will be the case. The lord of the XIIth afflicted by ♅, ♄ or ♂, and that infortune the ruler of the VIIIth, the quesited will die in prison.

A fixed sign ascending, and the lord of the XIIth a superior planet and angular, long imprisonment. The lord of the Ist being also lord of the XIIth, is symbolical of lasting misfortune in prison; likewise if the lords of the Ist and XIIth apply to a ☌ with each other, and the latter be the stronger and an infortune, a fatal imprisonment. If the lord of the Ist be cadent from his house of exaltation, and the ☽ in ♏ or ♒, long imprisonment. If the lord of the Ist or the ☽ apply to evil aspects of ♅, ♄ or ♂, particularly if the infortune be lord of the VIIIth or going into combustion without any good aspect of a benefic, or if ♂, ♄ or ♅ be in ☍ to the luminaries, or the ☽ or lord of the Ist be near any violent fixed stars, particularly Caput Algol, it denotes that the whole will end in a violent death, or at least that he will die in prison.

The Time of Release—May be known by observing the degrees of distance between the lord of the XIIth and the fortunes; or between the good aspects of the ☉ and the XIIth, according to the sign in which the applying significator is, as before described, whether it be common, fixed or moveable, according to paragraphs 231 and 232.

367. Of Sickness Generally
Query 1. What Part of the Body is Afflicted?

1. Notice the sign in which the ruler of the ascendant is located, and that will in part show the disease and the part of the body afflicted.
2. Notice the VIth, its cusp, its lord, and the planets therein, if any, and these will show the complaint chiefly.
3. Observe the sign in which the ruler of the VIth is, and that part will be afflicted.
4. Take notice of the place of the ☽, and that will in part be afflicted.

From the combination of the above you may come to the true disease; and then apply the remedy as laid down in my *Herbal Guide to Health*.

That planet which afflicts either the ascendant, its ruler, or the ruler of the VIth or the ☽, will declare the affliction in part.

If it should be ♅, you should then administer nervines. When ♄ or ☿ is the cause of disease, I should recommend stimulants, such as preparations of composition powers; see my *Herbal*, 238. When ♂ or the ☉ rules the complaint, I use cooling medicines or refrigerants, and those are generally of a purgative character, as *Herbal Guide*, 138. If a fever or inflammatory action, use febrifuges, 181, 182 or 183 in the *Herbal*.

When the ☽ or ♀ is the cause of the disease, diuretics are generally of great service; but as the diseases are various, they must be distinctly discovered; then apply according to the quality of the disorder, and this will be found under the head of various Recipes.

Query 2. Signs of Short Disease—When the ☽ is on the cusp of the VIth, and ruler of the Ist and VIth in ♈, ♋, ♎ or ♑, or the ruler of the Ist swift or near the end of a sign, so that it be not the sign of the VIth or XIIth. ♀ or ♃ in the VIth in ♎, ♓ or ♐ produces short sickness. The rulers of the VIth, Ist or the ☽, in good aspect of each other, denotes short.

Query 3. Signs of Long Disease—The ruler of the Ist, VIth or the ☽ in ♉, ♌, ♏ or ♒, long and tedious; and if these rulers be in bad aspect with each other, they denote the same.

Common signs ♊, ♍, ♐ and ♓ denote neither long nor short, but a few weeks; or, if the ☽, or ruler of the Ist or VIth be R., or slow in motion, will give rather a chronic and protracted illness.

If the ☽ be in ill aspect to the lord of the Ist, the disease will increase.

Evil planets in the VIth denote an ill end to the disease, and the ruler of the VIth afflicted in the VIth, VIIIth or XIIth.

The ruler of the VIth in ☌ of the ☉, or R., or in his fall, and in the VIIIth, in ☌, □, S□, or ☍ of ♅ or ♄ or ♂, you may fear that the disease will never leave the patient till death.

The ☉ and ☽ cadent and their dispositors with the ruler of the Ist and afflicted, denotes a long disease, although ♃ and ♀ may lend their aspects.

The ruler of the Ist in the VIth, and the ruler of the VIth in the Ist, is long.

Query 4. Prognostics of Life—If the ruler of the Ist be stronger than the lord of the VIth, VIIIth or XIIth, or ♃ be in ☌, ⚹ or △, of the lord of the VIth, and the ☉ and ☽ be free from affliction of ♅, ♄ or ♂—all these presage life.

Ruler of the Ist dispose of the lord of the VIIIth, it is very good; and ♃, or ♀ or ☉, or the ☽ in the Ist not afflicted by the ruler of the VIIIth, takes away all fear of death.

The ☽ in the Xth, in good aspect of ♅, ♄, ♂ and ☉, is a perfect signification of life; but it shows vomitings almost to distraction. In such cases medicine should be given to stay sickness.

The ☽ or ruler of the VIth separating from the ruler of the VIIIth, and immediately apply to good aspect of the ☉ in the Ist, VIIth, Xth or XIth, the sick will recover, and this recovery will be by means of medicine.

The ☽ in ♋, ♐, ♓, ♉ or ♎ and in good aspect of ♀ or ♃, takes away either the imagination or fear of death; also, if the ☉ or ☽, or ruler of the Ist, be free from affliction of the ruler of the VIIIth, or ♅, ♄ or ♂.

Examine all the significators; as the Ist and its lord; the VIth and its lord; the ☉ and ☽. If all these or the greater part of them be well configurated or posited, then certain recovery.

Query 5. Time of Recovery—When the chief significators are in good aspect in ♋, ♑, ♈ or ♎, say so many days as they are degrees to complete the aspect. If in ♉, ♌, ♏ or ♒, then say the sick will be so many months as there are degrees between the principal significators before he recovers to perfect health. If the chief significators be in ♊, ♍, ♐ or ♓, then so many weeks as there are degrees between them.

Query 6. Prognostics of Death—The ruler of the Ist and ☽ in conjunction of lord of the VIIth in the Ist, Xth, VIIth or IVth, especially if the ruler of the VIIIth be ♅, ♄ or ♂. If the ruler of the Ist separate from ☌ of the lord of the VIIIth by R. motion, when they come to ☌ by direct motion, the sick will die, unless the ☉ interpose his benefic beams before then.

The ruler of the Ist in ☌ of the ☉ in the Ist, or the lord of the VIIIth in the Xth, and the ruler of the Ist in the IVth, VIth or VIIIth R. and in conjunction of the ☽, or in □ or ☍ to her shows death.

The ☽ in the IVth, with ♂ or the ☉ therein with ♅ or ♄—death; also the ☽ on the cusp of the Ist in □ of ♂ from the IVth. The ☽ in ☌ of the ☉ in the VIIIth, or if lady of the VIth, and in ☌ of ☉ in the Ist or IVth, the same; and more especially if the lord of the VIIIth be afflicted.

The lord of the Ist with one evil planet, and another evil one in the Ist, destroys life without remedy.

Also if the lord of the Ist is in ☌, □ or ☍ of the lords of the IVth, VIth, VIIIth or XIIth.

The lord of the Ist under the earth, and in ill aspect to the ruler of the VIIIth, or if the two lords be in ☌ in the IVth, or the lord of the Ist and lord of the VIIIth both one planet, if he be cadent and afflicted by ♅, ♄, ♂ or ☉, is very dangerous.

The lord of the Ist and lord of the VIth in □ or ☌ from angles shows an incurable disease with great pain. Or the ruler of the VIth R., combust, detriment, or fall, in the VIIIth, in ☌ of ♅, ♄ or ♂, shows the disease will continue to death.

♃ ruler of the Ist in the VIIIth and ruler thereof R., the ☽ separating therefrom and applying to ♂, shows death. The ☉ ruler of the Ist and unfortunately placed in the VIIIth and behold ♄ from the IId.

The Cause of Disease—Look to the lord of the VIth or XIIth and to the planet from which the ☽ last separated from body.

If the ☽ separate from ♂ and he be lord of the XIIth or VIth, then by a strain, or bruise, or fall, or fire, or some sudden calamity.

If the ☽ separate from ♅ or ♂ in ♊, ♒, ♓ and ♀, lady of VIth, then by surfeit. If the ☽ separate from ♂ and apply to ♅, ♄ or ☿, and ♃ ruler of the XIIth in ♈, the party has overworked himself.

Query 7. Of Giving Medicine—Take medicine at the time the ☽ is in ♋, ♏, ♓; and if the lord of that sign be under the earth, then medicine will have good effect.

Do not purge if possible when the ☽ is in ♈, ♉ or ♑, but you may give emetics. But neither give vomit nor purge when the ☽ is in ♌.

Mark Well—Let not ♃ be ruler of the Ist when you give a purge, nor in ☌ or aspect with the ☽ or ♂, nor ♃ in the Ist, for these hinder all purges operating beneficially.

Medicine given when the lord of the Ist is retrograde, and the ☽ in ☌ or aspect in ♋, ♏, ♓, the party will vomit it up again.

POINTS IN GENETHLIACS

1. The ☽ passing through the twelve signs takes the character of each planet that has rule in the sign in which she happens to be. Thus if in the sign Aries, she becomes martial and masculine; if in Taurus, she is feminine and takes on the character of ♀; and so on for the other houses.

2. If the ☽ is aspected by any planet whatever she partakes of its nature.

3. If the ☽ ascend in ♉, the child then born will be effeminate and fond of pleasure.

4. If the ☽ ascends in ♈, the child then born will be a martial man, brave, but yet of a changeable mind.

5. ♀ or the ☽ in ♉ at the time of a birth denotes a fruitful person.

6. Every planet when in the house or exaltation of another partakes of the nature of that other.

7. The ☽ rules or governs existences, and without she be in power conjointly with ♀ there is no animal existence.

8. All animal copulation is in vain if the ☽ be not in power at the moment.

9. The periods of gestation and incubation in all animals, even to the human female, are exactly regulated by the periods of the ☽, and the moment of completed gestation strike, exactly as the tide flows, to the motion of the ☽.

10. The ☽ adversely aspected and evilly placed at the moment of birth of a child or animal, the progeny will never see the light.

11. The child born when the ☽ is in ♋ is easily brought forth.

12. When the ☽ is in ☍ to the ☉, the brain is nearest the top of the skull.

13. There are certain times in the day when it is most fortunate for an infant to be born, the cause of which is the particular position of the ☉. During the winter season from 11 to 12 o:clock in the morning, during the spring and autumn from 10:30 to 12 o:clock, in the summer from 10 to 12 o:clock; the ☉ is then in the Xth house, and will elevate the native, procure active honourable employment, generally under some public body. Females born near these times generally marry men above their own station in life.

14. Here is a fact—easily verified even if you are not an astrological student: females born between sunrise and noon, or sunset and midnight, usually marry early in life, or otherwise marry men younger than themselves;

while those born between noon and sunset, or midnight and sunrise, generally marry late in life, or to persons many years their senior. Of course, those born nearest to noonday, but not past it, are the most fortunate, for the solar influences are then most powerful. Note, this judgment by position must not be considered infallible, for aspects from the planets will accentuate or modify this, and if the ☉ is in evil aspect to either ♅ , ♄ or ♂, the parties may be very unfortunate.

15. If the native is a male, take the ☽ and judge in every respect relating thereto, as the ☉ in a female nativity.

16. Persons born with the sign ♋ ascending have always some defect, mole, mark, scar or disease in the breast.

17. The ☽ in ☌ , □ or ☍ of ♃ in the horoscope will cause either an illness or peculiar trouble near every 7th year of the native's life; this will be illness if the ☽ by hyleg.

18. The Sun in ☌ , □ or ☍ of ♃ in the horoscope will cause an illness or peculiar trouble near every 10th year of the native's life; if the ☉ is hyleg, it will be illness.

19. In a female horoscope the ☉ and ♀ in □ , ☌ or ☍ of ♂ will cause an evil love affair near 19 years of age, and danger of an illegitimate child.

In a male's, ♀ ☌ , □ or ☍ of ♂, same love, danger, and probabilities of an illegitimate child being laid to his charge.

The ✶ , △ will cause either a love affair or marriage, and with a female the ☉ and ♀ in ✶ , △ of ♂ brings a love affair or marriage.

20. The ascendant in a nativity is a very important quarter of the heavens, as it signifies the general health and disposition. It is the beginning; it is the individual.

21. The VIIth and Xth houses are extremely powerful. Powerful for good if the benefics are there, but if the malefics be there calamities are threatened. If the fortunes fall in the southern angle and the ☽ has good latitude, free from affliction, then the person will become eminent.

22. Several planets in sympathy or good aspect, continual success attends the efforts of the native.

23. The ☽ in the IId denotes mutability in circumstances or means, but if ♃ or ♀ ✶ or △ , it very much improves and gives wealth in the decline of life.

24. If ♃ and ☿ be well posited in a figure and in good aspect to the ☉ and ☽ , the native will be highly successful in his undertakings, have a good disposition with many friends, and be held in high esteem.

25. If at the birth of an individual ♅ , ♄ or ♂ be on the meridian and afflict the ☉ and ☽ , ill fortune and calamity will pursue the native through life, in whatever sphere he may be.

26. In a male horoscope should the ☉ be in ☌ of ♂ in ♈ or ♏ , the man will prosper and attain dignity in all martial concerns.

27. Should the ☉ be in ☌ of ☿ in ♊ or ♍ , the man will gain honor

by science or literature.

28. ☿ rules the brain, and accordingly as he is powerful in a nativity so will the mental quality of the native be. When in highest exaltation and power the native is remarkable for brain power and wisdom.

29. ♃ or ♀ in the ascendant, void of evil configurations, will make the mind just and upright; and such persons may be trusted in any position in which they may be placed.

30. If you find ♄ in the ascendant with other evil configurations, such persons are exceedingly mean and selfish, seek after other people's goods, and should not be placed in any position of trust.

THE DOCTRINE OF ELECTIONS

Elections are understood by astrologers as certain observations of days and hours, which times, by the motion of the stars and planets, are either known to be fortunate or unfortunate, as they agree or disagree with the nativities of persons who desire to have success in the business they are about to undertake, as the opening of a shop, marrying, travelling, selling, etc.

1. In the commencing of any enterprise, fortify the ☽ and the planet under which the querent was born. It is a good election when that sign ascends which was posited on the Ist at birth, provided it be not afflicted by the presence of an ill fortune. In electing a time for anything of a long continuance, place ♉, ♌, ♏ or ♒ on the Ist.

2. In making an election for anything connected with the IId house, fortify that planet which was lord of the Ist at birth, and ♃, and let either of them be in the IId unafflicted.

3. In all things relating to the IIId house fortify the lords of the Ist and IIId, the ⊕, ☽ and her dispositor; let planets be placed in the IIId which were fortunately posited and in aspect to the IIId at birth; let not those be the lords of the VIth, VIIIth or XIIth. Consider for what you take your journey, and let the lord of that which is significator of the business about which you go be unafflicted.

4. In elections belonging to the IVth house, fortify that planet which was ruler of the IVth at birth, the IVth of the figure with the ☽ applying to good aspect.

5. In elections appertaining to the Vth house, fortify the Vth in the Radix and place the lord thereof on the cusp of the IId; let ♃ or ♀ behold the cusp of the Vth; be careful not to afflict the Ist and its lord, debilitate the VIIth and its lord.

6. For the VIth house fortify the ☽ and let her be in ♉, ♊ or ♑, and the lord of the IId at birth in the VIth of figure in good aspect to Ist.

7. For the VIIth house fortify the Ist, lord thereof, the ☽, and these must not be afflicted by ♅, ♄ or ♂, or ☋; let ♌ or ♒ ascend.

8. For the VIIIth, fortify the Ist, its lord, and the ☽, and let lord of Ist and the ☽ apply to good aspect of ♄.

9. In elections of the IXth house, see that the lord of the IXth at birth and that of the figure be free from affliction.

10. For the Xth house, let the cusp of the Xth at birth be the cusp of the Ist of the figure, making the lord of the Xth, ☽, and lord of the Ist well situated.

11. For the XIth house, let ♃ and ♀ be therein, and the lord of XIth strong and in good aspect of lord of Ist at birth.

12. For the XIIth, let the lord of Ist and ☽ be free from affliction, in good aspect of lord of XIIth in the Radix.

By these short rules the student in astrology may give a correct judgment of the events of every undertaking in life.

Never begin any undertaking when the ☽ is going to be joined to any retrograde planet; it will soon be destroyed, and if there be other evil configurations at the same time it will put many other impediments in the way, and end in great mischief.

It is well not to lend or pawn anything when ♃ is under the sunbeams, for if he should be at the time, and not in good aspect of other planets, there will be little or no hopes of redemption.

368. Election for Receiving Your Wife's Portion—Let the lord of the ascendant and cusp thereof be well fortified, and let the lord of the VIIIth apply by ✶ or △ to the lord of the ascendant, or to the lord of the IId, and if they cannot be made to behold each other, then let them be in mutual reception. But for the making of wills and testaments, in order to continue long, let the ☽ be increasing in light and slow in motion, and let the lord of the ascendant and the ☽ apply to ✶ or △ of ♄ or ☿.

369. Election for Recovering Money Owing—Be sure to fortify that planet which was lord of the ascendant in the nativity, and also ♃, who is a natural significator of wealth and substance; and if possible, let either of them be placed in the IId house, or essentially dignified, in a good place of the figure, free from combustion or other application, and in good aspect to the fortunes that behold the IId house or lord thereof, by any good aspect at the hour of birth.

370. Election Concerning Friendship between Brethren, Kindred and Neighbours—Let the lord of the ascendant in the nativity be well fortified in the election and, if you can, let him apply to some good aspect of the lord of the IIId; otherwise let the lord of the ascendant and lord of the IIId be in reception and well posited in a hopeful place of the figure. Either of these observations will make a good and successful election.

371. Election for Buying or Taking Houses, Lands or Tenements—To perform this you must fortify that planet which was lord of the IVth in the geniture, and also the IVth house itself, together with the ☽, and let her apply to the ✶ or △ of the lord of the IVth and IId houses, and let as many of the significators be in reception as possible, and in good places of the figure, and let a fixed sign be on the ascendant.

372. Election for Finding Hidden Treasure—Before you make choice of a time to dig for hidden treasure, you ought first to view the party's nativity to see if there would be any probability that the native would be likely to find any hidden treasure. If you find the lord of the ascendant and the lord of the IVth well posited in the radix and in good aspect one to another, and both of them in good aspect to the cusp of the IId or its lord; it is an argument the native will be fortunate in finding riches in the earth. When you intend to search for it, fortify the lord of the ascendant and the ☽ , IVth house and lord thereof, and let them apply to a ✶ or △ of ♃ or ♀ ; also let the infortunes be cadent and the benevolent planets in angles.

373. Of Removing from Place to Place—The changing of houses, lodgings, etc., is best done when the ☽ is in a fixed sign, increasing in light, and at the same time in good aspect with fortunate stars in the IVth house or ascendant. The lord of the IId strong, and above the earth, and in ✶ or △ with the lord of the VIIth and VIIIth houses, for that is the place the party must go to for profit or penury.

374. Taking Possession of any House—In the performance of this, let the ☽ be in her greatest dignity, in good aspect of ♃ or ♀ and in no way afflicted by ♄ or ♂; let a fixed sign ascend, and both the cusp of the house and its lord be befriended by the good rays of the fortunes; let not ♄ nor ♂ be in the VIIth, and let the lord of the ascendant be in good aspect with the lord of the VIIth and, if possible, with reception also; let the luminaries also cast their friendly beams to the Ist and VIIth houses; but do not let the ☋ afflict any of the aforesaid houses or significators.

375. Election for Fishing—The most successful time to fish is when the ☽ is in ♋ or ♓ , in the Xth house, in ✶ or △ to ♀ in the VIIth, the ☽ applying and not separating from any planet in a watery sign. Let not the ☽ be afflicted by either ♄ or ♂ , neither let them be in angles of the figure, especially the first and seventh.

376. Elections for Engaging Servants—When you engage or receive servants into your house or employment, be sure to let the ☽ be strong, well aspected, and free from all manner of afflictions, and let the lord of the ascendant or lord of the IId in the radix be in good aspect to the lord of the VIth, or let the fortunate planets be placed in the VIth; provided they were lords of good houses in the geniture, or in good aspect to the lord of the ascendant; and let the ☽ be placed in ♉ , ♊ or ♍.

377. Election for Buying and Selling—He that buyeth anything when the ☽ being from the beginning of ♑ to the latter end of ♊ , buyeth dear and selleth cheap.

He that buyeth anything to sell again, the ☽ being from the beginning of ♋ to the latter end of ♐ , buys cheap and sells dear; especially if the ☽ at her entrance into ♋ be swift in motion, and in good aspect to ♃ or ♀.

The ☽ in her last quarter is good for him that buys any secret or hidden commodity, which he would conceal or not have known.

From the first quarter to the full is best for the seller; from the full to the last quarter of the ☽ is best for the buyer. Always remembering to let the ☽ at her entrance into the first quarter (as before hinted) be swift in motion and in ✶ or △ to ♃ or ♀.

The first 12 hours of the new moon are bad for the beginning of any undertaking, but from 12 hours to 72 hours are good and successful for the beginner, provided, as I said before, that the ☽ be well aspected and strong at her entrance into the beginning of the 13th hour.

378. Election for Setting up any Trade or Profession — Let the cusp of the Xth house in the nativity be the ascendant in the election, and let the lord of the ascendant and the ☽, not only be free from affliction but in ✶ or △ to the lords of the Xth and IId houses; and if possible, let the fortunes be angular and the infortunes cadent at the same time.

379. Election for Entering into any Place or Office Employment — Firstly, let the luminaries be in their dignities or at least not afflicted by infortunes; and secondly, let ♃ be in the ascendant, and the ☉ in the midheaven.

Let the VIIth and IId be strong and fortunate, for the one signifies money and the other counsellors and council to assist in public affairs; for if in these houses the unfortunate stars are placed, it shows much damage and hurt to those things, the more so if ♃ and ♀ do not cast their good aspects thither. But in all martial undertakings and offices, it is necessary that ♂ be well placed in the figure.

380. Election for Buying Horses and Oxen — Let the lord of the ascendant and ☽ be free from affliction, and in some of their essential dignities, also in good aspect to the lord of the XIIth in the radix and IId in the election. Let all the significators be in good houses in the figure and, if possible, let ♈, ♌, ♐ ascend, and let the lords of those signs be free from affliction.

381. Elections for Most Undertakings and First Journeys — The ☽ increasing in good aspect of the ☉ helps for journeyings. In all journeys the greatest impediment of a planet is to be peregrine or retrograde. It is bad in journeys to have ♂ in the IIId or IXth, but much worse to have him in the IId. The lord of the IXth or IIId in the Ist, the journey will be successful, but if strong and well aspected, the better. In all journeys view the ☽, for she is a genial significatrix of journeys.

382. Election for Marriage — In the marriages of men, let the ☽ and ♀ be strong and fortunate in good places of the figure, and in good aspect of ♃, he being the author of peace and wealth, and let him be in reception with one or both of them, and all in friendly aspect to the lord of the ascendant; and let the VIIth house and ☽, as also the ascendant, be free, and in such signs as favour marriage, as ♉, ♎, ♐, ♒ and ♓. But in marriages of women you must depute the ☉ and ♂ as before you did the ☽ and ♀.

In marriages, the ascendant stands for the man, the VIIth for the woman. In which of these parts good planets are, it will be best for them.

Let not the ☽ be combust on the marriage day, for that signifies the death of the man; nor in the combust way, for that signifies an ill end. It is very ill in marriages if the ☽ apply to ♄ or ♂, though the aspect be ever so good, for then there will be neither peace nor love between the contracting parties.

In all marriages let the ☽ increase in light and motion, and let her have no ill aspect to the ☉, nor any at all to ♄ or ♂.

♀ is the general significatrix in marriage, and therefore it is best to let the Moon apply to her by ☌, ✶ or △.

If the lord of the ascendant is weak, and the lord of the VIIth strong in the VIIth, and he a commanding planet, and in good aspect of ♂, the woman will want to be the master at all times, and endeavour to hold dominion over her husband.

* * * *

> Let exiled Reason be restored,
> > Just Education bear the sway,
> Let Nature's Empire be explored,
> > And Truth her volume wide display.
> Let Science 'luminate the mind,
> > The Mystic World her page unfold;
> Let Truth and Justice rule the world,
> > And knowledge teach to young and old.

TERMS USED IN THIS WORK

Abcission of light when a light planet goes to a ☌ of a ponderous planet, but before his ☌ of the ponderous planet goes to a more ponderous, whereby the light of the inferior is cut off.

Affliction a planet or cusp of a house, being in evil aspect to any planet, or in ☌ to a malefic.

Airy signs ♊, ♎ and ♒.

Angles the Ist, IVth, VIIth and Xth houses. When planets are therein, they are more powerful than in any other situation.

Application To apply. These terms mean the approach of any planet to the body or aspect of another, or to the cusp of any house.

Ascendant the Ist house, that space between the eastern horizon and one-third of the distance towards the meridian under the earth; also the cusp of that house which represents the party, as the cusp of the Vth is the ascendant for a child of the querent, the Xth for business, etc.

Ascending a term denoting any planet which is between the IVth houses, more especially when rising above the eastern horizon.

Aspects the being placed at certain distances from a planet, or the cusp of a house, as if ♃ be 60° from the ☽, then they are both said to be in sextile aspect to each other. They are zodiacal and mundane.

Barren signs ♊, ♌ and ♍.

Benefics the two planets ♃ and ♀, and sometimes ☿.

Bestial signs ♈, ♉, ♌, ♐ (the first half excepted) and ♑.

Besieged when a planet, fortunate by nature, is situated between two malevolent stars, as ♀ in 12° of ♋, ♄ in 15° and ♅ in 10° of the same sign, where she is in a state of "siege," and highly unfortunate. He whose significator it was, would be denoted thereby to be in "a great strait," and particularly "hemmed in," or surrounded with ill fortune.

Bicorporeal signs ♊, ♐ and ♓, because each contains two different animals.

Cadent houses so called because they are falling from the angles. These are the weakest of all the houses, and are the IIId, VIth, IXth and XIIth.

Cardinal signs ♈, ♋, ♎ and ♑.

Collection of light when a planet receives the aspects of any two others which are not themselves in aspect. It denotes that the affair will be forwarded by a third person, described by that planet; but not unless they both receive him in some of their dignities.

Combustion when a planet is posited within 8°30′ of the ☉, either before or after the ☉'s body. In horary questions, unless the ☉ be the chief significator, this is deemed unfortunate. The ☽ is singularly weak when so elongated.

Common signs ♊, ♍, ♐ and ♓.

Conjunction two planets being in the same longitude. If they be exactly in the same degree and minute, it is a partile conjunction and very powerful; if within the half of the sum of their two orbs, it is a platic conjunction and less powerful.

Culminate to arrive at the midheaven, meridian, or cusp of the Xth house.

Cusp the beginning of any house. Thus the eastern horizon is the cusp of the Ist house, and the meridian, where the ☉ is at noon is the beginning, or cusp of the Xth house.

Debilities a planet in a weak and afflicted position, as fall, detriment, etc.

Declination the distance any body is north or south of the equator. The ☉ has never more than 23°28′ of declination, which happens only when he is in ♋ or ♑.

Decreasing in light when any planet is past the ☍ of the ☉ it decreases in light; it is a testimony of weakness.

Decumbiture a laying down; the figure erected from the time of any person being first taken ill and taking to their bed.

Descendant the VIIth house or that space from the western horizon to one-third of the distance towards the meridian above the earth.

Destruction when three planets shall be in one sign, of which one planet is ponderous, the other two more light; then one of the light planets should pass the ponderous, the other tends to a ☌ with the ponderous; but before the ☌ is made the planet which passes the ponderous turns R., and is again joined to the ponderous, and from thence passes to the other light planet.

Detriment the sign opposite the house of any planet, as ♂ in ♎ is in his detriment; it is a sign of weakness, distress, etc.

Dignities are either essential or accidental. The former is when any planet is in its own house, exaltation, triplicity, joy; the other is when any planet is in an angle, and well-aspected, not afflicted. swift in motion, increasing in light, etc. The reverse of dignities is debilities.

Direct as applied to planets, denotes their moving in the true order of the celestial signs, as from ♈ to ♉, etc.

Dispose, Dispositor a planet disposes of any other which may be found in its essential dignities. Thus if ☉ be in ♈, the house of ♂, then ♂ disposes of ☉ and is said to rule, receive or govern him. When the disposer of the planet signifying the thing asked after is himself disposed of by the lord of the ascendant, it is a good sign. To dispose by house is the most powerful testimony, then by exaltation, then triplicity, then term, and lastly face, which is a very weak reception.

Doublebodied signs ♊, ♐ and ♓.

Dragon's head thus marked, ☊, is where the ☽ crosses the ecliptic into south latitude. It is always a good symbol denoting success, a good disposition, etc.

Dragon's tail thus marked, ☋, is where the ☽ crosses the ecliptic into south latitude or her south node (actually it is the point opposite the north node or Dragon's Head, and both are the plane of the ☽ crossing the ecliptic).

It is very evil, and in all things the reverse of the ☊. It diminishes the power of good, and increases that of evil planets.

Ephemeris a kind of almanack, containing the places of the planets, etc. The best is Simmonite's (now *American Astrology* is best) in which the aspects are also calculated to the minute, an acquisition almost invaluable to the student of astrology, astronomy, astrometeorology, astrobotany, astrophrenology, etc.

Equinoctial signs ♈ and ♎.

Exaltation an essential dignity, next in power to that of the house. If a planet be in that sign wherein he is exalted, you may consider him essentially strong. If the significator be in his exaltation and no way impedited, but angular, it represents a person of a haughty condition, arrogant, assuming more to himself than is due.

Fall a planet has its fall in the opposite sign to that in which it has its exaltation. In horary questions, a planet in its fall denotes a person unfortunate, despised, degenerated, mean, insolvent, or helpless; and the thing signified by it is in a helpless state, except some good aspect by application, or some translation of light happen, which will relieve it quite unexpectedly.

Feminine signs ♉, ♋, ♍, ♏, ♑ and ♓. These are the even signs; they are supposed to be weak and feminine on account of their passive qualities, coldness and moisture, and are supposed to render those they govern the same.

Fiery signs, fiery triplicity ♈, ♌ and ♐.

Figure the diagram which represents the heavens at any time; it is also called a scheme or horoscope.

Fortunate signs ♈, ♊, ♌, ♎, ♐ and ♒.

Fortunes ♃ and ♀, and ☉, ☽ and ☿, if aspecting them, and not afflicted are considered fortunate planets.

Fruitful signs ♋, ♌, and ♓. The ascendant, the ☉, or lord of the ascendant, in one of these signs, and strong, are symbols of children.

Frustration the cutting off or preventing anything shown by one aspect by means of another. Thus if ♀, lady of the ascendant, were hastening to the △ of ♂, lord of the VIIth, in a question of marriage, it might denote that the match would take place; but if ☿ were to form an opposition of ♂ before ♀ reached her △ of that planet, it would be a frustration and would show that the hopes of the querent would be cut off; and if ☿ were lord of the XIIth, it might denote that it would be done by a private enemy; if of the IIId, by means of relations, etc.

Horary questions so named from the Latin word hora, an hour, because the time of their being asked is noted, and a figure of the heavens for that time is taken by which to judge the result.

Horoscope the ascendant is sometimes so-called, but it is more generally a term for the figure of the heavens used by astrologers for predicting by nativities, mundane astrology and horary questions.

Houses the twelve divisions or compartments into which the circle of the heavens is divided; also, the signs in which any planet is said to have most influence.

Humane signs ♊, ♍, ♒ and the first half of ♐. They are said by Ptolemy to give the native a humane disposition, when the lord of the geniture or the ascendant is in one, otherwise he will be brutish and savage. He also says that the lord of an eclipse being in any humane sign, its evil effects will fall on mankind.

Increase in light when any planet is leaving the ☉ and is not yet arrived at the ☍, after which it decreases in light. The former is good, the latter an evil testimony, especially as regards the ☽.

Increasing in motion when any planet moves faster than it did on the preceding day.

Inferior planets ♀, ☿ and the ☽ are so-called because their orbits are inferior to that of the earth.

Infortunes ♅, ♄ and ♂, also ☿ when he is much afflicted.

Light of time the ☉ by day and the ☽ by night.

Lights the ☉ and ☽.

Lords the planets which have the most powerful effects in particular signs; thus if ♈ ascend in any figure, ♂, who rules this sign, is the lord of the ascendant.

Malefics ♅, ♄ and ♂, and ☿ in money, marriage and law.

Masculine signs the odd signs, viz., ♈, ♊, ♌, ♎, ♐ and ♒.

Medium coeli the midheaven.

Midheaven (M.C.) the south angle or cusp of the Xth house.

Moveable signs ♈, ♋, ♎ and ♑.

Mute signs ♋, ♏ and ♓.

Nativity the birth, the instant the native draws breath, or rather that when the umbilical cord is divided. It also signifies a figure of heaven from the time of birth.

Nodes the point where a planet crosses the ecliptic out of south into north latitude is called its north node, and where it crosses into south latitude its south node. (This is not technically correct, for the nodes are the "plane" of the planets crossing the ecliptic.) The Moon's north node is called the Dragon's Head, and is marked ☊; and her south node, the Dragon's Tail, and marked ☋. Their motion is retrograde, about 3' per day.

Northern signs ♈, ♉, ♊, ♋, ♌ and ♍. They are also called commanding signs because planets in them are said to command, and those in the opposite signs, to obey.

Opposition when two planets are distant 180°, or just half the distance of the zodiac apart, which places them in a diametrical radiation. This is considered an aspect of perfect hatred.

Orb the deferent of a planet, supposed by the ancients to fit into each other like the coats of an onion, and to carry the planets about with them. The word is now used to describe the distance at which a planet may operate from a partile aspect before it quite loses its effects. The orb of the cusp of any house, a fixed star, or ☉, is 5°.

Pars Fortuna   the Part of Fortune, ⊕.

Peregrine   a peregrine planet is one posited in a sign where it has no essential dignity of any kind. It is reckoned a debility of 5°. In questions of theft, a peregrine planet in an angle, or in the IId house, is the thief. No planet is reckoned peregrine if it be in mutual reception.

Ponderable planets   ♆, ♅, ♄ and ♃, so-called because they move slower than the rest.

Prohibition   the same as frustration; it indicates the state of two planets that are significators of some event, or the bringing of some business to an issue or conclusion, and are applying to each other by ☌, but before ☌ can be formed a third planet, by means of swifter action, interposes his body and destroys the expected ☌ by forming an aspect himself; and this indicates that the matter under contemplation will be greatly retarded or utterly prevented.

Querent   he or she who requires or asks the question, and desires the result of any event.

Quesited   the person or event concerning whom the question is asked.

Radical, radix   The figure at birth is the radix or root from which everything is judged, and the term radical refers to it.

Rays   in the common acceptation of the word, a ray is a beam of influence or sympathy which accompanies such ray, when two planets are within orbs of each other. The fixed stars have no distant influence by aspect, but only operate with a planet when joined to it from 2° to 5° of its body, according to the magnitude of the fixed star.

Reception   when two planets are mutually posited in each other's essential dignities; as ♃ in ♈, and the ☉ in ♋, where ♃, being in exaltation of the ☉, and the ☉ in the exaltation of ♃, both are in mutual reception; or the ☉ in ♈ and ♃ in ♌ are in reception, one by house (sign), the other by triplicity. This is accounted an aspect of singular amity and agreement.

Retrograde   when any planet is decreasing in longitude; it is a very great debility.

Retrograde application   when both planets are retrograde and move contrary to the order of the signs of the zodiac, applying to each other.

Separation   when an aspect is past, the planets, etc., are said to be separating from that aspect; and denotes that the influence is passing away.

Significator   the significator of any party is that planet which rules or has dominion by celestial house over that part of the figure or scheme peculiar to the business at hand. Thus, were the question about money, the lord of the IId house of heaven is the chief significator of the matter; and his good or evil aspects must be well observed ere the answer can be faithfully given. The lord of the ascendant is the general significator of the querent.

The ☉ is in general his co-significator.

Signs of voice   ♊, ♍, ♎. ♒ and the first part of ♐ ; because it is said if any of them ascend and ☿ be strong, the native will be a good orator.

Slow of course   when a planet moves slower than its mean motion. It is considered a great debility and it may be so in some cases of horary questions.

Stationary   when a planet is in its station and appears to stand still. The lights are never stationary.

Stations   those parts of the orbit of a planet where it becomes either retrograde or direct; because it remains for a while there stationary before it changes its course. The first station is when it becomes retrograde; the second station is after it has passed its perigee, and from retrogradation becomes direct.

Strong signs   ♌, ♏ and ♒ , because they are strong, athletic bodies.

Succeedent houses   so-called because they follow or succeed the angles. These houses are next in power to the angles and are the IId, Vth, VIIIth and XIth.

Swift in motion   when a planet moves quicker than its mean motion in 24 hours, and slow in motion when it moves less.

Violent signs   the houses or exaltations of the malefics, viz., ♈, ♎, ♏, ♑ and ♒ ; also those signs are called violent where there are any remarkably violent fixed stars, as ♉ for Caput Algol, etc. (We do not agree with the author that ♎ is a violent sign.)

Unfortunate signs   ♉, ♋, ♍, ♑ and ♓ . The natives are said to be unfortunate in the general tendency of the events of their lives. The most unfortunate of them all is ♑.

Watery signs or triplicity   ♋, ♏ and ♓ .

N.D. The student will do well to learn and digest the terms, as a correct knowledge of them is necessary.

INDEX

(References are to paragraph numbers rather than pages unless specifically indicated as pages.)

A

Abroad, Will husband, wife or lover return from? 347
Absent brothers, cousins, neighbours, children 280
Absent mother, Is she dead or alive? 299
Absent person, Welfare of 289
Advice, Is it good or bad? 310
Advice to students .... page 7
Agreement between brethren or neighbours 310
Antagonists in races, games or purchase of shares 291
Application, Orbs of 14
Armies, Whether two will fight or not 334
Article or thing missing will not be found 316
Aspects 6-13
Asteroids 4

B

Barrenness, Testimonies of 320
Benefice, Will the benefice be obtained? 348
Besieged places 334
Bills and promissory notes 292
Bills, Will it be safe to cash the person the bill? 340
Birth, Time when the birth will take place 320
Books, Of the success of a book or other literary undertaking 345
Borrowing money, Can I be successful in borrowing the money
    from a club, etc.? 300
Business, If the calling be a profession or an art 351
Business, Of the most appropriate 349
Business, Shall I prosper in? 350

C

Cattle (large), When to sell 329
Cattle (small) and dogs 324
Change, When can the querent expect? 285
Character produced by planets rising 144-160
Character produced by signs and planets rising 15-143

Chastity, The female is chaste 318
Child, Is the absconded child dead or alive? 365
Child, Whether the child will live 320
Child, Will the child be male or female? 320
Cities ruled by signs of zodiac 203-214
Collection of light 239
Colours represented by compound singificators 228
Colours represented by houses 230
Colours represented by planets 227
Colours represented by signs 229
Conception, The querent has just conceived 320
Countries and cities under the influence of the signs 203-214
Courtship, Dishonoured 318

D

Death, Shall we soon have death in the family? 341
Death, What kind of death the querent will die 337
Death, Whether the querent will suffer from what he fears 338
Debtor, Shall I be able to pass the insolvent court? 336
Debts, Of the recovery of 339
Detriment of planets 246
Dignity or debility of planets 246
Directions, geographically 233-234
Diseases, On giving medicine 367
Diseases, Prognostics of death 367
Diseases, Prognostics of life 367
Diseases, Signs of long 367
Diseases, Signs of short 367
Diseases, Time of recovery 367
Diseases, What part of the body is afflicted? 367
Dispositions produced by the influence of the planets 144-160
Dispositions produced by the signs and planets ascending ... 15-143
Distance of quesited 235
Dragon's Head and Tail, Indications of 247

E

Elections concerning friendship between brethren, kindred
    and neighbours 370
Elections, Doctrine of .... page 148
Elections for buying and selling 377
Elections for buying or taking houses, lands or tenements 371
Elections for buying horses and oxen 380

Elections for engaging servants 376
Elections for entering into any place or office employment 379
Elections for finding hidden treasure 372
Elections for fishing 375
Elections for marriage 382
Elections for most undertakings and first journeys 381
Elections for receiving money owing 369
Elections for receiving your wife's portion 368
Elections for removing from place to place 373
Elections for setting up any trade or profession 378
Elections, Taking possession of any house 374
Employments signified by the planets 161-170
Enciente, The time when she may become 320
Enemies, Description of the 335
Enemies, Has the querent any public? 335
Enemies, He has no private 364
Enemies, Of private 364
Enemies, What is the description of the foe? 364
Enemies, Will the enemies overcome? 335
Enemies, The power of their enmity 364
Enemies, The state and quality of the foe 364
Equating, Mode of equating the planets . . . . page 74
Essential fortitudes and debilities of the planets 246
Estates, Will the querent succeed to the estate of his father? 315
Event, The nature of events likely to take place 284
Event, When and what time will the event happen? 231
Exaltation of the planets 246
Exchanging of commodities 290
Exile, Whether an exile will be restored 362
Explanation of the diagram (horoscope) . . . . page 63

F

Fall of the planets 246
Feminine houses 230
Figure of the heavens, How to erect 249
Finding, How to find the places of the planets 250
Fortitude or debility of the planets 246
Friends, Is the quesited a friend to me? 363
Friends, What kind of person I ought to trust as a 363
Frustrated, How persons and things are 241

G

Gender of houses	230
General judgment	251-274
Genethliacs, Points in	page 146

H

Home, Am I likely to stay at home with parents?	342
Honesty, The servant, apprentice or lodger will be honest	322
Hopes and wishes	293
Horary figure, Of the time of erecting	243
House rulerships of parts of human body	276
Houses, Diagram of the principal signification of the houses	page 62
Houses, Geographical directions indicated by	234
Houses, Miscellaneous signification of the	230
Houses, Signification of the twelve	215-226
Horoscope	page 74
Horoscope, Example of	page 88

I

Illegitimate children	318
Imprisonment or banishment	366
Insert, How to insert the signs in the figure	249
Insurance, Shall I be able to effect an?	344

J

Journey, Issue of a long	297
Journey, Short	311
Joys of the planets	246
Judgment of the horoscope, General	251-274

L

Lawsuits, Shall I have a?	332
Lawsuits, Who conquers in the	332
Lawsuits, Who will be most ready to agree?	332
Lawsuits, Will the judge, lawyer, etc., proceed fairly?	332
Legacy, Will the querent obtain the expected?	343
Letters, Anonymous	312
Life, Of the good or evil attending	286
Life, How long is it probable querent will live?	282

Life, Signs of long or short 281
Life, What portion of querent's life is likely to be most fortunate? 283
Life, Will the querent's be long? 281
Local places ruled by the planets 183-192
Local places ruled by the signs 171-182
Long journey, Of the issue of a 297
Lords of houses 246
Lost, The place where a thing may be 316
Lottery, Will a ticket in a lottery be blank or a prize? 307

M

Man's body, Signs and houses ruling 276
Manufactures and other articles affected by the planets 170-177
Marks, moles or scars 275, 277
Marriage, A woman leaving her husband 326
Marriage, Election for 382
Marriage, Has he another lover? 326
Marriage, Has the gentleman another lover? 326
Marriage, Has the lady another lover? 326
Marriage, How the parties will agree in 326
Marriage, No great gains by 326
Marriage, Of the circumstances of the husband or wife 326
Marriage, Of the time of 326
Marriage, Persons and means hindering 326
Marriage, Prevention of, and its cause 326
Marriage, She will marry this lover 326
Marriage, The expected falls away 326
Marriage, The husband described 326
Marriage, What distance is the fugitive? 326
Marriage, Whether man or wife die first 326
Marriage, Which of the two is best connected? 326
Marriage, Will querent marry more than once? 326
Marriage, Will the absconded husband return? 326
Marriage, Will the man or woman marry? 326
Marriage, Will wife or husband be a stranger? 326
Masculine houses 230
Matter, Is the matter good or evil? 245
Messenger, Character of the 321
Messenger, Of a messenger sent on important business 321
Messenger, Time of the messenger's return 321
Messenger, What business is effected by him? 321
Messenger, What takes place on the journey of the 321
Method, General, to be observed in all questions 240

Mislaid, Of an article, how and where to find it 316
Moles, marks or scars on individuals 275
Moles, General remarks on the moles of the quesited 277
Money lost, Will the querent obtain the? 308

N

Names of the querent and quesited 278

O

Obtaining money, debt, goods, etc. 300-302
Offspring generally 320
Orbs of application 14

P

Parliament, Member re-elected or restored 358
Parliament, Whether a petition to, will succeed 352
Part of Fortune, Portents of the 248
Part of Fortune, To find its place .... page 74
Partnership, How shall we agree? 331
Partnership, If we disagree, what will be the cause? 331
Partnership, It will prosper 331
Partnership, May I enter a, or society? 331
Partnership, Shall we succeed in business? 331
Partnership, Which will be the best affected? 331
Persons described by the twelve signs and the planets 15-143
Physiological rulerships of signs and houses 276
Place, The kind of, where the things are 316
Places ruled by the planets 183-192
Places ruled by the signs 171-182
Planetary orbs 14
Planets, Indications of colours 227-228
Planets, Judgment of, in houses 251-274
Planets, Rulerships, dignities and debilities 246
Points in genethliacs .... page 146
Poverty, The cause of, or hindrance to gain 303-306
Pregnancy, If a man ask unknown to the woman 320
Pregnancy, The length of time she has been pregnant 320
Property, Of letting 327
Property, Of making purchases or sales of 328
Property, Of succeeding to 315
Property, Shall I purchase the? 313

Property, What is the quality of the? 313
Property, Will it be dear or cheap? 313

Q

Quesited, At what distance is the? 235
Quesited, Where and in what place is the? 233
Questions 300
Questions, General method to be observed 240
Questions, Is the answer good or evil? 244
Questions, Is the report true or false? 245
Questions, Whether the question is radical or fit to be judged 242

R

Racing, Ruler for winning or losing 291
Radical, Whether the question be 242
Removals, Astrological judgments on 314
Removing, About what time shall I remove? 314
Removing, Is it better for querent to remove? 314
Removing, Is it well to remove from one house to another? 314
Removing, To which quarter should I remove for better success? 314
Removing, What afflicts in my present place, etc.? 314
Removing, What would afflict whither I would remove? 314
Report, Is the, true or false? 245
Riches, By what means will querent obtain? 304
Riches or gain 303
Riches, The time when querent may obtain 306

S

Scars, marks or moles 275, 277
Science, Will the querent profit by the? 336
Servants, Do not engage the, or apprentice 322
Servants, When is the best time for engaging? 322
Ship at sea and its voyage 294
Short journey, Is it well to go on my? 311
Sickness generally 367
Signs, Geographical directions by 234
Signs, The twelve 2
Situation, Shall I be restored to my? 358
Situation, Shall I continue my present? 354-355
Situation, Shall I obtain the, desired? 353
Situation, What will be the cause of my leaving? 357
Situation, When shall I leave my? 356
Situation, When shall I obtain a? 298

Small cattle and dogs, Dealing in them, buying and selling 324
Stolen, The nature of the article, or missing 316
Strayed cattle or servant, Which way is he or it gone? 325
Strayed cattle or servant will be found 325
Subject of inquiry, Is it to be or not? 236
Success, Which way must I steer for better? 288

T

Table of the fortitudes and debilities of the planets 246
Table of the measure of time 232
Tenants, On removal of 323
Terms used in this work . . . . page 153
Testimonies, Doubtful 315
Testimonies, Losing 291
Theft, All manner of questions relating to, or thief 330
Things ruled by the planets 193-202
Time for erecting horary figure 243
Timing events 231-232
Translation of light 238
Treasures, Mines, Whether recoverable or not 317
Triplicities 246
Twins, There will be 320

V

Vocations shown by the planets 161-170
Voyage, Will it be long or short? 296
Voyage, Will it prove prosperous? 295

W

Wages, Shall I get my, advanced? 359
Wages, Will the querent receive his, or salary? 309
War, Shall I return safe from the? 333
Wealth, Persons or means hindering property 343
Wealth, Will the husband or wife be well off? 343
Will, What will be the purport of the sick person's? 343
Will, Will the wife's or husband's portion be obtained? 343
Wishes, Shall I obtain my 293
Woman enquiring, She is enciente 320
Woman enquiring, She is not enciente 320

Work, Will it be well to engage in this? 360
Workman, Is the, servant, etc., faithful? 322
World, What part of the, is most prosperous for the querent? 287

Z

Zodiac, Signs of colours 229
Zodiac, Signs of rulership of countries and cities 203-214
Zodiac, Signs of rulership of distances 235
Zodiac, Signs of rulership of geographical directions 234
Zodiac, Signs of rulership of parts of human body 276
Zodiac, Signs of rulership of places 171-182

* * * * * *